The Lean Years of the Yankees, 1965–1975

The Lean Years of the Yankees, 1965–1975

ROBERT W. COHEN

McFarland & Company, Inc., Publishers

Jefferson, North Carolina, and London

LIBRARY OF CONGRESS CATALOGUING-IN-PUBLICATION DATA

Cohen, Robert W.
    The lean years of the Yankees, 1965–1975 / Robert W. Cohen.
        p.   cm.
    Includes bibliographical references and index.

    ISBN 0-7864-1846-X (softcover : 50# alkaline paper) ∞

    1. New York Yankees (Baseball team)— History — 20th century.
I. Title.
GV875.N4C65   2004
796.357'64'097471— dc22   2004005132

British Library cataloguing data are available

Cover photograph: Clete Boyer, third baseman for the Yankees, traded to
the Braves for outfielder Bill Robinson in 1966.

Manufactured in the United States of America

McFarland & Company, Inc., Publishers
    Box 611, Jefferson, North Carolina 28640
        www.mcfarlandpub.com

In loving memory of Rusty
the best friend I ever had,
who passed away
during the writing of this book

Acknowledgments

I wish to thank the following people, who, in one way or another, assisted in the production of this book:

Bill Burdick of the National Baseball Hall of Fame Library in Cooperstown, New York, who assisted me in acquiring some of the photographs used in this book.

Mike Yasdah, who is affiliated with the Sacramento River Cats of the Triple-A Pacific Coast League, and who provided me with the necessary contact information for getting in touch with Roy White.

Roy White, former Yankee stand-out, who provided his insight into the players and events of the era, and who carries himself with the same dignity and class off the field as he always did on it.

Teri, LJ, Len, and the rest of the gang at the office who helped me make it through the difficult days following the loss of my closest friend.

Nancy and Phil, who supported my efforts and encouraged me to do my best.

Mom and Dad, from whom I drew strength during my darkest hour, and whose love I know is always with me.

In addition, some of the information used in this book was obtained free of charge from and is copyrighted by Retrosheet. Interested parties may contact Retrosheet at 20 Sunset Rd., Newark, DE 19711.

Contents

Introduction

The history of the New York Yankees is filled with stories of great achievements, outstanding performances, and overwhelming success. No other team has captured the imagination and interest of fans all over the world the way the Yankees have. They are probably the nation's most beloved sports franchise; yet they are also probably the most hated. The reason for both is simple: people enjoy rooting for a winner, but success also breeds envy and contempt.

For more than 40 years, Yankees fans had a great deal to cheer about. From 1921 to 1964, New York won 29 pennants and 20 world championships—a truly amazing record. They featured great players such as Babe Ruth, Lou Gehrig, Joe DiMaggio, Mickey Mantle, Bill Dickey, Yogi Berra, and Whitey Ford. Yankees fans walked around with their chests out, swelling with pride over the accomplishments of their team. Yankee haters perceived the franchise and their fans as arrogant, and waited endlessly for the demise of the seemingly unbeatable team from New York.

Then a strange thing happened. After 44 years of winning, the Yankees began to flounder. From 1965 to 1975, they didn't win anything. The team finished with a winning record only six times during that eleven-year period, finished as high as second place only twice, and experienced their longest pennantless drought since the earliest days of their existence. They reached their nadir in 1966, when they finished in tenth and last place in the American League, 26½ games behind the pennant-winning Baltimore Orioles.

During this period, fans of the team had little to cheer about and were constantly harassed by those Yankee haters who finally had their moment of glory. Yet, in their mediocrity, the team and its players somehow acquired a more endearing quality that previously had not existed. The great New York Yankees had become fallible and, as a result, more lovable. A team that had once fielded players like Babe Ruth, Lou Gehrig, Joe

1

DiMaggio, and Bill Dickey now offered their fans Bill Robinson, Danny Cater, Jerry Kenney, and Jake Gibbs.

There were some outstanding players who performed during this era, however. There were Bobby Murcer, Mel Stottlemyre, Thurman Munson, and Roy White. Munson and White were fortunate enough to make it through these "lean years" and last into the next period of Yankee excellence. Stottlemyre experienced only two months of Yankee glory, after he was brought up from the minor leagues during the 1964 campaign. Murcer was traded away during this period, but returned later after the Yankees had once again risen to the top of the standings. However, all of these players experienced first-hand the frustration and disappointment that one generation of Yankee players and fans had to live through.

This book is written for that generation of Yankee players. It is for Bobby Murcer, Mel Stottlemyre, Thurman Munson, Roy White and the other players who excelled during this era. It is also for Horace Clarke, Gene Michael, Jake Gibbs, Ron Blomberg, Stan Bahnsen and the other players whose names became synonymous with this period of Yankee mediocrity. However, it is also for Mike Ferraro, Frank Fernandez, Jim Lyttle, Ron Woods, Joe Verbanic and all the other players from that era, long-forgotten by most fans, who were an integral part of what that team went through. But, more than anyone, it is for the Yankees fans from that era who, like myself, continued to root for their team even though there was little to root for.

ONE

The Yankee Legacy

The New York Yankees are the most prestigious and storied franchise in the history of professional sports. Their level of success is unmatched by any other major sports team. Having completed, in 2002, their 100th season in the American League, New York has won an astounding 38 pennants and 26 world championships—figures not even approached by most other sports franchises. While the Boston Celtics dominated the National Basketball Association for much of the 1950s and 1960s, winning 11 titles in 13 seasons from 1957 to 1969, they were unable to sustain that level of dominance beyond that timeframe. They did win two more championships during the 1970s and another three during the 1980s, but their total of 16 NBA titles pales by comparison to New York's total. In the National Hockey League, the Montreal Canadiens won five consecutive Stanley Cups, from 1956 to 1960, and another four in succession during the 1970s, but have won only two in the last 23 seasons. Their total of 24 Stanley Cups is certainly quite impressive, but still falls short of the Yankees' total of 26 world championships.

In baseball, there have been other successful franchises. The Brooklyn/Los Angeles Dodgers have won the most pennants of any other National League team (18), but have won only six world championships. The New York/San Francisco Giants have won 17 N.L. pennants, but have won only five championships, while the St. Louis Cardinals have won 15 N.L. pennants and have come out on top in the World Series nine times. In the American League, the Philadelphia/Oakland Athletics franchise has amassed 14 pennants and nine world championships. However, New York's total of 38 pennants more than doubles the total of this closest rival, and their 26 World Series triumphs almost triples the number attained by their closest competitors. Perhaps even more impressive is the fact that the Yankees won their first American League pennant in 1921. That means that they have won 38 of the last 82 A.L. pennants, or almost 50 percent. During that same time, they have also been World Series victors 26 times, or almost once out of every three years. Such long-term dominance is truly a remarkable achievement, and is something that even their detractors must marvel at.

However, while the Yankees have been baseball's dominant team throughout much of their existence, there have been a few periods during which their level of performance has not been quite up to the high standards that they have set for themselves, and that their fans have come to expect from them.

The first of these "down" periods came during the team's formative years, from 1903 to 1919. New York entered the American League in 1903, in the league's third season in existence. The team originally played its home games at Hilltop Park, so named because it was built on a tract of land in Washington Heights, on Manhattan Island's most elevated point. As a result, they were initially dubbed the *Highlanders*. They remained there through 1912, but abandoned Hilltop Park at the end of that season and moved into the Polo Grounds as tenants of the National League's New York Giants. It is unclear when, how, and where their name was changed to the *Yankees*, but one thing is very clear: through the 1919 season, the franchise experienced very little success. In their first 17 seasons in the American League, New York finished with a winning record only six times. They finished in second place three times, but also came in last three times.

Nevertheless, during this period, the team did have its fair share of outstanding performers. During the first decade of the 20 century, there were first baseman Hal Chase, outfielder Wee Willie Keeler, and pitcher Jack Chesbro. Chase was a marvelous fielder and baserunner, who was the finest first baseman of his time. Unfortunately, he was also a heavy gambler who had a reputation for betting against his own teams and then making sure they lost by throwing games. Keeler was a Hall of Fame outfielder who had his finest seasons in the National League, prior to the turn of the century. However, after jumping to the rival American League in 1903, he still had enough left to lead New York in batting its first three seasons, with averages over .300. Chesbro was a Hall of Fame pitcher who had previously pitched for the National League's Pittsburgh Pirates. However, he had his greatest season with New York in 1904, when he won an American League record 41 games.

In the century's second decade, New York featured first baseman Wally Pipp, third baseman Frank "Home Run" Baker, and pitcher Bob Shawkey. Pipp led the American League in home runs twice, but is better known for being the man who Lou Gehrig eventually replaced at first base for the Yankees. Baker was a Hall of Famer who had his finest seasons with

Connie Mack's Philadelphia Athletics teams, from 1909 to 1914. However, after sitting out the 1915 season over a bitter contract dispute with Mack, Baker was dealt to New York in 1916. While he was not the same player he had been with Philadelphia, Baker was still a solid performer for the next few years. Shawkey was an outstanding righthander who pitched into the 1920s and won more than 20 games four times for the Yankees.

It wasn't until 1920, however, when New York purchased Babe Ruth from Boston, that they started to build their legacy as the game's dominant team. Over the next 16 seasons, from 1920 to 1935, they won seven pennants, finished second six times, and came in third twice. The only time they finished out of the first division during that period was in 1925, when Ruth missed a good portion of the season due to a serious illness. New York was particularly dominant from 1921 to 1928, when they won their first six pennants and three world championships. Many people still feel that the *Murderers' Row* Yankee team of 1927 and 1928 was the greatest ever, and with good reason. Featuring six future Hall of Famers in Ruth, Gehrig, centerfielder Earle Combs, second baseman Tony Lazzeri, and pitchers Herb Pennock and Waite Hoyt, along with rifle-armed left-fielder Bob Meusel, the Yankees swept through the World Series both years, devastating the Pittsburgh Pirates in 1927 and the St. Louis Cardinals in 1928.

Although New York's offense remained potent the next three seasons, the combination of their aging pitching staff and a superb Philadelphia Athletics team kept them out of the World Series. In 1932, however, re-tooled with the arms of Hall of Fame pitchers Lefty Gomez and Red Ruffing, and featuring that same potent offense that had added catcher Bill Dickey behind the plate and Joe Sewell at third base, the Yankees returned to the Series and, once again, swept the opposition, this time defeating the Chicago Cubs in four straight games. So, that made 12 consecutive victories in World Series games and three consecutive four-game sweeps, a record unmatched, to this day. Still, the best was yet to come.

With an aging Ruth, the Yankees failed to win the pennant in 1933, 1934, and 1935. However, in 1936, they added Joe DiMaggio to a lineup that already featured a still dominant Lou Gehrig, Bill Dickey, who was just reaching his peak, and a young third baseman named Red Rolfe, who was just coming into his own. The next few seasons saw them add young players such as second baseman Joe Gordon and outfielders Charlie Keller and Tommy Henrich. The result was a team that went on to win four successive world championships, from 1936 to 1939, losing only three World Series games in the process. The Yankees took the cross-town rival New York Giants in six games in 1936, then needed only five games to dispose of them the following season. They swept the Chicago Cubs again in 1938, and did the same to the Cincinnati Reds the next year.

After failing to win the American League pennant in 1940, New York returned to the top of the league standings in 1941 and went on to defeat the Brooklyn Dodgers in the World Series, four-games-to-one. The Yankees won the pennant in each of the next two seasons, dropping the Series in five games to the Cardinals in 1942, and returning the favor the following year. With most of the game's best players in the military during the war, New York did not win the pennant again until 1947, when they, once again, faced the Dodgers in the World Series. This time, they needed seven games to defeat Brooklyn, and it appeared that they were starting to become slightly more vulnerable. The starting outfield of DiMaggio, Keller, and Henrich was aging, Dickey was gone, and the starting pitching needed some reinforcements. Yet, there were still some young and talented players on the roster such as Phil Rizzuto, Yogi Berra, Hank Bauer, and Gene Woodling, who would help form the team's nucleus over the next several seasons. In addition, the front office was able to swing deals to bring in veteran starters Vic Raschi, Allie Reynolds, and Ed Lopat. These players, along with future stars Whitey Ford and Mickey Mantle, would enable New York to run off five consecutive world championships, from 1949 to 1953, a feat that has yet to be replicated.

When all was said and done, this generation of Yankee players had accomplished something that even their New York predecessors would have been proud of. In the 18 years, from 1936 to 1953, they had won 13 pennants and 12 world championships, and never finished out of the first division. Though there was much tinkering done with the roster during this period, and different players came and went, there were several constants. For one thing, there were always at least two or three great players on the team. At the start of this era, the team was led by Gehrig, DiMaggio, and Dickey. Later, DiMaggio and Berra were the backbone, and, at its conclusion, Mantle, Berra, and Ford provided leadership. There was also always the presence of a great player patrolling centerfield in Yankee Stadium. From 1936 to 1951, it was DiMaggio. Then, after he retired, Mantle settled nicely into the position. There were always role players, such as Rizzuto, Henrich, Bauer, Woodling, and George Stirnweiss, who were good in their own right, but who were happy to have more of a supporting role to the DiMaggios, Berras, and Mantles in order to increase the team's chances of winning. Then, there was the solid pitching and defense that came to be synonymous with the Yankee teams of this era. While most people tend to associate the great Yankee teams of the forties and fifties with power and run production, it was actually their pitching and defense that set them apart from other clubs. With DiMaggio in center, Dickey and, later, Berra behind the plate, Rizzuto at short, and Gordon, and, later, Stirnweiss and Jerry Coleman at second, New York always had excellent defense up the middle — so important to any pennant contender. And, as for their pitching, it was undoubtedly the quartet of Reynolds, Raschi, Lopat, and Ford that allowed them to win five consecutive world championships, from 1949 to 1953. In three of those World Series, they faced a Brooklyn Dodger team that, quite possibly, with players such as Duke Snider, Roy Campanella, Jackie Robinson, Gil Hodges, and Pee Wee Reese, had a starting lineup that was superior to their own. However, the Yankees' starting four, team depth, and professionalism allowed them to prevail each time.

New York failed to win the pennant in 1954, in spite of the fact that they won 103 games (Cleveland won 111 games that year). However, over the next ten seasons, from 1955 to 1964, the Yankees were able to come away with nine more pennants and four world championships, failing to finish first in the American League in only 1959. They lost the 1955 World Series to the Dodgers in seven games, then came back the following year to beat Brooklyn in seven. They dropped the 1957 Series to the Braves in seven games, then returned the favor the following year. In the memorable Series of 1960, they lost to the Pirates on Bill Mazeroski's ninth inning homer in Game Seven, despite outscoring Pittsburgh in the Series, 55 to 27. The Yankees returned to dominance in 1961, establishing a then major league record of 240 home runs, while Roger Maris and Mickey Mantle waged their own personal battle in attempting to break Babe Ruth's cherished record of 60 home runs in a season. After finishing off the Cincinnati Reds in the Series that year, four-games-to-one, they returned in 1962 to edge out the San Francisco Giants in seven games. However, that would turn out to be the Yankees' last world championship for quite some time because they would be swept in the Series by the Los Angeles Dodgers the following year, and would lose in seven games to the St. Louis Cardinals in 1964.

TWO

New York's Downfall

During this latter period, it started to become more and more apparent that the rest of baseball was starting to catch up to the Yankees. While they remained the American League's dominant team, they were no longer easily able to dispose of their National League counterparts in the World Series as they had in past seasons. There were several reasons for this. For one thing, the farm system, so rich in talent for so many years, was beginning to dry up. Due to economic constraints, over the last five years, both a double-A and a triple-A team had been eliminated, leaving the organization with only about one-half of the previous number of players in its system. One of New York's greatest strengths had always been its ability to either dip down into the minors and call up a top prospect to replace one of its aging veterans, or to deal a minor leaguer or two for a veteran player who could put the team over the top in its run towards another pennant. However, with fewer minor leaguers now in the system, the number of top prospects was dwindling. With several veteran players beginning to show their age, it was becoming more difficult to replace them in the everyday lineup, and the team's depth was not what it had once been.

More important, however, was the fact that New York had always been extremely reluctant to sign the top black and Hispanic talent that was available. This stemmed partly from the fact that the extremely conservative George Weiss, who served as General Manager throughout the 1940s and 1950s, not only did not like the idea of dark-skinned players donning the Yankee pinstripes, but was concerned about offending the predominantly white upper-middle class fan base that frequented most of his team's home games.

Top Yankee scout Tom Greenwade, who is best known for having signed Mickey Mantle to his first contract, had worked for the Brooklyn Dodgers and Branch Rickey prior to joining the Yankee organization. While with Brooklyn, he had scouted much of the top black talent playing in the Negro Leagues and, therefore, could have been invaluable to the Yankees had they elected to go in that direction. However, in his first organizational meeting with George Weiss in 1945, the latter told Greenwade, "Now, Tom, I don't want you sneaking around down any back alleys and signing any niggers. We don't want them."[1] As a result, New York never even made an attempt to sign players such as Hank Aaron and Ernie Banks, whose abilities they were keenly aware of.

Unfortunately, this lack of interest in black players was symbolic of the overall arrogance of Yankee ownership and management, as well as their prevailing racial attitudes. For the most part, they believed many of the existing stereotypes about black players—that they were lazy and that they would not play well under pressure. Since the team continued to win, for the most part, without black players, they felt that it was unnecessary to go in a direction they really did not want to go in. Casey Stengel, who managed the team from 1949 to 1960, was also reluctant to change with the times, and frequently showed his insensitivity. Early in Elston Howard's career, Stengel said of the first black player to wear a Yankee uniform, "Well, when they finally get me a nigger, I get the only one who can't run."[2]

The Yankee front office's attitude towards black players in those days could perhaps best be seen in its treatment of Vic Power, an outstanding black Puerto Rican player who came up in the Yankee farm system. Power was an excellent fielding first baseman, and a solid hitter as well. He batted .294 with Syracuse of the International League in 1951. The following season, he was promoted to New York's top minor league team in Kansas City, where he batted .331. Instead of being brought up to the major league club in 1953, where he would have competed with and probably beaten out incumbent first baseman Joe Collins for the first base job, he was assigned to Kansas City again. There, he led the league with a .349 batting average, only to be traded to the Philadelphia Athletics in the off-season for very little. The reason for Power's mishandling—he did not fit the Yankee mold. On the ball field, he was flashy and eye-catching, drawing attention to himself with his fancy glove work and exuberant style of play. Off the field, he was New York's worst nightmare—a black man who flaunted his success and dated white women. While in the minor leagues, he drove a Cadillac convertible, often accompanied by white women in the front seat. On several occasions, representatives of the major league team spoke to him about changing his ways, telling him they were not going to bring him up unless he did, but Power would tell Hector Lopez, his roommate at the time, "They can tell me a lot of things. They can tell me to play first base or the outfield, and how to hit, and whether they want me to pull or not, but they cannot tell me which women I can go out with."[3]

As a result, Power was traded to the Athletics. He would go on to play 12 years in the major leagues, compiling a lifetime .284 batting average, winning seven Gold Gloves, and being elected to four All-Star teams. Instead, the Yankees opted for the more sedate and non-confrontational Elston Howard to be their first black player.

In the end, the only ones who were hurt by this attitude were the Yankees. By ignoring, to a large extent, a major segment of the talent pool, they prevented themselves from fielding the best possible team, reduced the depth of their major league roster, and permitted other teams to reach, and, eventually, surpass their level. Things began to improve somewhat in 1960, when Weiss was fired as GM and was replaced briefly by Roy Hamey, who was less reluctant to sign black players. (Hamey would eventually be replaced as GM by Ralph Houk after the 1963 season, after the latter had served as manager the previous three seasons.) But the damage had already been done. The Yankees were no longer in a class by themselves, they were starting to show signs of aging, and their minor league system was not what it once was.

New York's position was damaged even further after the 1964 season when, for the first time, the major leagues instituted a draft for new players signing their first contracts.

This draft was designed specifically by other owners to limit the huge bonuses being paid to untried players. However, it hurt the Yankees more than any other club because they were no longer free to sign the best young players available. Previously, the Yankees had been able to lure many a young talent into their fold, at times for less money than other clubs were offering, by using the Yankee *mystique* as a bargaining tool. In addition, they could offer the likelihood of playing in the World Series almost every year and receiving the Series paycheck that went along with it.

Amidst all this, on August 13, 1964, the news leaked out that, after nineteen years of ownership, Dan Topping and Del Webb had sold the Yankees to CBS. It was a two-part sale: in stage one, CBS bought 80 percent for $11.2 million, with an option to buy the remaining 20 percent.

So, the end of the 1964 season appeared to be ushering in a great deal of change for a team already in a state of flux. While New York had finished the 1964 season with a record of 99–63, and had come within one game of winning the World Series, they were clearly not the same team they had been just two or three years earlier. They had finished just one game ahead of the Chicago White Sox and just two ahead of the Baltimore Orioles in the final standings, and it had taken a late-season surge to accomplish that. Following their World Series loss to the St. Louis Cardinals, the front office decided to fire manager Yogi Berra and replace him with Johnny Keane, who the Cardinals' brass had decided to replace with Red Schoendienst, in spite of the fact he had just led his team to the world championship. There was some young talent on the roster in players like Joe Pepitone, Tom Tresh, Mel Stottlemyre, and Al Downing, but many of the players who had contributed so much to the success of the team in recent years were showing signs of wear and tear. Mantle, Maris, Ford, Howard, and Kubek were clearly on the downside of their careers, and there didn't appear to be anyone at the minor league level capable of eventually stepping in and replacing them when the time came. Such was the overall state of affairs as the 1965 season approached.

THREE

1965: The Dynasty Ends

The Yankees went to spring training prior to the opening of the 1965 season feeling pretty good about their chances of repeating as American League champions. After all, on paper, this was essentially the same team that had won the pennant the previous year and come within one game of winning the World Series. New York had captured the last five American League flags and still featured many of the same players from all or some of those pennant-winning teams.

Joe Pepitone was back at first base, and he was coming off an All-Star season in which he had hit 28 home runs and driven in 100 runs. Steady Bobby Richardson was back at second after making his third successive All-Star appearance and winning his fourth consecutive Gold Glove Award the previous year. Third baseman Clete Boyer was coming off a sub-par season in which he had hit only eight home runs, driven in only 52 runs, and batted an abysmal .218. However, better things were expected from him, and he was needed more for his great glove work anyway. Tony Kubek returned at shortstop after suffering through an injury-plagued 1964 season that saw him appear in only 106 games and bat a career-low .229. It was a season he clearly wanted to forget.

Behind the plate once again was Elston Howard who had led the team in batting the previous season, with a mark of .318, driven in 84 runs, played in his eighth consecutive All-Star game, won his second Gold Glove Award, and finished third in the American League MVP voting. He was now looked upon, along with Mantle, as the team leader.

The starting outfield would once again consist of Tom Tresh in left, Mickey Mantle in center, and Roger Maris in right. Tresh had failed to make the All-Star team the previous year for the first time in his three-year career, finishing with only 16 home runs and a .246 batting average. However, he was expected to bounce back. Mantle had led the team with 35 home runs and 111 runs batted in, while batting .303, and was still considered to be one of the most dangerous hitters in the game. Maris had driven in only 71 runs the previous year, but had batted .281, and his 26 home runs placed him third on the team behind Mantle and Pepitone. In addition, he had been extremely productive the last month-and-a-half, driving in 24 runs in his last 41 games during the Yankees' stretch drive to the pennant. It was, therefore, assumed he would be productive again in 1965.

There was some talent on the bench as well. Reserve infielder Phil Linz had filled in admirably for Kubek at shortstop the previous year, even hitting a home run off Bob Gibson in Game Seven of the World Series. He was expected to fill in for Richardson at second, Kubek at short, and Boyer at third.

Hector Lopez would, once again, serve as the primary backup in the outfield. The versatile Panamanian had started his career with the Kansas City Athletics in 1955, playing mostly third base with the team and batting as high as .294 in 1957. The Yankees had acquired him in a trade early during the 1959 season and Lopez had been their regular third baseman for much of that year, hitting a solid .283. However, his glove was somewhat suspect and, with the arrival of Clete Boyer, New York had moved him to the outfield in 1960. Although slow afoot, Lopez was a decent outfielder, and he had provided timely hitting off the bench and, occasionally, as a starter on the last five pennant-winning teams. In the 1961 World Series against Cincinnati, he had filled in for an injured Mickey Mantle and driven in seven runs in the five game series.

Elston Howard would be backed up behind the plate by veteran Johnny Blanchard and youngster Jake Gibbs. Blanchard had been with the team since 1959 and was considered to be a defensive liability. However, he had good power and, in 1961, had excelled in a part-time and pinch-hitting role. That year, he hit 21 homers in only 243 at-bats and batted a career-best .305. He also tied a major league record in July of that year by hitting home runs in four consecutive at-bats, two of which came as a pinch-hitter.

Gibbs was a former University of Mississippi All-American quarter-back and third baseman who had been drafted by the AFL Houston Oilers and NFL Cleveland Browns. However, the Yankees had signed him to a $105,000 bonus, converted him into a catcher in the minor leagues, and brought him up to the big club for the first time for a brief trial in 1964.

Other reserves included Ross Moschitto and Art Lopez in the outfield, Duke Carmel at first base, and Pedro Gonzalez in the infield.

The starting rotation appeared to be solid. Once again, it would be headed by Whitey Ford, who had finished with a record of 17–6 and an

ERA of 2.13 the previous year. He would be followed in the rotation by Jim Bouton, Mel Stottlemyre, Al Downing, and Bill Stafford.

Bouton had won 18 games the previous year, and two more in the World Series, after winning 21 games in 1963. He was rapidly becoming one of the most dependable, steadiest, and finest pitchers in the American League.

Stottlemyre, after being called up from the minors in August of 1964, had gone 9–3 with a 2.06 ERA. He had shown remarkable composure for a rookie, especially considering the circumstances surrounding his call-up. The Yankees were in the middle of a pennant race and he had conducted himself like a veteran, giving them the lift they needed to edge out Chicago and Baltimore. He had even beaten Bob Gibson in Game Two of the World Series. It appeared that he might be ready for stardom.

Downing had won 13 games in each of the past two seasons and had led all American League pitchers with 217 strikeouts in 1964. His control and composure were still somewhat suspect, but he had a live arm and an outstanding fastball. If he could gain better control of the strike zone, it was thought he could be a big winner.

Stafford appeared to be the one question mark in the rotation. He had finished 14–9 for the Yankees in both 1961 and 1962, and had finished second in the league in earned run average in 1961, with a mark of 2.68. However, in his first start of 1963, on a particularly cold night, he had injured his arm and was able to start only 14 games that season. He finished with a record of 4–8 and an ERA of 6.02, but was more effective the following year. Pitching mostly in relief, Stafford had finished the 1964 season with a record of 5–0 and an ERA of 2.67. New York was counting on him to, once again, assume a regular spot in the starting rotation and return to his form of 1961 and 1962.

The bullpen appeared to be strong as well. Cuban-born right-hander Pedro Ramos would be relied upon heavily. Ramos had been a starting pitcher for much of his career on losing teams in Washington and Cleveland. In fact, he had led all American League pitchers in losses four straight years, from 1958 to 1961, as the Senators finished last in 1958 and 1959, and below .500 the other two years. He had also led the league in starts in two of those years, once setting a then single-season A.L. record by surrendering 43 home runs. However, Ramos was dealt to the Indians prior to the start of the 1962 season for Vic Power and Dick Stigman. During the 1964 campaign, he was converted into a relief pitcher by Cleveland, and he was dealt to the Yankees on September 5 of that year for pitchers Ralph Terry, Bud Daley, and $75,000. After the trade, he proved to be invaluable to New York during its stretch run, going 1–0 with a 1.25 ERA, and saving eight games.

Ramos would be joined in the Yankee bullpen by left-hander Steve Hamilton and right-handers Pete Mikkelsen and Hal Reniff. The stocky Reniff had been an effective reliever for New York in each of the two previous seasons, saving 18 games in 1963 and nine more in 1964, while winning another six. Hamilton was a tall, gangly left-hander with a sweeping curveball, who was usually brought in only to pitch to left-handed batters. While he generally struggled somewhat against right-handed hitters, because of his exaggerated sidearm motion and unusually sharp-breaking curveball, lefties found him almost impossible to hit. Mikkelsen was a sinkerballer who, pitching strictly in relief, had won seven games and saved twelve others the previous year. The battle for the last bullpen spot would be between youngsters Gil Blanco, Jack Cullen, and Roland Sheldon. The latter had started for the team sporadically in 1961, 1962, and 1964 with a fair amount of success. However, with the arrival of Stottlemyre the previous year, he was now being looked upon more as a reliever.

So, on the surface, there appeared to be enough talent for the Yankees to make a strong bid to win their sixth consecutive American League pennant. However, troubles were looming on the horizon.

For one thing, during the off-season, Bobby Richardson and Tony Kubek had both begun to think about retirement. Although both players were less than 30 years of age, they each had legitimate reasons for wanting to leave the game. Richardson, an extremely religious and moral man, had more important things he wanted to do with his life. He had also grown tired of the constant travel and of being away from his family.

Kubek had been badly injured playing touch football while in the army in 1962, had suffered cracked vertebrae, and had never fully recovered. By 1964, he was experiencing constant back and neck problems and doctors warned him that he would have to retire or risk permanent damage to his spinal column. The Yankees' double play combination discussed things prior to the start of the 1965 season and decided that it would be unfair to the team to leave at the same time. Therefore, even though they both wanted to play just one more year, they decided that it would be best if Kubek retired at the end of 1965 and Richardson quit after the 1966 season.

In addition, the team had a group of veteran stars that was aging and could no longer perform at their highest level. Mickey Mantle had been playing with injuries throughout his entire career and was in constant pain. He could no longer be counted on to play every day, and he was no longer the player he once was. During the latter stages of the 1964 season, and in the World Series, Mantle had been shifted to right field, with Roger Maris moving to center, to save the wear and tear on Mantle's injured legs.

In Tony Kubek's nine seasons with the Yankees, they won seven pennants and three world championships. When Kubek retired prematurely at the end of the 1965 season, New York sorely missed his leadership.

Even though he had finished the season with impressive offensive numbers, he was finding it increasingly difficult to perform at optimum proficiency. He had missed huge chunks of both the 1962 and 1963 seasons, and, in 1964, had failed to finish the season with at least 500 official at-bats for the third year in a row. That year would prove to be his last hurrah, and he would never again put up huge offensive numbers.

Whitey Ford had reached a point in his career where he was getting by more on guile and courage than on sheer ability. Beginning in 1964, he was experiencing circulatory problems in his left (pitching) shoulder that were causing him constant pain. He could no longer throw the ball with the same velocity he once did and he now had to rely on wit, trickery, and doctoring the ball to get opposing hitters out.

Elston Howard had only been a full-time player for the last four seasons, finally supplanting Yogi Berra as starting catcher in 1961, but he had turned 36 during the off-season. The combination of Berra's presence and the Yankees' unwillingness to allow their first black player to develop rapidly into the star he undoubtedly would have been on most other teams had slowed down the progression of his career. Yet, he had clearly established himself as one of the team's best and most important players. However, age and injuries would soon begin to take their toll on him.

Only four years earlier, Roger Maris had established a new single-season home run mark with his *61 in '61*. However, he had suffered through an injury-plagued 1963 season in which he had appeared in only 90 games and finished with a total of just 312 official at-bats. Although he had rebounded somewhat in 1964, he often played hurt and was clearly no longer the player he once had been.

Therefore, as the team broke training camp and the regular season began, things were actually quite a bit more ominous than they appeared to be on the surface.

The Yankees lost their season opener to the Minnesota Twins in Metropolitan Stadium, 5–4 in 11 innings, with neither starter—Jim Bouton for New York or Jim Kaat for Minnesota—involved in the decision. After Whitey Ford started and lost the season's second game in California to the Angels, the Yankees got their first win of the season against the Angels the next day on a Mel Stottlemyre shutout. New York won each of its next two contests against the Kansas City Athletics, behind Al Downing and Jim Bouton, respectively, but, sadly, at 3–2, that would prove to be the only time all season the Yankees would have a winning record. They would reach the .500 mark a few times, but would fail to surpass it again.

The onset of injuries that would plague the team for much of the year began in early May, when Elston Howard injured his elbow. The injury required surgery and Howard was lost to the team for one month. He wound up playing in only 110 games and coming to the plate just 391 times. Howard finished the season with only 9 home runs, 45 runs batted in, and a .233 batting average. To compensate for their starting catcher's loss, on May 3 the Yankees traded Johnny Blanchard and pitcher Roland Sheldon to Kansas City for catcher Doc Edwards. Edwards went on to appear in 45 games and come to the plate a total of 100 times, but finished the season with only a .190 batting average.

On May 10, feeling the need for another left-handed bat coming off the bench, the Yankees traded minor league infielder Pedro Ramos to the

Cleveland Indians for backup first baseman Ray Barker. Later in the season, in June, Barker would go on to tie a major league record by hitting two consecutive pinch-hit home runs.

On May 17, after dropping their eleventh game in sixteen decisions, the Yankees' record stood at 12–18, they were in eighth place, ten games out of first, and, for all intense purposes, had been eliminated from the pennant race.

More than one month later, on June 22 during a doubleheader split with the Athletics, Mickey Mantle attempted to score from second base on a wild pitch and ended up pulling an upper-thigh hamstring. As a result, he was lost to the team for three weeks.

However, this was just one of a string of injuries that would, once again, keep Mantle out of the starting lineup for much of the season. He went on to start only 108 games and accumulate only 361 official at-bats. His totals at season's end: 19 home runs, 46 runs batted in, and a .255 batting average.

Things only got worse one week later when, after sitting out several games with a mysterious hand injury, Roger Maris discovered he had bone chips in the heel of his right hand. He would be out of the lineup for the next 49 games and would wind up appearing in only 46 games the whole season. In 155 at-bats, he hit 8 homers, knocked in 27 runs, and batted .239.

To compound matters, several key veterans were having off years. Joe Pepitone, who just one year earlier had played at an All-Star level, was starting to let his earlier success go to his head and was no longer applying himself the way he needed to in order to get the most out of his God-given talent. He finished the season with only 18 home runs, 62 runs batted in, and a .247 batting average. Bobby Richardson was his usual steady self at second base but, his heart no longer in the game, finished the season batting only .247. Tony Kubek, in considerable pain and thinking about retirement, appeared in only 109 games and finished the season with a .218 batting average.

On the pitching staff, Whitey Ford was able to take his regular turn in the rotation but, with the circulation in his left arm continuing to bother him, finished only 16–13, with a 3.24 ERA. Al Downing won only 12 games, while losing 14, and continued to struggle with his control, walking one batter per every two innings of work. Jim Bouton, for the first time in his career, started to experience arm problems, and finished with a won-lost record of 4–15 and an ERA of 4.82. In addition, Bill Stafford was unable to regain his earlier form and won only 3 of his 15 starts.

Nevertheless, in mid-July, with New York in seventh place, 14½ games out of first, five Yankees were selected to the American League All-Star team — Mantle, Pepitone, Richardson, Howard, and Stottlemyre. Needless to say, those selections, with the exception of Stottlemyre and, perhaps, Richardson, were based strictly on reputation, past performance, and the Yankee aura that still existed at that time.

New York continued to struggle after the All-Star break, reaching the .500 mark only four times during the second half of the season, with the last time coming on September 3, when their record stood at 68–68. With the Yankees clearly out of the pennant race much earlier than they expected to be, and with many of their veteran players missing large portions of the season due to injury, several minor league prospects were called up during the second half of the season.

The first to join the big club was a highly-touted left-handed hitting outfielder named Roger Repoz. Repoz was a big kid, with a big swing, whose left-handed power stroke was thought to be perfect for Yankee Stadium. He showed some promise that year, hitting 12 home runs and knocking in 28 runs in only 218 at-bats. However, he had a difficult time making contact, batting only .220 and striking out 57 times.

Another call-up was a young infielder from the Virgin Islands named Horace Clarke. Filling in at second, short, and third, the switch-hitting Clarke showed some promise as well, batting .259 in 108 at-bats and exhibiting good speed on the bases.

Also making their first appearances in a Yankee uniform were two youngsters who New York was looking towards for big things in the future — Roy White and Bobby Murcer. The switch-hitting White was a converted outfielder who had originally played second base in the minor leagues. However, with the presence of Bobby Richardson on the big club, Manager Johnny Keane had moved him to the outfield. In 42 at-bats with the Yankees, he batted .333. The lefty-swinging Murcer was a young shortstop who had been signed by Tom Greenwade, the same scout who had signed Mickey Mantle. Although only 19 at the time, he was already being projected as the next great Yankee player. He could hit, run, and throw, and seemed to have the kind of talent that would help New York continue its winning tradition. In 37 at-bats, he hit his first major league home run and batted .243.

Nothing seemed to help the Yankees' plight, though. They won only 9 of their final 26 games and finished the season with a 77–85 record, in sixth place, 25 games behind the pennant-winning Minnesota Twins.

The Yankee pitching staff had a decent season, with the starters combining for 41 complete games, tying them for second in the league. The team ERA of 3.28 was good enough for fifth in the league. However, the offense did not fare quite as well. Although New York finished a respectable fifth in the league in home runs, with 149, they finished seventh in runs scored, and their .235 team batting average was ninth best in the league, seven points below the league average of .242. There were a few bright spots, however.

Tom Tresh had, perhaps, his finest all-around season in the majors and led the team in virtually every offensive category. The switch-hitting outfielder finished first in homers (26), runs batted in (74), batting average (.279), runs scored (94), and base hits (168). While those numbers may not, on the surface, appear to be overly impressive, it should be remembered that this was 1965, right in the middle of a pitcher's era. Tresh finished among the league leaders in numerous categories. He was fifth in home runs, tenth in batting average, fourth in doubles, third in runs scored, fourth in base hits, and second in total bases. His .279 batting average was 37 points higher than the league average of .242 that year. In addition, he played a superb left-field and was awarded a Gold Glove at the end of the season. Tresh finished ninth in the league MVP voting and was arguably, along with Tony Oliva, league MVP Zoilo Versalles, Rocky Colavito, and Brooks Robinson, one of the five best all-around players in the American League that year.

On the Yankees, Tresh was followed in home runs by Mantle (19), Pepitone (18), and Boyer (18). Pepitone's 62 RBIs were second on the team, and Richardson finished second in runs scored (76) and base hits (164).

Mel Stottlemyre established himself as the ace of the pitching staff, leading the team in almost every pitching category. His 20 wins (against 9 losses) were the second highest total in the American League, and he finished sixth in earned run average (2.63), tied for second in shutouts (4), and led the league with 291 innings pitched and 18 complete games. Stottlemyre finished fourteenth in the league MVP voting, and, had each league presented its own Cy Young Award, he most likely would have won it in the A.L. Although Jim "Mudcat" Grant won 21 games that year, he pitched for the pennant-winning Minnesota Twins and had a much better offensive team playing behind him. The Minnesota lineup featured Tony Oliva, who won his second consecutive batting title that year with an average of .321, led the league in hits, and also finished in the top five in runs batted in, runs scored, doubles, total bases, and on-base percentage. Grant also received support from league MVP Zoilo Versalles, who had a career-year, leading the league with 126 runs scored, 12 triples, and 308 total bases, and finishing among the league leaders with 45 doubles and 182 base hits. Minnesota's powerful lineup also included sluggers Harmon Killebrew, Jimmie Hall, and Bob Allison, and produced a league-leading 774 runs—163 more than the Yankees' total of 611. That means, in essence, that the Twins scored one run more a game than the Yankees did. Yet Stottlemyre won only one game less than Grant and finished ahead of him in virtually every other pitching category. Unfortunately for the Yankee right-hander, in 1965, just one Cy Young Award was presented to the best pitcher from both leagues combined, and Sandy Koufax was named the unanimous winner.

Al Downing finished fifth in the league, and led the team with 179 strikeouts, while Ford finished second on the team to Stottlemyre in wins (16), ERA (3.24), and innings pitched (244), and runner-up to Downing in strikeouts (162).

In the bullpen, Pedro Ramos picked up right where he had left off the previous year. In 65 relief appearances—at that time, a record for a Yankee right-hander—he won 5 games, saved 19 others, and finished with a 2.92 ERA. Steve Hamilton excelled in his role as left-handed specialist by going 3–1, with a 1.39 ERA and 5 saves.

As for post-season honors, along with Tresh in the outfield, Pepitone, at first base, and Richardson, at second, were awarded Gold Gloves. In fact, Pepitone's .997 fielding percent that year remains the highest ever by a Yankee first baseman. Stottlemyre and Richardson were named to *The Sporting News* All-Star team at the end of the year.

Sadly, however, at the age of 29, Tony Kubek had played his last game of major league baseball. In the off-season, he would officially announce his retirement.

Tony Kubek came up to the Yankees in 1957 and almost immediately became one of manager Casey Stengel's favorites. Stengel always had a fondness for platooning players, and also enjoyed playing them at multiple positions—especially in the infield. Kubek's versatility and athleticism allowed Stengel to move him around quite a bit and, early in his career, he saw extensive playing time at his natural position of shortstop, third base, and in the outfield. Kubek was rewarded for his .297 batting average and fine all-around play at the end of the 1957 season by being named the American League Rookie of the Year. In the third game of the World Series that year, playing in his hometown of Milwaukee against the Braves, Kubek hit two home runs.

The following season, Kubek supplanted Gil McDougald as the Yankees' everyday shortstop and was selected to the American League All-Star

Team for the first time. Although frequently moved around in the field by Stengel once again in 1959, Kubek made his second All-Star game appearance, batting .279 and leading the league with 13 sacrifice bunts. Back at shortstop in 1960, Kubek had perhaps his most productive season, establishing career highs in home runs (14) and runs batted in (62), while batting .273.

When Ralph Houk took over as Yankee manager in 1961 he wanted to create a greater sense of stability on the team. To that end, one of the first things he did was to insert Bobby Richardson as the everyday second baseman and Kubek as the everyday shortstop, batting one and two in the lineup. Kubek responded by setting career highs in hits (170), at-bats (617), and runs scored (84), finishing second in the league with 38 doubles, and being selected to *The Sporting News* All-Star team. In spite of his two home runs in Game Three of the 1957 World Series, Kubek has always maintained that the greatest thrill he ever got from baseball was batting second in the 1961 Yankee lineup, just ahead of Roger Maris and Mickey Mantle.

While Kubek was a modest man who always thought of himself as being just a small piece of the puzzle, his double play partner Bobby Richardson realized how important Kubek was to the team. Richardson says, "Tony was underrated as a player. He was not a flashy player, but he made all the plays. When he was in the lineup the Yankees won. He could go in the hole, he could make the double play, he got on base. He was just a team leader in every sense. He could have played any position."[4]

With Kubek in the army for much of the 1962 season, Yankee rookie Tom Tresh saw extensive action at shortstop, as well as in the outfield. Tresh describes Kubek as, "A great shortstop who was a bit unorthodox in his style. He wasn't as fluid or as smooth as some guys, but he was very efficient and very fast, with a strong arm. He made all the plays, and he was a good clutch hitter."[5]

There were clearly more talented players than Kubek on the Yankee teams of the late 1950s and early 1960s. However, while those teams were known more for their power and pitching, most astute baseball people felt that the core of their success, as it always had been, was in the strength of their middle infield. The combination of Kubek at short and Richardson at second was as solid as one could find anywhere, and many, such as relief pitcher Steve Hamilton, felt that they were the heart and soul of the team during that period.[6] Kubek, in particular, played with a tremendous determination and inner toughness that his teammates seemed to feed off of and that generally permitted him to perform his best in big games. Hamilton felt that this toughness and desire to win might well have made him the most important player on the team.[7] Kubek's teams had always done well in the minor leagues, and he expected to win at the major league level as well. Despite his choir boy looks and clean-cut image, no player on those Yankee teams was any tougher, or more confrontational, than Kubek.

Kubek's inner toughness can best be exhibited by two recollections that teammate Bobby Richardson had of their minor league days together in Denver. The first incident involved Eddie Stanky, a former big league player who was then the opposing team's manager. There was an argument at second base and Stanky came out of the dugout and, with his yelling and screaming, attempted to intimidate both the umpire and the Denver players alike. Kubek simply drew a line in the dirt and told Stanky, "Cross that line and I'll knock you on your ass." Stanky, surprised that a twenty year-old youngster like Kubek would have the temerity to make such a statement to a tough veteran like himself, did not accept the challenge.[8]

Another incident in Denver occurred when a pitcher named Frank Barnes threw at him and Kubek immediately laid down a bunt so that he could nail Barnes at first.[9]

It was this mental toughness and desire to win, as much as Kubek's playing ability that the team missed when he was prematurely forced into retirement at the age of 29 with severe neck and back problems. While Kubek went into a very successful career as a television baseball analyst, New York fielded many shortstops in the ensuing years, attempting to find one with the kind of leadership qualities, inner toughness, and desire to win that he had always exhibited. Finally, after 30 years, they were able to find one in Derek Jeter.

Season Highlights, Outstanding Performances, and Memorable Moments:

April 9   The Houston Astrodome opens for the first time when the Astros host the Yankees in an exhibition game. Houston wins 2–1 in 12 innings, but Mickey Mantle hits the first home run in the new park.

April 25   At Yankee Stadium, New York sweeps the California Angels in a doubleheader, winning the first game, 3–2, and the second, 1–0. In the nightcap, Mel Stottlemyre and Rudy May lock up in a pitching duel that sees Mickey Mantle score the only run of the game with a fourth inning home run into the left field bleachers.

June 5   At Yankee Stadium, Mel Stottlemyre goes 10 innings to win 4–3 over the White Sox. Stottlemyre also hits a fourth inning homer, for the first Yankee score in 24 innings. Mickey Mantle adds a homer in the sixth inning, and Elston Howard, recovering from elbow surgery a month earlier, wins the game with a single in the tenth.

June 6   At Yankee Stadium, New York sweeps a doubleheader from the White Sox, winning the first game, 6–1, and the second, 12–0. In the opener, Whitey Ford bests Tommy John, while, in the nightcap, Al Downing throws his first shutout of the season. Tom Tresh hits four home runs on the day-three in game two.

June 18   At Yankee Stadium, New York routs the first-place Minnesota Twins, 10–2 on four homers. Mickey Mantle cracks a grand slam in the first inning, and his replacement, Ross Moschitto adds his first and only major league home run.

June 22   At Yankee Stadium, New York and Kansas City split a doubleheader, but Ray Barker ties a major league record with his second consecutive pinch-hit home run. He would hit three for the season.

June 28   In Washington, New York sweeps a doubleheader from the Senators, winning the opener, 3–0, behind Mel Stottlemyre, and the nightcap, 4–3. The two victories extend the Yankees' winning streak to five games, the longest they would have all year.

July 20   At Yankee Stadium, during a 6–3 victory over Boston, Mel Stottlemyre becomes the first pitcher in 55 years to hit an inside-the-park grand slam home run.

Sept. 21   At Yankee Stadium, New York defeats the Cleveland Indians, 9–4 for Mel Stottlemyre's 20 victory of the season.

Oct. 3   In the final game of the season, and in Tony Kubek's last in the majors, the Yankees defeat Boston at Fenway Park, 11–5. Kubek goes 3–for–4 and clouts a ninth-inning homer off Dick Radatz in his final major league at-bat.

1965 American League Final
Team Standings and Offensive Statistics

TEAM	G	W	L	PCT	GB	R	H	2B	3B	HR	BB	SO	SB	AVG	OBP	SLG
MINN	162	102	60	.630	—	774	1396	257	42	150	554	969	92	.254	.327	.399
CHI	162	95	67	.586	7	647	1354	200	38	125	533	916	50	.246	.317	.364
BAL	162	94	68	.580	8	641	1299	227	38	125	529	907	67	.238	.309	.363
DET	162	89	73	.549	13	680	1278	190	27	162	554	952	57	.238	.314	.374
CLE	162	87	75	.537	15	663	1367	198	21	156	506	857	109	.250	.317	.379
NY	162	77	85	.475	25	611	1286	196	31	149	489	951	35	.235	.300	.364
CAL	162	75	87	.463	27	527	1279	200	36	92	443	973	107	.239	.300	.341

TEAM	G	W	L	PCT	GB	R	H	2B	3B	HR	BB	SO	SB	AVG	OBP	SLG
WASH	162	70	92	.432	32	591	1227	179	33	136	570	1125	30	.228	.306	.350
BOSTON	162	62	100	.383	40	669	1378	244	40	165	607	964	47	.251	.329	.400
KC	162	59	103	.364	43	585	1294	186	59	110	521	1020	110	.240	.311	.358
TOTAL						6388	13158	2077	365	1370	5306	9634	704	.242	.313	.369

1965 American League Team Pitching and Fielding Statistics

TEAM	CG	SH	SV	IP	H	HR	BB	SO	ERA	FA	E	DP
MINN	32	12	45	1457	1278	166	503	934	3.14	.973	172	158
CHI	21	14	53	1481	1261	122	460	946	2.99	.980	127	156
BAL	32	15	41	1477	1268	120	510	939	2.98	.980	126	152
DET	45	14	31	1455	1283	137	509	1069	3.35	.981	116	126
CLE	41	13	41	1458	1254	129	500	1156	3.30	.981	114	127
NY	41	11	31	1459	1337	126	511	1001	3.28	.978	137	166
CAL	39	14	33	1441	1259	91	563	847	3.17	.981	123	149
WASH	21	8	40	1435	1376	160	633	867	3.93	.977	143	148
BOSTON	33	9	25	1439	1443	158	543	993	4.24	.974	162	129
KC	18	7	32	1433	1399	161	574	882	4.24	.977	139	142
TOTAL	323	117	372	14359					3.46	.978	1359	1453

1965 New York Yankee Pitching Statistics

PLAYER	W	L	ERA	G	GS	CG	SHO	SV	IP	H	R	ER	BB	SO
Mel Stottlemyre	20	9	2.63	37	37	18	4	0	291	250	99	85	88	155
Whitey Ford	16	13	3.24	37	36	9	2	1	244	241	97	88	50	162
Al Downing	12	14	3.40	35	32	8	2	0	212	185	92	80	105	179
Jim Bouton	4	15	4.82	30	25	2	0	0	151	158	89	81	60	97
Bill Stafford	3	8	3.56	22	15	1	0	0	111	93	45	44	31	71
Pedro Ramos	5	5	2.92	65	0	0	0	19	92	80	34	30	27	88
Hal Reniff	3	4	3.80	51	0	0	0	3	85	74	40	36	48	74
Pete Mikkelsen	4	9	3.28	41	3	0	0	1	82	78	40	30	36	69
Jack Cullen	3	4	3.05	12	9	2	1	0	59	59	22	20	21	25
Steve Hamilton	3	1	1.39	46	1	0	0	5	58	47	12	9	16	51
Rich Beck	2	1	2.14	3	3	1	1	0	21	22	6	5	7	10
Gil Blanco	1	1	3.98	17	1	0	0	0	20	16	10	9	12	14
Bob Tiefenauer	1	1	3.54	10	0	0	0	2	20	19	10	8	5	15
Roland Sheldon	0	0	1.42	3	0	0	0	0	6	5	1	1	1	7
Mike Jurewicz	0	0	7.71	2	0	0	0	0	2	5	2	2	1	2
Jim Brenneman	0	0	18.00	3	0	0	0	0	2	5	5	4	3	2

1965 New York Yankee Hitting Statistics

PLAYER	AB	R	H	2B	3B	HR	RBI	BB	SO	SB	OBP	SLG	AVG
Bobby Richardson	664	76	164	28	2	6	47	37	39	7	.287	.322	.247
Tom Tresh	602	94	168	29	6	26	74	59	92	5	.348	.477	.279
Joe Pepitone	531	51	131	18	3	18	62	43	59	4	.305	.394	.247

PLAYER	AB	R	H	2B	3B	HR	RBI	BB	SO	SB	OBP	SLG	AVG
Clete Boyer	514	69	129	23	6	18	58	39	79	4	.304	.424	.251
Elston Howard	391	38	91	15	1	9	45	24	65	0	.278	.345	.233
Mickey Mantle	361	44	92	12	1	19	46	73	76	4	.379	.452	.255
Tony Kubek	339	26	74	5	3	5	35	20	48	1	.258	.295	.218
Phil Linz	285	37	59	12	1	2	16	30	33	2	.281	.277	.207
Hector Lopez	283	25	74	12	2	7	39	26	61	0	.322	.392	.261
Roger Repoz	218	34	48	7	4	12	28	25	57	1	.298	.454	.220
Ray Barker	205	21	52	11	0	7	31	20	46	1	.326	.410	.254
Roger Maris	155	22	37	7	0	8	27	29	29	0	.357	.439	.239
Horace Clarke	108	13	28	1	0	1	9	6	6	2	.296	.296	.259
Doc Edwards	100	3	19	3	0	1	9	13	14	1	.289	.250	.190
Mel Stottlemyre	99	8	13	2	1	2	8	1	43	0	.140	.232	.131
Whitey Ford	82	4	15	1	0	0	4	5	26	0	.230	.195	.183
Al Downing	74	4	8	2	0	1	7	3	30	0	.143	.176	.108
Jake Gibbs	68	6	15	1	0	2	7	4	20	0	.267	.324	.221
Art Lopez	49	5	7	0	0	0	0	1	6	0	.160	.143	.143
Jim Bouton	43	1	4	0	0	0	2	5	24	0	.204	.093	.093
Roy White	42	7	14	2	0	0	3	4	7	2	.404	.381	.333
Bob Schmidt	40	4	10	1	0	1	3	3	8	0	.302	.350	.250
Bobby Murcer	37	2	9	0	1	1	4	5	12	0	.333	.378	.243
John Blanchard	34	1	5	1	0	1	3	7	3	0	.286	.265	.147
Bill Stafford	29	2	0	0	0	0	1	0	12	0	.000	.000	.000
Ross Moschitto	27	12	5	0	0	1	3	0	12	0	.179	.296	.185
Jack Cullen	20	0	3	0	0	0	1	0	9	0	.150	.150	.150
Archie Moore	17	1	7	2	0	1	4	4	4	0	.524	.706	.412
Pedro Ramos	12	0	1	0	0	0	0	0	8	1	.083	.083	.083
Pete Mikkelsen	10	0	1	0	0	0	0	0	6	0	.100	.100	.100
Duke Carmel	8	0	0	0	0	0	0	0	5	0	.000	.000	.000
Rich Beck	7	0	0	0	0	0	0	1	4	0	.125	.000	.000
Steve Hamilton	6	0	1	0	0	0	0	1	2	0	.286	.167	.167
Pedro Gonzalez	5	0	2	1	0	0	0	0	2	0	.400	.600	.400

FOUR

1966: A New Low Point

While the 1965 season had been greeted with much anticipation and high expectations by the Yankees and their fans, the outlook prior to the opening of spring training in 1966 was a far different one. There was much uncertainty surrounding the team, and a number of questions needed to be answered.

The first of these was whether the previous season was merely an aberration, or a portent of things to come. Was New York's sixth-place finish in 1965 simply the result of the inordinately large number of major injuries sustained by key members of the team, or was it a sign that the core group of aging veterans, led by Mantle, Maris, Howard, and Ford, was no longer capable of performing at the high level that they had been accustomed to? Mantle had missed large portions of the four previous seasons, and was succumbing more and more to the injuries that had plagued him throughout much of his career. Maris had not been a dominant player since 1962, was frequently injured himself, and, although only 32, was already starting to think about retirement. Howard's injury was the first major one he had sustained during his Yankee career, but he was now 37 years old and it was not known if he would be able to return to top form. Ford had been experiencing discomfort in his left shoulder due to circulatory problems for the last two years and, unfortunately, the pain had not subsided over the winter. It appeared that his career might be coming to a close.

Another issue was whether or not the younger veterans who had experienced poor seasons in 1965 could bounce back and be more productive this year. Joe Pepitone had hit 28 home runs and driven in 100 runs in 1964. However, last year, he had hit only 18 homers and knocked in just 62 runs. After winning a total of 39 games over the previous two seasons, Jim Bouton had won only 4 in 1965. Could he make a comeback? Al Downing, after showing so much promise the previous two years, had finished with a record of only 12–14 last year. Could he bounce back?

27

Then, there was the situation in the middle infield. Second baseman Bobby Richardson had already decided that this was going to be his last season. He had informed Yankee management during the off-season that he would not play beyond 1966, and it was now up to them to find his eventual replacement, either somewhere in the system, or from another team. Perhaps Horace Clarke, who had been brought up from the minors the previous season, would be groomed as his replacement.

During the off-season, New York had dealt utility infielder Phil Linz to the Philadelphia Phillies for veteran shortstop Ruben Amaro. The latter was a weak hitter, but was an exceptional fielder who had won the National League Gold Glove for his defensive work at shortstop just two years earlier. He was expected to replace Tony Kubek at the position.

Third base and left field were really the only positions that did not have huge question marks surrounding them. Slick-fielding Clete Boyer returned at third, after having one of his better offensive seasons a year earlier. In 1965, he had matched his career-high in home runs, with 18, and had knocked in 58 runs and batted .251—decent numbers, for him. Tom Tresh was coming off a fine all-around season that saw him lead the team in virtually every offensive category. He would, once again, play left-field.

Reserves included Ray Barker at first base, Horace Clarke as the utility infielder, Jake Gibbs behind the plate, and Hector Lopez in the outfield. New York had also acquired reserve outfielder Lou Clinton from the Cleveland Indians during the off-season in a deal for backup catcher Doc Edwards. Outfield prospects Roy White and Roger Repoz would battle it out for the last roster spot.

On the pitching staff, right-hander Mel Stottlemyre had been one of the few bright spots on the team the previous year. It was expected that he would be solid once again. Stottlemyre would be joined in the starting rotation by Ford, Downing, and two pitchers who were new to the team. One of these was a young left-hander named Fritz Peterson, who had performed well in the minor leagues in 1965. Although he was not blessed with a blazing fastball or particularly sharp-breaking curveball, Peterson had excellent control and a great deal of poise for a rookie. The Yankees felt he was ready to play at the major league level. The other was veteran right-hander Bob Friend, who had been obtained during the off-season from the Pittsburgh Pirates in a deal for relief pitcher Pete Mikkelsen and cash. Friend had once been a solid pitcher for Pittsburgh, winning 22 games in 1958 and being selected to a couple of All-Star teams. However, he was now in the twilight of his career and was expected to remain in the starting rotation only as long as it took Jim Bouton to recover from the arm problems he had experienced throughout much of the previous season.

The bullpen would, once again, be headed by veteran Pedro Ramos, who had been the Yankees' closer since being obtained for the pennant drive towards the end of the 1964 season. He would be joined by left-hander Steve Hamilton, and right-handers Hal Reniff, Jack Cullen and Dooley Womack, who was a youngster brought up from the minor leagues.

The season got off to an inauspicious start when the Yankees lost their first three games, at home, to the Detroit Tigers. Whitey Ford lost the opener to Mickey Lolich by a score of 2–1, while Mel Stottlemyre and Bob Friend were the victims in a doubleheader sweep by Detroit two days later. The Yankees finally won their first game when Fritz Peterson defeated the Baltimore Orioles in New York's fourth game of the season. However, they went on to lose their next seven games and, 11 games into the season, their record stood at 1–10 and they were in tenth and last place, 8½ games out of first.

To make matters worse, the Yankees were forced to compete without some of their key players for extended periods of time. Jim Bouton had been very slow in recovering from his arm problems, and he was lost to the team for the first two months of the season. Whitey Ford was pitching at less than 100 percent, and it appeared to be just a matter of time before he would have to be removed from the starting rotation. In addition, a little over a week into the season, starting shortstop Ruben Amaro suffered a serious injury when, chasing after a pop fly, he collided with left-fielder Tom Tresh. Amaro missed the remainder of the season and, as a result, New York was forced to use a combination of Horace Clarke and regular third baseman Clete Boyer at the position for the rest of the year.

After 20 games, the Yankees' record stood at a dismal 4–16, and GM Ralph Houk decided to fire manager Johnny Keane and install himself as manager. The move seemed to pay off as the team went on a surge that saw them win 13 of their next 17 games, but, with their record standing at 17–20, that would be as close as they would get to the .500 mark all season. After the team's initial spurt following the managerial change, New York, once again, fell into a pattern of losing. They dropped 28 of their next 47 games and, at the All-Star break, their record stood at 36–48 and they were 20 games behind the first place Baltimore Orioles.

Two Yankees were selected to the American League All-Star team — an unusually low number, for them. Second baseman Bobby Richardson made his seventh and final All-Star appearance, and pitcher Mel Stottlemyre his second.

Shortly after the break, the Yankees went on another surge, winning a season-high six consecutive games at one point, to close to within six games of .500, at 43–49. However, the success was short-lived and the team struggled throughout the remainder of the season.

Although there was frequent tinkering with the roster throughout the year, nothing seemed to help. In mid-May, the Yankees purchased light-hitting shortstop Dick Schofield from the San Francisco Giants, but he had little impact and was eventually traded to the Dodgers on September 10.

On June 10, New York dealt pitchers Bill Stafford and Gil Blanco, and promising outfielder Roger Repoz to Kansas City for pitcher Fred Talbot and reserve catcher Billy Bryan. Talbot was a journeyman right-hander who had originally come up with the Chicago White Sox in 1963. After spending all of 1964 with the Sox, Talbot was dealt to the Athletics, for whom he finished 10–12 in 1965. Prior to his trade to the Yankees, Talbot had compiled a 4–4 record and 4.79 ERA for Kansas City. He was inserted into the starting rotation to replace the ailing Whitey Ford but finished with a very mediocre 7–7 record and 4.13 ERA for New York. In 69 at-bats, Bryan hit 4 home runs, knocked in 5 runs, and batted .217.

With regular third baseman Clete Boyer splitting time at shortstop with Horace Clarke, left-fielder Tom Tresh was given extensive playing time at third base. On those days when Tresh played third, his spot in left was taken by Roy White, who struggled in his first real opportunity to make an impression. After starting off the season strong, White ended up hitting 7 home runs, knocking in 20 runs, and batting only .225 in 316 at-bats. He did, however, lead the team with 14 stolen bases.

There were also several minor league call-ups, necessitated by the many injuries that had hit the team once more. Outfielders Steve Whitaker and John Miller joined the big club for the first time. Whitaker was a left-handed hitter with a big swing who the team hoped would be able to hit for power in Yankee Stadium. Although he frequently failed to make contact, striking out 24 times in only 114 at-bats and batting only .246, he did show some power, hitting 7 home runs and driving in 15 runs. Miller saw very limited action, coming to the plate only 23 times and getting only two hits. However, one of those hits was a home run that came in his very first major league at-bat, making him the first Yankee in history to accomplish the feat.

Two other late-season call-ups who would figure rather prominently in the Yankees' future were shortstop Bobby Murcer and pitcher Stan Bahnsen. Murcer batted only .174 in 69 at-bats, but continued to be heralded as the next great Yankee. Bahnsen was a hard-throwing right-hander who went 1–1 in his three starts, but who made quite an impression in his major league debut. On September 9, during a 2–1 Yankee victory at Fenway Park, pitching in relief, Bahnsen came in and struck out the side. Two of his victims were Boston sluggers Carl Yastrzemski and Tony Conigliaro.

Unfortunately, as had happened the previous season, many key players either had bad years or missed extensive playing time due to injuries. Tom Tresh, the team's best player in 1965, managed to hit 27 home runs but knocked in only 68 runs and batted just .233. Catcher Elston Howard, now being rested more frequently in favor of backup Jake Gibbs, finished with only 6 home runs and 35 runs batted in, along with a .256 batting average, in 410 at-bats.

In an all-too-familiar scenario, Mickey Mantle and Roger Maris both missed large portions of the season with injuries. Mantle was effective when he played, hitting 23 homers, driving in 56 runs, and batting .288 in only 333 at-bats. The problem was, it had become quite clear that he could no longer play everyday. At one point, he missed two weeks due to a hamstring pull; at another, he missed 12 games with a bad knee. Mantle now hobbled more noticeably than ever both in the field and on the bases. His range in the outfield was very limited, and he could no longer steal bases or take the extra base the way he once did.

Maris came to the plate only 348 times and finished with just 13 home runs, 43 runs batted in, and a .233 batting average. He had not fully regained the strength in his right hand following his 1965 injury and was no longer able to hit for power on a regular basis. In addition, the media had painted a very negative picture of him and the fans believed most of what they read. As a result, Maris—never a fan favorite to begin with—had become one of the most hated men in New York. He was booed mercilessly by the fans every time he came to the plate, and it had become apparent that his days in New York were numbered.

The pitching staff experienced its share of problems as well. Whitey Ford's circulatory problem had worsened and he was removed from the starting rotation in mid-May. Although he pitched fairly effectively out of the bullpen for much of the season, he was finally forced to have shoulder surgery on August 25. Ford finished the season with a 2–5 record and a 2.47 ERA.

Mel Stottlemyre, the ace of the staff a year earlier, had experienced adversity for the first time in his young career. He seemed to be having a difficult time getting his sinker-ball, which was his best pitch, to break down to opposing hitters the way he wanted it to. In particular, he struggled in the early innings of games when he was perhaps a bit too strong.

Stottlemyre found that, as the game wore on and he grew a bit tired, his ball had more of a tendency to break downward. If he was able to make it through the first couple of innings unscathed, he was usually able to pitch a good game. However, all too often in 1966 that was not the case. Stottlemyre finished the season with a record of 12–20 and an ERA of 3.80.

Al Downing, once again, failed to perform at the level the Yankees expected him to. His control improved somewhat, but his record didn't. He finished the season with a record of 10–11 and a 3.56 ERA. Jim Bouton returned to the starting rotation in June but was unable to return to his earlier form. Still experiencing soreness in his right (pitching) shoulder, he finished only 3–8, but did compile a rather impressive 2.69 ERA. And, in the bullpen, Pedro Ramos was not the stopper he had been since the Yankees had obtained him late in 1964. He finished the season with a record of 3–9, only 13 saves, and an ERA of 3.61.

While most of his teammates were struggling through sub-par seasons, Bobby Richardson decided to officially announce his retirement on August 31. He finished the season with 7 home runs, 42 runs batted in, 71 runs scored, and a .251 batting average, and was the only Yankee selected to The Sporting News All-Star team.

Yet, there were a few players on the team who had good seasons. Joe Pepitone was far more productive than he had been in 1965. Although he batted only .255, he led the team with 31 home runs, 83 runs batted in, and 85 runs scored. His 31 homers were good enough for fifth in the American League and, at the end of the season, he was awarded his second consecutive Gold Glove for his outstanding work at first base. On the Yankees, Pepitone was followed by Tresh (27) and Mantle (23) in homers, and by Tresh in both runs batted in (68) and runs scored (76). Mantle led the team in hitting, with a .288 average, while Richardson led in base hits, with 153.

On the mound, rookie Fritz Peterson was the most consistent Yankee starter, finishing 12–11, and leading the team with 11 complete games and an ERA of 3.31. In spite of his off year, Stottlemyre led the team with 3 shutouts and 251 innings pitched, while Downing led in strikeouts, with 152. In the bullpen, rookie Dooley Womack was outstanding. In 42 appearances, he compiled a 7–3 record, with 4 saves and a 2.64 ERA. Steve Hamilton, once again, excelled in his role as left-handed specialist, finishing with a record of 8–3, saving 3 games, and even throwing a complete game shutout in one of his three starts.

Nevertheless, the bad far outweighed the good and, by season's end, the Yankees had compiled the worst record in the American League, winning only 70 games, while losing 89, and finishing 26½ games behind the pennant-winning Baltimore Orioles. New York's performance against the American League champions that year, in head-to-head competition, was particularly embarrassing as Baltimore won 15 out of the 18 contests between the two teams. Of course, the Orioles had the best player in baseball that year in the great Frank Robinson, who won the league's triple crown, hitting 49 home runs, knocking in 122 runs, and batting .316.

Ironically, the Yankees ended up scoring the exact same number of runs (611) as they had the previous season, and hit 13 more home runs (162), finishing third in the league in that category. They also batted .235 as a team again, but that was only seventh best in the league and five points below the league average. In addition, the pitching staff's ERA was 3.41—13 points higher than it had been in 1965, and their 29 complete games were down 12 from the previous year, and only the seventh highest total in the league.

When all was said and done, the team that had come within one game of winning the World Series just two years earlier was now arguably the worst team in baseball. Like a captain deserting his sinking ship, on September 19, Dan Topping sold his 10 percent stock interest in the team to CBS and resigned as club president. He was to be succeeded by CBS executive Mike Burke, whose first move it was to hire Lee MacPhail as the team's new GM.

In addition to the retirement of Bobby Richardson, 1966 marked the last time either Clete Boyer or Roger Maris would wear a Yankee uniform. They would both be dealt to other teams during the off-season.

Casey Stengel once said of Bobby Richardson, "He don't smoke, he don't drink, and he still can't hit .250."[10]

That remark exemplifies the kind of relationship Richardson had with Stengel, who actually dealt with many of his players in the same manner. In comparing what it was like playing for Stengel to his years under Ralph Houk, the man who succeeded him as Yankee manager, Richardson stated, "Casey would get the most out of you, but he would do it in such a way that he would make you so mad you wanted to go out and prove him wrong. Ralph treated his players differently, and I enjoyed playing for him much more."[11]

Another reason why Richardson preferred playing for Houk was that the latter played him much more frequently. After late-season call-ups in both 1955 and 1956, Richardson came up to the Yankees for good in 1957.

However, at that time, the team had a glut of middle infielders that were capable of playing second base. Among others, there were Gil McDougald, Billy Martin, and Jerry Lumpe. As a result, Bobby saw only limited action at second base, starting sporadically, and being pinch-hit for frequently. However, after Lumpe and Martin were traded away, Richardson began to get more playing time in 1959. That season, he batted .301 in 469 at-bats.

However, it wasn't until Houk became manager in 1961 that Richardson became a full-time regular. Houk preferred to go with more of a set lineup than did Stengel, and one of the first things he did was to insert Tony Kubek at short and Richardson at second on an everyday basis, and place them both at the top of the batting order. The end result was the best double-play combination in the American League, with Richardson becoming one of the most durable players in the game.

From 1961 to 1966, Richardson missed only 31 of his team's 1,028 games and, in each of those seasons, amassed more than 600 at-bats and was selected to *The Sporting News* All-Star team. During that period, he led American League second basemen in double-plays four times and in putouts twice, and his 136 double-plays in 1961 are among the highest ever totaled by a second baseman. He won the Gold Glove award each year, from 1961 to 1965, and was selected to the American League All-Star team a total of seven times.

Friend and former teammate Tony Kubek showed his appreciation for what Richardson meant to the team when he said, "Bobby was really the leader of our infield. He was the guy who played every day, and played hurt. Bobby had as good a range as anybody in the game, turned two on the double-play as well as anybody, and had the leadership qualities that were admired by everybody in the clubhouse."[12]

The admiration and respect that Richardson's teammates had for him went beyond his playing ability. Although foul language between teammates has long-been an accepted practice, the other Yankee players knew how religious Bobby was and generally chose their words carefully around him. On one occasion, Moose Skowron was having a particularly difficult afternoon at the plate, and, after striking out for the third time in the game, let loose with a string of obscenities after entering the Yankee dugout. Yet, he had the presence of mind to interject an "Excuse me, Bobby" as he passed Richardson on the bench, before resuming his tirade as he continued on his way down to the other end of the dugout.[13]

Mickey Mantle was another who had a great deal of respect for Richardson. After he was voted the American League's Most Valuable Player in 1962, Mantle said that he thought the award should have gone to Richardson instead. Bobby, in his finest season, finished runner-up to

From 1961 to 1966, no one in baseball was more durable than Yankee second baseman Bobby Richardson. Always a clutch performer, Richardson was at his best in
post-season play.

Mickey in the voting. That year, Richardson established a Yankee record
with 692 at-bats, led the league with 209 hits, and finished seventh in batting average (.302), fourth in runs scored (99), fourth in doubles (38), and
ninth in total bases.

Mantle, in fact, often said that, if the game were on the line and the

Yankees needed a hit, the player he would want up was Richardson. Perhaps it was the latter's World Series record that prompted Mantle to feel that way because, although he was never thought of as being one of the more potent hitters in the Yankee lineup, Richardson was always at his best in the fall classic.

In 1960, against the Pirates, after hitting one home run and driving in only 26 runs in 150 games during the regular season, Richardson batted .367 with 11 hits, a grand slam, and eight runs scored. He set World Series records with 12 total RBI and 6 RBI in Game Three. In the process, he became the only player in baseball history to play on the losing team and still be voted Series MVP. The following year, against Cincinnati, Richardson established a record for most hits (9) in a five-game Series, while batting .391. Then, in the 1964 Series against the Cardinals, he tied the record for most hits in a seven-game Series (13). Overall, in 36 World Series games, Richardson batted .305, 39 points higher than his career batting average of .266.

When he retired at the end of the 1966 season, the Yankees sorely missed Richardson's consistency and leadership. He was only 31 years old and probably could have played another four or five seasons. However, as was mentioned earlier, he had grown weary of the constant travel associated with playing ball professionally and wanted to spend more time with his family. He also had other, more important interests. For awhile, he coached baseball at the University of South Carolina, and he eventually went into the ministry.

Of all the players on the Yankee pennant-winning teams of the early 1960s, none was more overlooked or underrated than Clete Boyer. There are a number of reasons why he was, for the most part, passed over, but Boyer was an integral part of the team that made it into the World Series each year, from 1960 to 1964, and was one of the finest third basemen of his day.

After spending parts of three seasons with the Kansas City Athletics, Boyer was traded to the Yankees prior to the start of the 1959 season. With Gil McDougald and Andy Carey already on the team, Boyer saw very limited action his first two seasons, shifting back and forth between third base and shortstop. However, once Ralph Houk took over as manager in 1961, he handed the third base job to Boyer. Over the next six seasons in New York, he established himself as one of the best third basemen in the game. He had his finest season with the Yankees in 1962, when he hit 18 home runs, knocked in 68 runs, scored 85 others, and batted a career-high .272. He also batted .318 against the Giants in the World Series that year and helped to win Game One with a seventh-inning home run.

However, Boyer always had the misfortune of being compared to, perhaps, the two finest third basemen of his time—Brooks Robinson and Ken Boyer. Brooks also played in the American League, was a better hitter than Clete, was generally considered to be a better fielder, and won the Gold Glove award annually. Brother Ken played in the National League, mostly with the Cardinals. Although not quite the fielder that Clete was, Ken was a much better hitter and, therefore, also received far more recognition.

Another reason why Clete was never given the credit he deserved was that the Yankee teams he played on had so many stars it was easy not to notice him. Mantle, Maris, Howard, Berra, and Skowron were more productive hitters and were far more glamorous. In addition, Boyer, a right-handed batter, was playing half his games in Yankee Stadium, with its *Death Valley* in left and left-center field. As a result, his power numbers and run production were reduced significantly from what they would have been had he played in almost any other ballpark.

Yet Boyer's teammates were well aware of what his contributions to the team were. In particular, they knew what an outstanding defensive third baseman he was. Although he was always ranked behind Brooks Robinson as a fielder, some of his teammates didn't agree.

In his book *Few And Chosen*, Whitey Ford describes Boyer as, "... the best third baseman I've seen, including Brooks Robinson."

Mickey Mantle said, "Cletis Boyer, I think, was as good a third baseman as Brooks Robinson, and I thought Brooks Robinson was great."[14]

While Robinson may have had a slight edge in quickness and reflexes, Boyer had something that Robinson lacked—a powerful throwing arm. Robinson always got rid of the ball quickly to make sure he got the out at first base, but didn't have a particularly strong arm. However, Boyer's arm was so strong that he frequently threw runners out from his knees. He could dive either into the shortstop hole, or down the third base line, and throw a base-runner out from a kneeling position.

Robinson himself said, "I've seen a lot of great third basemen, but none better than Clete Boyer. In the sixties, I thought Boyer was the best I ever played against."[15]

After being traded to the Braves after the 1966 season, Boyer had his most productive offensive season. Away from Yankee Stadium and its far-reaching fences, he established career-highs in home runs (26) and runs batted in (96) in 1967. Two years later, he won the only Gold Glove of his career.

After five seasons with the Braves, he played for Hawaii in the Pacific Coast League, where he became the first American professional to be traded

Perhaps the most underrated of all the players on the Yankees' championship teams of the early 1960s, Clete Boyer was considered the equal of Brooks Robinson, defensively, by some of his teammates. It took New York seven years to find a suitable replacement for Boyer at third base after he was traded to the Braves for outfielder Bill Robinson at the end of the 1966 season.

to a Japanese league when he was dealt to the Tayio Whales. After his career was over, Boyer coached for both the Oakland A's and Yankees during the 1980s.

Roger Maris may very well have been the most misunderstood and misrepresented athlete of his time. While he was portrayed by the media as being sullen, moody, and arrogant, he, in reality, was someone who was quiet, shy, painfully honest, and completely unpretentious.

Maris was a small-town boy who was originally from Fargo, North Dakota. In 1953, he signed with the Cleveland Indians right out of high school for a $5,000 bonus after turning down an athletic scholarship from the University of Oklahoma. At Keokuk, in 1954, manager Jo Jo White taught him to pull, and Maris hit 32 home runs. He broke into the major leagues with the Indians by going 3–for-5 on Opening Day 1957 against the White Sox, and the next day hit his first big league home run, a grand slam game-winner, in the top of the 11th inning. He went on to hit 14 home runs in his rookie year, but was traded prior to the start of the 1958 season after alienating the Cleveland front office by refusing to play winter ball at the end of the 1957 season. He was acquired by the Kansas City Athletics, along with

Preston Ward and Dick Tomanek, for All-Star first baseman Vic Power and slugging outfielder Woody Held.

Maris thrived in Kansas City, hitting 28 home runs his first year there and making the All-Star team his second. He was very happy playing in the small midwestern town and expected to spend the remainder of his career there. However, in those days, the Yankees dealt with Kansas City quite frequently, practically treating them as their minor league affiliate. The New York brass looked at the short, compact swing of the left-handed, pull-hitting Maris and

Just five years after breaking Babe Ruth's single-season home run record and winning his second consecutive American League MVP award, Roger Maris was traded to St. Louis for journeyman third basemen Charley Smith. Maris went on to help the Cardinals to two pennants and one world championship in his final two seasons.

felt that it would be perfect for the short right-field porch in Yankee Stadium. So, after finishing third in 1959, the Yankees obtained Maris from Kansas City, along with backup first baseman Kent Hadley and utility infielder Joe DeMaestri, for Don Larsen, Hank Bauer, Marv Throneberry, and Norm Siebern.

Upon his arrival in the big city, the always honest Maris immediately alienated much of the New York press corps by telling them, in no uncertain terms, that he had been quite happy in Kansas City and really did not want to leave. Nevertheless, the lopsided deal paid huge dividends for the

Yankees as Maris hit 39 home runs in his first year with the team and edged out teammate Mickey Mantle by three points in the league MVP voting. Maris also led the league in runs batted in (112) and slugging percentage (.581), finished second in runs scored (98), and won a Gold Glove for his outstanding play in right-field.

However, a strange thing happened that year. Up until then, as great as he was, Mickey Mantle had been booed by the New York fans for much of his career. He had so much natural ability, the fans always expected him to produce, and they frequently jeered him after he struck out, something he did more frequently than any other player had, up to then. But, during the 1960 season, a home run race developed between the two, with Mantle's final total of 40 edging Maris out by 1 for the league lead. Many of the fans chose sides, and, with Mantle being the "home-grown Yankee," he suddenly became the fan favorite. The situation was exacerbated even further the following year when the two men waged their assault on Babe Ruth's single-season home run record of 60. Most of the New York fans, and even the players, felt that Mantle should be the one to break the record since he had been with the team for so long. In addition, many people felt that this .260–.270 hitter was unworthy of breaking the great Babe Ruth's record. He had been cast as an outsider and as a usurper, and no matter what he did from that point on, it would not have been good enough.

In that 1961 season, Maris led the American League with 61 home runs, 142 runs batted in, and 132 runs scored, and won his second consecutive MVP Award. However, many people thought it was a fluke, and when Maris hit "only" 33 home runs the following year, they were vindicated, and he became the object of their wrath. However, there were other factors that greatly contributed to the lack of popularity that Maris experienced with the fans.

During that 1961 season, as Maris drew closer and closer to Ruth's cherished record, the pressure he endured intensified tremendously, and the number of interview requests he had to comply with became almost unbearable. Over the years, Mantle had become accustomed to dealing with the constant media attention that came with being a New York sports hero. In fact, he had even come to enjoy it. He had reached a point where he knew the kinds of answers the press was looking for, and he graciously accommodated them. Maris, however, never felt comfortable in the spotlight. He was shy, quiet, unassuming, and lacked Mantle's charisma. He was a ballplayer, and that was all he wanted to be. When he was asked questions by the media, he gave them short, honest answers. If he thought that the question asked of him was a stupid one, he would say so. He felt extremely uncomfortable being questioned by large groups of reporters, and was much better in one-on-one interviews. But, he always remembered if a reporter had written something about him that he felt had misquoted, or misrepresented him. Once that happened, he would no longer speak to the reporter. As a result, some members of the press started to portray him as being a sullen and moody snob.

To make matters worse, the Yankees, completely unprepared for the media circus, gave him no help, offered no protection, and set no guidelines. As Maris would say in later years, the Yankee public relations department, basically, let him hang out to dry. Maris, stubborn, suspicious, and lacking tact, was ill prepared for the entire ordeal, and did not know how to deal with it. As he became more and more irritable, he became more suspicious and granted fewer interview requests. However, when he snubbed powerful sportswriter Jimmy Cannon, who was extremely influential, Cannon wrote a scathing article on Maris, causing much of the public to view him inaccurately.

It was, therefore, not very difficult for the New York fans to become suspicious of Maris when it came to the severity of his injuries. In June of 1965, he broke his hand sliding into home plate and lost much of the strength in the hand. X-rays taken did not show the break, and Maris was subsequently listed as day-to-day. When he sat on the bench, unable to play, the fans began to question his injury, and the already antagonistic press only added fuel to the fire. Maris also felt that club officials minimized the severity of that, and other injuries he had sustained, and sometimes did not even seem to believe he was hurt. Finally, another X-ray was taken that showed a small fracture of a bone in the hand that required surgery at the end of the season. However, the damage had already been done, and Maris' relationship with the fans, the press, and the Yankee front office was even worse than it had been before.

However, Maris' teammates had a different perception of the man. Bobby Richardson, who played with Maris for seven seasons, said, "He was the most reserved, quiet individual I think I ever knew, so the press' portrayal of him was not the real Roger Maris."[16]

Clete Boyer said of his former teammate, "The guy was a great player. They like to say that 1961 was a fluke, but Roger hit 39 homers and was the American League MVP in 1960. Not too many stiffs become back-to-back MVPs."[17]

In his book *Few And Chosen*, Whitey Ford discusses Maris: "He was fast, and he was a great base-runner with excellent instincts when it came to taking the extra base. And he was as good as I've seen at breaking up the double play."

Moose Skowron said of Maris: "He could run, he could throw, he could hit ... great defensive outfielder. He did the little things to win a ballgame ... and the writers crucified him ... no way."[18]

In speaking of Maris, Mickey Mantle said, "When people think of Roger, they think of the 61 home runs, but Roger Maris was one of the best all-around players I ever saw. He was as good a fielder as I ever saw, he had a great arm, he was a great base-runner—I never saw him make a mistake on the bases—and he was a great teammate. Everybody liked him."[19]

Perhaps Gil McDougald said it best when he said, "Roger was the everyday ballplayer that every manager would like to see on a ballclub."[20]

One more thing about Maris—he was a winner. He played in more World Series than any other player in the 1960s. In addition to his five World Series appearances with the Yankees, he helped the St. Louis Cardinals to both the 1967 and 1968 pennants. In fact, in the Cardinals' seven-game victory over the Boston Red Sox in the 1967 Series, Maris batted .385, with 10 hits and 7 runs batted in.

After staying away from Yankee Stadium for more than a decade, declining numerous invitations to Old-Timer's Day, Maris agreed to come back when George Steinbrenner donated money to build a stadium in Gainesville, Florida, where the former player had been residing. He made his return on opening day, 1978, fittingly raising the Yankees' 1977 championship flag with Mickey Mantle, and being given a standing ovation when he was introduced to the crowd.

Maris was, once again, cheered loudly by the Yankee Stadium crowd in 1984, when he had his number retired, along with that of former teammate Elston Howard. During his acceptance speech, he showed the kind of emotion that he had never shown to the public before, and that they had always wanted to see from him.

Just one year later, shortly before his death from lymph-gland cancer in 1985, he said, "I always came across as being bitter. I'm not bitter. People were very reluctant to give me any credit. I thought hitting 60 home runs was something. But everyone shied off. Why, I don't know. Maybe I wasn't the chosen one, but I was the one who got the record."[21]

Season Highlights, Outstanding Performances, and Memorable Moments:

May 9   At Minneapolis, the Yankees edge the Twins, 3–2. Roger Maris, Mickey Mantle, and Joe Pepitone, with the game-winner in the ninth inning, hit homers for New York. The win marks the third consecutive victory for the team under new manager Ralph Houk.

May 22   At Yankee Stadium, New York completes a four-game sweep over the defending American League champion Minnesota Twins by winning both ends of a doubleheader, 5–3 and 2–1. In the first game, Mel Stottlemyre defeats Jim Mudcat Grant, while, in the second, Fritz Peterson bests Jim Merritt. The sweep gives the Yankees five straight victories.

May 25   At Yankee Stadium, the Yankees defeat the California Angels, 11–6, as Mickey Mantle hits two home runs, one off Dean Chance and the other off reliever Lew Burdette.

June 29   At Fenway Park, Mickey Mantle hits a three-run homer in the first inning, then sandwiches a homer between round trippers by Bobby Richardson and Joe Pepitone in the third inning in New York's 6–5 win over Boston. The consecutive trifecta was last done for the Yankees in 1947, when Charlie Keller, Joe DiMaggio, and Johnny Lindell accomplished the feat. Richardson finishes the game 5–for-5, while Mantle's two homers tie him with Babe Ruth for the most home runs (38) hit by a Red Sox opponent at Fenway Park.

July 3   At Robert F. Kennedy Stadium in Washington D.C., Mickey Mantle hits a first inning homer, and, for the second time in less than a week, hits three home runs in consecutive times at bat. New York squanders a 5–0 lead in the eighth inning as the Senators storm back, but Bobby Richardson's home run in the eleventh inning gives the Yankees a 6–5 victory.

July 7   At Yankee Stadium, New York scores two runs in the bottom of the ninth inning to tie Boston, 2–2. Then, with two men out and two men on, Mickey Mantle breaks a 1–for-17 slump with a three-run home run into the right-field stands to give the Yankees a 5–2 win.

July 8   Mickey Mantle stars in a doubleheader split with the Senators at Yankee Stadium. The Yankees lose the first game, 7–6, but come back to win the nightcap, 7–5. Mantle goes 5–for-8 in the doubleheader, hitting a homer in each game. The second home run, off Jim Hannan, clears the 461–foot sign behind the monuments in dead center-field and lands in the bleachers.

July 21   At Yankee Stadium, New York defeats the Athletics, 4–3, behind Fritz Peterson. The victory is the Yankees' sixth consecutive, which will turn out to be the longest winning streak the team will put together all year.

July 23   At Yankee Stadium, New York celebrates Old-timers' Day but loses to the Angels, 7–6, despite a grand slam by Mickey Mantle. The slam is the ninth of his career. Mantle also ties Babe Ruth in games played as a Yankee.

July 24   At Yankee Stadium, the Yankees sweep a doubleheader from the Angels, winning the first game, 9–1, behind Mel Stottlemyre, and the second, 4–1, with Steve Hamilton going the distance. Mickey Mantle hits his second home run in two days, and the 493rd of his career, tying him with Lou Gehrig for sixth place on the all-time list.

July 29   At Comiskey Park, the Yankees defeat the White Sox, 2–1, on Mickey Mantle's 14th homer in 24 games. The blast is the 494 of his career, and puts him ahead of Lou Gehrig into sixth place on the all-time list.

Sept. 11   In a 4–2 victory over the Red Sox at Fenway Park, rookie outfielder John Miller becomes the first Yankee in history to hit a home run in his first major league at-bat.

1966 American League Final Team Standings and Offensive Statistics

TEAM	G	W	L	PCT	GB	R	H	2B	3B	HR	BB	SO	SB	AVG	OBP	SLG
BAL	160	97	63	.606	—	755	1426	243	35	175	514	926	55	.258	.325	.409
MINN	162	89	73	.549	9	663	1341	219	33	144	513	844	67	.249	.319	.382
DET	162	88	74	.543	10	719	1383	224	45	179	551	987	41	.251	.323	.406
CHI	162	83	79	.512	15	574	1235	193	40	87	476	872	153	.231	.299	.331
CLE	162	81	81	.500	17	574	1300	156	25	155	450	914	53	.237	.299	.360
CAL	162	80	82	.494	18	604	1244	179	54	122	525	1062	80	.232	.305	.354
KC	160	74	86	.463	23	564	1259	212	56	70	421	982	132	.236	.295	.337
WASH	159	71	88	.447	25.5	557	1245	185	40	126	450	1069	53	.234	.296	.355
BOSTON	162	72	90	.444	26	655	1318	228	44	145	542	1020	35	.240	.312	.376
NY	159	70	89	.440	26.5	611	1254	182	36	162	485	817	49	.235	.302	.374
TOTAL						6276	13005	2021	408	1365	4927	9493	718	.240	.308	.369

Team Pitching and Fielding Statistics

TEAM	CG	SH	SV	IP	H	HR	BB	SO	ERA	FA	E	DP
BAL	32	13	51	1466	1267	127	514	1070	3.32	.981	115	142
MINN	21	11	28	1438	1246	139	392	1015	3.13	.977	139	118
DET	32	11	38	1454	1356	185	520	1026	3.85	.980	120	142
CHI	45	22	34	1475	1229	101	403	896	2.68	.976	159	149
CLE	41	15	28	1467	1260	129	489	1111	3.23	.978	138	132
CAL	41	12	40	1457	1364	136	511	836	3.56	.979	136	186
KC	39	11	47	1435	1281	106	630	854	3.56	.977	139	154
WASH	21	6	35	1419	1282	154	448	866	3.70	.977	142	139
BOSTON	33	10	31	1463	1402	164	577	977	3.92	.975	155	153
NY	18	7	32	1415	1318	124	443	842	3.41	.977	142	142
TOTAL	334	118	364	14492					3.44	.978	1385	1457

1966 New York Yankee Pitching Statistics

PLAYER	W	L	ERA	G	GS	CG	SHO	SV	IP	H	R	ER	BB	SO
Mel Stottlemyre	12	20	3.80	37	35	9	3	1	251	239	116	106	82	146
Fritz Peterson	12	11	3.31	34	32	11	2	0	215	196	89	79	40	96
Al Downing	10	11	3.56	30	30	1	0	0	200	178	90	79	79	152
Fred Talbot	7	7	4.13	23	19	3	0	0	124	123	59	57	45	48
Jim Bouton	3	8	2.69	24	19	3	0	1	120	117	49	36	38	65
Hal Reniff	3	7	3.21	56	0	0	0	9	95	80	37	34	49	79
Steve Hamilton	8	3	3.00	44	3	1	1	3	90	69	32	30	22	57
Pedro Ramos	3	9	3.61	52	1	0	0	13	89	98	43	36	18	58
Dooley Womack	7	3	2.64	42	1	0	0	4	75	52	25	22	23	50
Whitey Ford	2	5	2.47	22	9	0	0	0	73	79	33	20	24	43
Bob Friend	1	4	4.84	12	8	0	0	0	44	61	25	24	9	22
Stan Bahnsen	1	1	3.52	4	3	1	0	1	23	15	9	9	7	16
Jack Cullen	1	0	3.97	5	0	0	0	0	11	11	5	5	5	7
Bill Henry	0	0	0.00	2	0	0	0	0	3	0	0	0	2	3

1966 New York Yankee Hitting Statistics

PLAYER	AB	R	H	2B	3B	HR	RBI	BB	SO	SB	OBP	SLG	AVG
Bobby Richardson	610	71	153	21	3	7	42	25	28	6	.280	.330	.251
Joe Pepitone	585	85	149	21	4	31	83	29	58	4	.290	.463	.255
Tom Tresh	537	76	125	12	4	27	68	86	89	5	.341	.421	.233
Clete Boyer	500	59	120	22	4	14	57	46	48	6	.303	.384	.240
Elston Howard	410	38	105	19	2	6	35	37	65	0	.317	.356	.256
Roger Maris	348	37	81	9	2	13	43	36	60	0	.307	.382	.233
Mickey Mantle	333	40	96	12	1	23	56	57	76	1	.389	.538	.288
Roy White	316	39	71	13	2	7	20	37	43	14	.308	.345	.225
Horace Clarke	312	37	83	10	4	6	28	27	24	5	.324	.381	.266
Jake Gibbs	182	19	47	6	0	3	20	19	16	5	.327	.341	.258
Lou Clinton	159	18	35	10	2	5	21	16	27	0	.288	.403	.220
Hector Lopez	117	14	25	4	1	4	16	8	20	0	.268	.368	.214
Steve Whitaker	114	15	28	3	2	7	15	9	24	0	.306	.491	.246
Mel Stottlemyre	80	8	11	1	1	1	7	4	31	0	.176	.213	.138
Ray Barker	75	11	14	5	0	3	13	4	20	0	.225	.373	.187
Al Downing	70	4	7	0	1	0	7	4	30	0	.149	.129	.100
Bill Bryan	69	5	15	2	0	4	5	5	19	0	.270	.420	.217
Bobby Murcer	69	3	12	1	1	0	5	4	5	2	.219	.217	.174
Fritz Peterson	67	4	15	5	0	0	0	2	19	0	.246	.299	.224
Dick Schofield	58	5	9	2	0	0	2	9	8	0	.265	.190	.155
Roger Repoz	43	4	15	4	1	0	9	4	8	0	.396	.488	.349
Mike Hegan	39	7	8	0	1	0	2	7	11	1	.326	.256	.205
Jim Bouton	38	1	4	0	0	0	4	1	23	0	.128	.105	.105
Fred Talbot	35	4	5	0	0	0	3	5	15	0	.268	.143	.143
Mike Ferraro	28	4	5	0	0	0	0	3	3	0	.281	.179	.179
Ruben Amaro	23	0	5	0	0	0	3	0	2	0	.217	.217	.217
John Miller	23	1	2	0	0	1	2	0	9	0	.087	.217	.087
Steve Hamilton	19	1	1	0	0	0	1	0	2	0	.053	.053	.053
Whitey Ford	18	0	0	0	0	0	0	1	6	0	.053	.000	.000
Hal Reniff	14	1	4	0	0	0	2	0	8	0	.286	.286	.286
Pedro Ramos	13	0	2	0	0	0	0	0	8	0	.154	.154	.154

PLAYER	AB	R	H	2B	3B	HR	RBI	BB	SO	SB	OBP	SLG	AVG
Bob Friend	11	0	0	0	0	0	0	0	5	0	.000	.000	.000
Stan Bahnsen	7	0	1	0	0	0	0	0	5	0	.143	.143	.143
Dooley Womack	5	0	1	0	0	0	0	0	0	0	.200	.200	.200

FIVE

1967: Farewell Ellie and Whitey

If nothing else, the Yankees' disastrous 1966 season proved that 1965 was no fluke. The dynasty was over, and the team was old and lacking in many areas. Of the eight position players who had been in the starting lineup on Opening Day in 1966, only Joe Pepitone and Tom Tresh were under 30 years of age. Mantle, Maris, Howard, and Ford were clearly in the twilight of their careers. Bobby Richardson had retired, shortstop Ruben Amaro had missed all but 14 games due to injury, and he was a light hitter to begin with. After a brilliant 1965 season, Mel Stottlemyre had struggled through much of 1966, losing 20 games. Al Downing had suffered through his second consecutive season with a losing record, and Jim Bouton continued to be plagued by arm problems. The team needed help, but there appeared to be little on the horizon. Other than Stottlemyre and Fritz Peterson, none of the younger players the team had promoted to the big club over the last three seasons had given any indication that they were capable of succeeding at the major league level. Something definitely needed to be done if the Yankees were, once again, going to be competitive.

The changes started early in the off-season when, on November 29, the Yankees traded third baseman Clete Boyer to the Braves for top outfield prospect Bill Robinson. Robinson was a right-handed hitter with good power and speed who had a strong and accurate throwing arm. After the Yankees acquired him, they began touting him as "the next Mickey Mantle."

A little over a week later, on December 8, New York attempted to fill the vacancy left at third base with the departure of Boyer by making a trade with the St. Louis Cardinals for journeyman third baseman Charley Smith. Smith's best season had come in 1964 when he had hit 20 home runs and knocked in 58 runs, but batted only .238 for the Mets. He had been traded from the Mets to the Cardinals, along with left-handed pitcher Al Jackson, following the 1965 season for 1964 National League MVP Ken Boyer. With St. Louis in 1966, Smith had hit only 10 home runs and driven in just 43 runs, while batting .266 in 391 at-bats. To obtain Smith, however, the Yankees parted with Roger Maris, which is a rather good indication of how far the latter's value had dropped in the eyes of his employers in recent years, and, also, of how desperate both sides were to part ways.

Just two days later, the team dealt former bullpen closer Pedro Ramos to the Phillies for right-handed starter/reliever Joe Verbanic. The wheeling and dealing continued on December 20 when New York acquired infielder Dick Howser from Cleveland for minor leaguer Gil Downs and cash. In 1961, as a member of the Kansas City Athletics, Howser had been named the American League's Rookie of the Year when he batted .280, stole 37 bases, and scored 108 runs. However, since then, he had been a regular player only one other season, and the Yankees intended to use him more as a utility player.

So, the Yankee team that entered spring training in 1967 was a far different one from just a year earlier. In addition, after the players arrived in Florida, manager Ralph Houk announced that he was going to try an experiment that would shift Mickey Mantle to first base and Joe Pepitone to centerfield. The idea was to save wear and tear on Mantle's oft-injured legs, allow his bat to remain in the lineup more often, and prolong his career, since it had become quite clear that he could no longer play the outfield on a regular basis. Mantle had never played the position before, but was receptive to the idea. Pepitone had shown earlier in his career, when he had been asked to occasionally play there, that he was quite capable of playing the outfield. Therefore, the adjustment would be a lesser one for him. The experiment seemed to work as both players handled themselves admirably at their new positions. Mantle showed soft hands and good footwork around the bag, and Pepitone had good speed and a strong throwing arm. Yet, several other questions still needed to be answered prior to the start of the regular season.

The first of these was whether or not the team would be able to find a suitable replacement for Bobby Richardson at second base. The plan was to give Horace Clarke a shot at the job, but he had played mostly shortstop the prior two seasons and had never played regularly at the major league level before. Would he be able to get the job done?

At shortstop, Ruben Amaro was attempting a comeback from an injury that had sidelined him for most of the 1966 season. How would he perform? How much would the team miss Clete Boyer at third base? Could Charley Smith hit and field well enough to justify the trade that brought him here?

Behind the plate, the intent was to give Jake Gibbs more playing time in order to give the 38 year-old body of Elston Howard more rest. The hope was that, with more days off, Howard would be more productive at the bat than he had been the previous year, when he hit only 6 home runs and drove in just 35 runs in 410 at-bats.

Tom Tresh would be back in left-field and it was hoped that he would perform better than he had last year, when he batted only .233. The Yankees were counting on a return to his 1965 form. Pepitone would be in center, and it was hoped that either Bill Robinson or Steve Whitaker, who had shown some power potential the previous year, would lay claim to the right-field job. Reserves would include Ray Barker at first base, Dick Howser in the infield, Billy Bryan at catcher, and Roy White in the outfield.

On the mound, New York was looking for Mel Stottlemyre to bounce back from his sub-par 1966 season, and for Fritz Peterson to continue with his progression. The team was also hoping that Al Downing would finally live up to his potential and that Whitey Ford would be able to return to the starting rotation after his season-ending surgery. The team was not as optimistic about the return of Jim Bouton, however, who was still struggling to regain the strength in his right arm. If he could not make it back, his spot in the rotation would be taken by Fred Talbot.

In the bullpen, with Pedro Ramos gone, New York was counting heavily on the combination of Hal Reniff, Steve Hamilton, and Dooley Womack, the right-hander who had performed so admirably in his rookie season. Youngsters Joe Verbanic and Thad Tillotson would complete the staff.

The Yankees got off to a good start in the regular season, defeating the Washington Senators at RFK Stadium, 8–0, on a two-hit shutout by Mel Stottlemyre. After dropping their next two decisions, New York won their next three, leaving their record at 4–2. The team continued to play well through the first two weeks of the season, compiling a record of 9–5 after 14 games.

However, the optimism that was created by the fast start soon faded as the team started to slump. After losing 8 of their next 12 games, the Yankees' record stood at a decidedly mediocre 13–13. The team continued to play .500 ball over the next few weeks, and, after 50 games, their record was 25–25, and they were 5½ games out of first place. However, that would be the last time all year their winning percentage would be as high as .500. After dropping 10 of their next 13 decisions, including 5 successive losses to the White Sox and Red Sox, the Yankees' record was 28–35, and they were 10½ games out of first place and, ostensibly, eliminated from the pennant race. At the end of play on July 9, prior to the All-Star break, New York's record stood at 36–45.

Two Yankees were selected to the American League All-Star team. Al Downing, who was having a fine season, was selected for the first time in his career. Mickey Mantle was also selected, but that was more out of respect than anything else since he was not having an All-Star type of season. He would finish the year with only 22 home runs, 55 runs batted in, and a .245 batting average, although he did manage to finish second in the league, with 107 walks.

Several things happened during the first half of the season to contribute to New York's lack of success. To begin with, several players who the team was counting on to perform well were not doing as well as expected. Joe Pepitone, who one year earlier had led the team with 31 home runs and 83 runs batted in, was slumping. He finished the season with only 13 home runs and 64 runs batted in. Tom Tresh continued his downward spiral, hitting only 14 homers, driving in just 53 runs, and batting only .219 for the season. Ruben Amaro provided adequate defense at shortstop, but brought little to the offense, batting only .223, with just 1 home run and 17 runs batted in all year.

While Roger Maris had a good year for the St. Louis Cardinals, helping them win the National League pennant, Charley Smith — the man he was traded for — did little to justify the deal from the Yankees' perspective. He hit 9 home runs, drove in 38 runs, and batted .224 on the season.

However, an even bigger disappointment was outfielder Bill Robinson. He seemed to struggle tremendously with his self-confidence, and with the pressure he put on himself to live up to the hype that his new team had given him. In 342 at-bats, he hit only 7 homers, drove in just 29 runs, and batted a meager .196. By season's end, he was usually benched in favor of either Steve Whitaker or Roy White, neither of whom was particularly impressive either. Whitaker, in 441 at-bats, hit 11 homers, knocked in 50 runs, and batted .243. White, in just 214 at-bats, hit 2 homers, drove in 18 runs, and batted .224.

The Yankees' pitching wasn't bad. The team ERA of 3.24 was fourth best in the league. However, the team's offense was anemic. While offensive productivity was down slightly from the previous year throughout all of baseball, the Yankees' disparity was greater. Their 522 runs scored were 89 less than they had scored in 1966 and were the lowest total in the league. Their 100 home runs were down 62 from the previous year and placed them eighth in the A.L., while their .225 team batting average was down ten points from 1966, tied them for eighth best in the league, and was eleven points below the league average.

The saddest thing, though, was that two players who had meant so much to the Yankees over the years wound up playing their final games with the team. On May 30, Whitey Ford, nearing 41, announced that he was retiring from baseball due to an elbow injury. Ford had pitched effectively during the season, when he was able to pitch, going 2–4, with a 1.64 ERA in his seven starts. However, the pain in his pitching arm had become too great and he knew that the time had come for him to walk away from the game.

In addition, on August 3, the Yankees traded Elston Howard to, of all teams, the Boston Red Sox for cash and two players to be named later. In 199 at-bats with New York, Howard had hit 3 home runs, driven in 17 runs, and batted just .196. He wound up hitting just .147 for the Red Sox over the last two months of the season, but provided leadership and guidance for their pitching staff in helping them to the A.L. pennant. Of course, the key to the Red Sox' success in 1967 was left-fielder Carl Yastrzemski, who won the league's triple crown by hitting 44 home runs, driving in 121 runs, and batting .326 on his way to being named league MVP. One of the players the Yankees received in exchange for Howard was catcher Bob Tillman, who hit .254 with 2 homers and 9 runs batted in for New York, in 63 at-bats.

Other disappointments were Jim Bouton and Fritz Peterson. Due to the persistent arm problems he had been experiencing, Bouton was able to appear in only 17 games all year, and started only one of those. He finished the season with a 1–0 record and a 4.57 ERA, and it looked like his brief career might be drawing to a close. Peterson, after leading the team in wins and ERA in his rookie season, finished with a record of 8–14 and an ERA of 3.47.

The Yankees tried to compensate for the losses of Ford and Bouton by inserting other pitchers into their spots in the starting rotation. However, none of those men fared particularly well. Fred Talbot, in his 22 starts, finished 6–8, with a 4.22 ERA.

Steve Barber was acquired during the first half of the season from the Baltimore Orioles. The hard-throwing left-hander had originally come up with the Orioles in 1960 and had had some fine seasons in Baltimore. In 1961, he finished 18–12, with a 3.33 ERA. Two seasons later, he had his best year as he compiled a record of 20–13, with an ERA of 2.75 and 180 strikeouts. In fact, as recently as 1965, Barber had gone 15–10, with a 2.69 ERA. However, since then he had developed control problems, and, in just 75 innings of work with Baltimore prior to the trade, had walked 61 batters and compiled a 4–9 record and 4.10 ERA. He fared no better in New York, making 17 starts in a Yankee uniform and finishing 6–9, with a 4.05 ERA, while walking 54 batters in only 97 innings.

Thad Tillotson, pitching both in relief and as a starter, finished 3–9, with a 4.03 ERA. At one point, after winning his first three decisions, Tillotson tied Bill Hogg's 1908 Yankee record for consecutive losses by dropping nine straight.

Bill Monboquette, however, fared slightly better . Monboquette, earlier in his career, had been the ace of weak Red Sox teams, winning as many as 20 games in 1963 and being selected to four All-Star teams. In fact, even though he was not a fastball pitcher, relying more on changing speeds and good control, he had once struck out 17 Washington Senators in a nine-inning game, in 1961. After the Yankees acquired him from the Detroit Tigers during the season, he assumed a dual role as a starter/reliever and compiled a 6–5 record and a 2.36 ERA in 10 starts and 23 relief appearances.

Other players who joined the team during the season included infielders John Kennedy and Jerry Kenney, first basemen Mike Hegan and Frank Tepedino, catcher Frank Fernandez, and outfielder Tom Shopay. Kennedy was acquired via a trade, while the others were all minor league call-ups.

Kennedy and Hegan were the only members of the group that saw a significant amount of playing time. Kennedy filled in at shortstop and third base and, in 179 at-bats, hit one home run, drove in 17 runs, and batted .196. Hegan, the son of then Yankee bullpen coach and former big league catcher Jim Hegan, was an excellent-fielding first baseman who, in 118 at-bats, hit 1 home run, drove in 3 runs, and batted .136.

Kenney was a young shortstop who had come up through the minor league system. He was a left-handed batter with exceptional running speed. He showed some potential following his late-season call-up, hitting .310 in 58 at-bats, stealing two bases, and hitting an inside-the-park home run.

Tepedino was a left-handed batter with a sweet swing. While most reports on him said "good hit, no field," he was still considered to be a top prospect since he had hit well at every level in the minors. In very limited duty, he batted .400, totaling 2 hits in 5 at-bats.

Fernandez was a powerfully-built right-handed hitting catcher who the Yankees hoped would eventually be able to take over most of the catching duties. The biggest concern regarding him, though, was his inability to make consistent contact at the plate. In his 28 at-bats with the big club he struck out 7 times, batted .214, and hit his first major league home run.

Shopay was a smallish outfielder with pretty good speed and a nice left-handed swing. He was not considered to be an upper echelon prospect, but the Yankees hoped that he might eventually develop into a good platoon player. He showed some potential, hitting 2 home runs, driving in 6 runs, and batting .296 in his 27 at-bats.

None of these additions seemed to help at all, though, as the Yankees continued to flounder during the second half of the season. New York won only 36 of its remaining 81 games to finish with a final record of 72–90, in ninth place in the American League standings, 20 games behind the first place Boston Red Sox. In head-to-head competition with the league champions, the Yankees finished a dismal 6–12. However, they were even worse against the Orioles, who once again dominated the season series against New York, winning 13 of their 18 games. Yet, there were some solid performers on the team.

While Mickey Mantle led the team with 22 home runs and Joe Pepitone finished first in runs batted in, with 64, Horace Clarke led in most other offensive categories. He led the team in batting average (.272), runs scored (74), base hits (160), and stolen bases (21). In addition, in 140 games at second base he committed only 8 errors, for an outstanding .990 fielding percentage. It appeared that he had staked his claim as the Yankees' second baseman of the future.

In addition, starting pitchers Al Downing and Mel Stottlemyre had outstanding seasons. Downing, apparently, had finally conquered the inconsistency and control problems that had plagued him for much of his career. Still possessing an excellent fastball, he had learned more how to change speeds and was no longer relying strictly on his fastball to get batters out in important situations. The results were obvious. In 201 innings of work, he surrendered just 158 hits and 61 walks, while striking out a team-leading 171 batters. He also led the staff with a 2.63 ERA, 4 shutouts, and 10 complete games. He finished the season with a won-lost record of 14–10, in spite of the fact he pitched for a team that scored the fewest runs in the American League.

Stottlemyre led the team with 15 wins and 255 innings pitched. He finished second to Downing on the team in ERA (2.96), and tied him for the team lead in shutouts and complete games. Although Stottlemyre's 15–15 record, on the surface, may not seem overly impressive, it must once again be stressed that the Yankees scored the fewest runs of any team in the league that year. Their 522 runs scored were *200 less* than the 722 scored by the highest scoring team in the league, the Boston Red Sox. Had either Downing or Stottlemyre pitched for a better team that year and received just an average amount of run support, there is a strong possibility that either man would have won 20 games.

In the bullpen, Dooley Womack assumed the role that Pedro Ramos had filled the prior two seasons, matching his then Yankee record of 65 total relief appearances. He finished the season with a 5–6 record, a 2.41 ERA, and 18 saves, good enough for fourth in the American League.

Right-hander Joe Verbanic also did well in his dual role as starter/reliever. In his 28 appearances—six as a starter—he compiled a 4–3 record, with a 2.80 ERA, 1 complete game, 1 shutout, and 2 saves.

Overall, though, the 1967 season was not a good one for the Yankees or their fans. Yet, in spite of the team's ninth-place finish, 1967 should be remembered mostly as having been a season of change, with the greatest of those changes being the departures of two longtime Yankees—Elston Howard and Whitey Ford.

It was Elston Howard's honor, and burden, to be the first black player to put on a New York Yankee uniform, for, while, in the world of black baseball, the honor of being the first black to play for the Yankees was a considerable one, it was also fraught with many obstacles and pitfalls.

The Yankees first purchased Elston Howard from the Kansas City Monarchs of the Negro Leagues in July of 1950, when he was 21 years old. However, Howard's road to the major leagues proved to be a long one as the Yankee front office was extremely hesitant to promote him to the big league club. In fact, they seemed more interested in slowing down his progression than anything else. It was not until 1953, when Howard was already 24 years old and playing at the Triple A level, that the organization decided to convert him into a catcher. The move was clearly designed to prolong his minor league career and make his path to success at the major league level a more difficult one since, not only would the transition to catcher be a difficult one, but, if successful, he would have to contend with future Hall of Fame catcher Yogi Berra for the starting job once he was finally called up by the big club. However, Howard, as he did with most things, took the move in stride because, more than anything, he wanted to play for the Yankees.

It was this desire to play for New York, and this ability to hold his anger inside of him and to control his emotions that made Elston Howard the perfect man to break the color barrier for the Yankees. While some men, such as former Yankee prospect Vic Power, who the team had traded away in 1953, were more outspoken and confrontational on matters of race, Howard preferred to walk away from controversy and keep everything bottled up inside. This had to make his career with the Yankees extremely unpleasant at times, but he always carried himself with dignity and class, and never let others see how much the injustices that he constantly had to endure bothered him inside.

As hard as the Yankee front office tried, though, by 1955, they could no longer delay his arrival to the major league club. That year, with Toronto of the International League, Howard hit 22 home runs, drove in 109 runs, and batted .330. He was finally called up to the Yankees that season and spent most of the next six seasons splitting time between catcher, first base, and the outfield, but never attaining full-time status. In fact, in only one season during his entire career was he able to accumulate as many as 500 official at-bats.

But his teammates saw the kind of ability he had, and knew how good he would have been had he been given more of an opportunity to play. Bobby Richardson, who spent his entire career playing with Howard, said, "I knew that Elston would have been a star on any other ballclub. When I first saw Elston and saw the tools that he had, I thought to myself, 'My goodness, the Yankees are certainly fortunate to have him'."[22]

It wasn't until 1961 that Howard was finally able to supplant Yogi Berra as the team's number one catcher. That year, in 446 at-bats, Howard hit 21 home runs, knocked in 77 runs, batted a career-high .348, and finished tenth in the league MVP voting. The following year, he hit another 21 home runs and knocked in a career-best 91 runs. By 1963, Howard had become quite possibly the best and most valuable player on the team. He had the admiration and respect of everyone on the team, and, at season's end, his leadership qualities were recognized when he was voted the American League's Most Valuable Player for his role in helping the Yankees to the A.L. pennant, even though they had been forced to play without Mantle and Maris for much of the season. Of course, he also put up good numbers that year, hitting 28 home runs, knocking in 85 runs, and batting .287. He also finished third in the voting the following year, when he batted .313 and drove in 84 runs.

Howard was selected to the American League All-Star team nine consecutive seasons, from 1957 to 1965, and was chosen for *The Sporting News* All-Star team at the end of the 1961, 1963, and 1964 seasons. He also won two Gold Glove Awards and was considered to be a superb handler of pitchers. In fact, even though he batted only .147 for the Red Sox in 1967 after they acquired him from the Yankees for their pennant drive, he was widely credited with stabilizing the team's pitching staff and providing much-needed leadership.

Tony Conigliaro, the former Boston outfielder who played with

Howard briefly, said, "I don't think I ever saw a pitcher shake off one of his signs. They had too much respect for him."[23]

Former Yankee relief pitcher Hal Reniff said of Howard, "Unless you pitched to him, you didn't know how good he was ... how agile he was behind the plate."[24]

Ex-reliever Bill Fischer said, "Ellie Howard was a winning player, an All-Star. He was probably overlooked because of those great Yankee teams he played on. He was a leader; he took charge."[25]

Roy White spoke of Howard's leadership qualities, and of the influence he had on him early in his career: "Ellie was great. Just a great guy ... a great gentleman; always going out of his way to give you some advice, or to help you; where to get around, where to go, how to dress. He never had anything bad to say about anybody."[26]

More than anything, though, Howard was a man of great inner strength, and with an undeniable ability to deal with adversity. Several years after he had joined the Yankees, Elston and his wife Arlene were at a dinner with Jackie and Rachel Robinson. Jackie, who had always resented the Yankees for their lack of interest in signing black players, told Elston how bigoted he felt the Yankees were as an organization and how he thought that, in some ways, what Ellie was going through was as hard or harder than

Despite having his New York arrival prolonged by the Yankees' front office during the 1950s, Elston Howard eventually became a true team leader and the best catcher in the American League.

what he had endured. At least Robinson had always known that the Dodger front office was behind him, whereas Howard knew that the Yankee front office had brought him up reluctantly.[27]

When Howard died in 1980 at just 50 years of age, the Yankee manager at the time was Dick Howser, who had both played and coached with Howard on the Yankees. In tribute to his former friend and colleague, Howser said, "Elston exemplified the Yankee class of the 1950s and 1960s. Class was the way to describe the guy. He epitomized the Yankee tradition. Everybody in baseball respected him."[28]

Whitey Ford was the greatest pitcher in New York Yankee history. He won more games (236), threw more shutouts (45), struck out more batters (1,956), and pitched more innings (3,171) than any other Yankee pitcher, and his .690 career winning percentage is the third highest in major league history, and the best among modern pitchers with 200 or more wins. It is just a shame that, during this period in Yankee history, he was merely a shell of his former self, and that the fans of my generation, who started watching the team during the mid-1960's, never got to see him at his best. For much of the 1950's and early 1960's, he was perhaps the finest pitcher in the American League and one of the very best in baseball.

Ford joined the Yankees for the first time during the 1950 season, when the team was in the middle of its run that would bring home a record five consecutive world championships. He won his first nine decisions before finally losing his first game, and finished the season with a 9–1 record and 2.81 ERA. In the World Series that year, he pitched 8⅔ innings without allowing an earned run to win the fourth game of a Yankee sweep over the Philadelphia Phillies. He spent 1951 and 1952 in the service, but returned to post 18–6 and 16–8 marks in 1953 and 1954.

Early in his career, Ford was fortunate enough to pitch for a team that already had three other outstanding starting pitchers on its staff in Allie Reynolds, Vic Raschi, and Eddie Lopat. As a result, manager Casey Stengel was able to work him into the rotation gradually and not put too much pressure on the youngster. Ford learned a great deal from these veteran pitchers and, in particular, fellow lefty Eddie Lopat was able to teach him many tricks of the trade.

However, by 1955, Ford had established himself as the Yankees' top pitcher, and as one of the best in the game. That year, his 18–7 record tied him for the league lead in wins, he led in complete games (18), was second in ERA (2.63), and he was selected to *The Sporting News* All-Star team for the first of four times during his career. In fact, that year, during the month of September, he pitched consecutive one-hitters.

Over the course of his career, Ford led American League pitchers in wins three times, ERA twice, innings pitched twice, shutouts twice, and complete games once. He was selected to the American League All-Star team eight times, finished in the top five in the league MVP voting twice, and won the Cy Young Award once.

Yet, had manager Casey Stengel not limited his starts for much of his career, there is a good chance that Ford's numbers would have been even better. Stengel preferred to start Ford every fifth or sixth day, manipulating his rotation so that the left-hander would be ready to start against the better teams in the league.

As Ford himself tells it, "Casey and Jim Turner (former Yankee pitching coach) … there were certain clubs they wanted me to pitch against. I know I would never miss Chicago, Cleveland, or Detroit. If I had to rest an extra day, they would do it in order for me to pitch against certain clubs."[29]

Another reason why Ford received more rest was that, in those days, the Yankees were so dominant that they could win the American League pennant and limit their players' statistics at the same time. Frequently, late in the season, if a pitcher was nearing 20 victories, either he would receive an inordinate amount of rest between starts, or the team that would be put behind him in the field was not the best the team had to offer. That way, his chances of winning 20 games would be greatly reduced, and the front office — notoriously cheap under then-GM George Weiss — would have more negotiating power at season's end when it came time to discuss next year's contract. The team usually had a sizeable lead in the pennant race by September, so it could usually afford to adopt this policy without jeopardizing its chances of going to the World Series. As a result, in his first nine big league seasons, Ford failed to win as many as 20 games even once.

However, when Ralph Houk took over as manager in 1961, he installed a regular four-man rotation and Ford started pitching on just three days' rest. That season, Ford made 39 starts, instead of the 30 or so he was accustomed to making. The result was the first 20–win season of his career, as he finished the season 25–4 and won the Cy Young Award. He also finished 24–7 in 1963 to win 20 games for the final time in his career.

Unfortunately, by 1964, Ford began experiencing circulatory problems in his pitching arm. Even though he had a fine season, going 17–6 with a 2.13 ERA, he was no longer able to do the things he had once done, and was forced to get by more on guile and courage than anything else. His inability to make more than one start in the World Series that year was a large part of the reason the Yankees wound up losing to the Cardinals, as Mel Stottlemyre was forced to make three starts, the last on only two days' rest.

Ford still had something left in 1965, going 16–13 that year, but, by 1966, the pain in his pitching arm had gotten so bad he could no longer pitch regularly. After undergoing shoulder surgery that year, he attempted a comeback in 1967 but realized that his pitching days were over. He announced his retirement during the season and was admitted to the Hall of Fame in 1974, with his close friend and teammate Mickey Mantle.

The reason Ford was able to get by as long as he

The greatest pitcher in Yankees history, Whitey Ford was forced to retire during the 1967 campaign due to persistent problems with his pitching arm.

could without his best stuff was that, even when he was at his best, he had always depended more on his intelligence and resourcefulness to get opposing batters out than on sheer physical ability. At 5'10" and 180 pounds, he was never a particularly hard thrower. But he handled himself on the mound like a surgeon, controlling games with his mastery of the mental aspects of pitching and with his pinpoint control. Batters had to deal with his wide variety of pitches, ranging from his outstanding changeup to his excellent curve and good fastball. He also had one of the league's best pick-off moves, and was an excellent fielder.

In speaking of one of the techniques he used to get opposing hitters out, Ford said, "You would be amazed how many important outs you can get by working the count down to where the hitter is sure you're going to throw to his weakness, and then throw to his power instead."[30]

As for his purported use of the spitter, Ford said, "I never threw the spitter, well maybe once or twice when I really needed to get a guy out real bad."[31]

Former manager Ralph Houk had high praise for the left-hander: "Whitey was the greatest pitcher that I ever managed, and, I think, one of the greatest pitchers that there's been around. He could make the hitter do almost anything he wanted him to do. He could throw his curveball, changeup, slider — anything he wanted, on any count."[32]

His teammates had the utmost confidence in his abilities. Johnny Blanchard, who occasionally caught Ford when neither Yogi Berra or Elston Howard did, said, "When you had Whitey bases loaded and nobody out, you were in trouble. That's how tough he was."[33]

Mickey Mantle said of him, "I don't care what the situation was, how high the stakes were — the bases could be loaded and the pennant riding on every pitch, it never bothered Whitey. He pitched his game. Cool. Crafty. Nerves of steel."[34]

Mantle added, "If the World Series was on the line and I could pick one pitcher to pitch the game, I'd choose Whitey Ford every time."[35]

Season Highlights, Outstanding Performances, and Memorable Moments:

April 10   On Opening Day at RFK Stadium in Washington, Mel Stottlemyre tosses a two-hit shutout as the Yankees defeat the Senators, 8–0. Bill Robinson collects two hits, including his first homer, and drives in two runs in his Yankee debut. Elston Howard also homers.

April 14   At Yankee Stadium, in New York's home opener, Red Sox rookie Bill Rohr debuts by taking a no-hitter into the 9th inning. Elston Howard spoils the no-hit bid by lining a 3–2 pitch for a single into right-center with two men out. The Red Sox win, 3–0, with Whitey Ford getting the loss.

April 15   After throwing a two-hit shutout against the Senators in Washington on Opening Day just five days earlier, Mel Stottlemyre tosses his second consecutive shutout. This time, the place is Yankee Stadium, the victims are the Boston Red Sox, who total just four hits, and the final score is 1–0.

April 16   At Yankee Stadium, the Red Sox and Yankees struggle for 18 innings before New York finally prevails, 7–6, in a game that lasts five hours and 50 minutes. Carl Yastrzemski and Tony Conigliaro of Boston each have five hits, but it is Joe Pepitone's two-out single that beats Lee Stange. Al Downing picks up the win in relief.

April 25   At Yankee Stadium, Whitey Ford beats the White Sox and Tommy John, 11–2, giving up eight hits to go 2–1 on the season. New York's offense is led by Charlie Smith, who collects four hits, and Dick Howser, who adds three. The win will turn out to be the last of Ford's career.

April 30   In the first game of a doubleheader at Yankee Stadium, Mickey Mantle breaks a 1–1 tie in the 10th inning with a three-run homer to give New York the victory. The Yankees drop the second game 4–2, but Mantle gets a pinch-hit double in the ninth inning to give him 2,215 career hits, one more than Joe DiMaggio.

May 14   In a 6–5 victory over the Baltimore Orioles at Yankee Stadium, Mickey Mantle becomes the sixth member of the 500–home run club. The historic blow comes batting left-handed off Stu Miller.

May 21   In the first game of a doubleheader split with Detroit at Tiger Stadium, Mickey Mantle hits his fifth homer in six games. However, the Yankees lose the game, 9–4, as Whitey Ford appears in his last major league game.

May 24   At Baltimore's Memorial Stadium, the Yankees defeat the Orioles, 2–0, on a two-hit shutout by Al Downing. The only runs of the game come in the third inning on a two-run homer by Mickey Mantle.

June 7   With the first pick of the free-agent draft, the Yankees select Georgia native Ron Blomberg.

July 7   At Baltimore's Memorial Stadium, the Yankees defeat the Orioles, 3–0, behind Al Downing, who goes the distance, allowing just 4 hits while striking out 12. Joe Pepitone's two-run homer in the eighth inning provides added insurance.

July 25   At Yankee Stadium, American League home run leader Harmon Killebrew gives the Twins a 1–0 lead with a 1st inning homer off Al Downing. Jim Kaat holds New York scoreless until two outs in the 9th inning when Mickey Mantle, batting right-handed, hits a ball over the 457–foot mark in left-center field to tie the score. The game is rained out with the score 1–1 and will be replayed on August 18. New York will win the replay, 1–0.

August 11 At Cleveland's Municipal Stadium, the Yankees sweep a doubleheader from the Indians, winning the first game, 5–3, behind Al Downing, and taking the nightcap, 4–1, with Mel Stottlemyre getting the best of Luis Tiant. In the 2nd inning of the first game, Downing strikes out the side on just nine pitches.

August 29 At Yankee Stadium, the Yankees and Red Sox tie a 62–year old American League record by playing 29 innings in a doubleheader. Boston wins the first game, 2–1, with eventual Cy Young Award winner Jim Lonborg out-dueling Mel Stottlemyre, but New York comes back to win the nightcap, 4–3, in 20 innings. Horace Clarke gets the game-winning single. The contest lasts 5:15 and is the third game this year of 18 innings or more for the Yankees.

Sept. 2   At Yankee Stadium, Washington's Bob Priddy loses his 1–0 lead to the Yankees in the 8th inning when Mickey Mantle hits a 2–run pinch-hit home run. The Yankees win the game, 2–1, as Mel Stottlemyre scatters six hits and does not walk anyone. It is Mantle's 14th game-winning hit of the year, eight of them home runs.

1967 American League Final Team Standings and Offensive Statistics

TEAM	G	W	L	PCT	GB	R	H	2B	3B	HR	BB	SO	SB	AVG	OBP	SLG
BOSTON	162	92	70	.568	—	722	1394	216	39	158	522	1020	68	.255	.323	.395
MINN	162	91	71	.562	1	671	1309	216	48	131	512	976	55	.240	.310	.369
DET	162	91	71	.562	1	683	1315	192	36	152	626	994	37	.243	.327	.376
CHI	162	89	73	.549	3	531	1209	181	34	89	480	849	124	.225	.293	.320
CAL	161	84	77	.522	7.5	567	1265	170	37	114	453	1021	40	.238	.302	.349
WASH	161	76	85	.472	15.5	550	1211	168	25	115	472	1037	53	.223	.289	.326
BAL	161	76	85	.472	15.5	654	1312	215	44	138	531	1002	54	.240	.313	.372
CLE	162	75	87	.463	17	559	1282	213	35	131	413	984	53	.235	.295	.359
NY	162	72	90	.444	20	522	1225	166	17	100	532	1043	63	.225	.298	.317
KC	161	62	99	.385	29.5	533	1244	212	50	69	452	1019	132	.233	.297	.330
TOTAL						5992	12766	1949	365	1197	4993	9945	679	.236	.305	.351

Team Pitching and Fielding Statistics

TEAM	CG	SH	SV	IP	H	HR	BB	SO	ERA	FA	E	DP
BOSTON	41	9	44	1459	1307	142	477	1010	3.36	.977	142	142
MINN	58	18	24	1461	1336	115	396	1089	3.14	.978	132	123
DET	46	17	40	1443	1230	151	472	1038	3.32	.978	132	126
CHI	36	24	39	1490	1197	87	465	927	2.45	.979	138	149
CAL	19	14	46	1430	1246	118	525	892	3.19	.982	111	135
WASH	24	14	39	1473	1334	113	495	878	3.38	.978	144	167
BAL	29	17	36	1457	1218	116	566	1034	3.32	.980	124	144
CLE	49	14	27	1477	1258	120	559	1189	3.25	.981	116	138
NY	37	16	27	1480	1375	110	480	898	3.24	.976	154	144
KC	26	10	34	1428	1265	125	558	990	3.68	.978	132	120
TOTAL	365	153	356	14601					3.23	.979	1325	1388

1967 New York Yankee Pitching Statistics

PLAYER	W	L	ERA	G	GS	CG	SHO	SV	IP	H	R	ER	BB	SO
Mel Stottlemyre	15	15	2.96	36	36	10	4	0	255	235	96	84	88	151
Al Downing	14	10	2.63	31	28	10	4	0	201	158	65	59	61	171
Fritz Peterson	8	14	3.47	36	30	6	1	0	181	179	88	70	43	102
Fred Talbot	6	8	4.22	29	22	2	0	0	138	132	78	65	54	61
Bill Monbouquette	6	5	2.36	33	10	2	1	1	133	122	39	35	17	53
Thad Tillotson	3	9	4.03	43	5	1	0	2	98	99	52	44	39	62
Steve Barber	6	9	4.05	17	17	3	1	0	97	103	47	44	54	70
Dooley Womack	5	6	2.41	65	0	0	0	18	97	80	33	26	35	57
Joe Verbanic	4	3	2.80	28	6	1	1	2	80	74	27	25	21	39
Steve Hamilton	2	4	3.48	44	0	0	0	4	62	57	25	24	23	55
Jim Bouton	1	0	4.67	17	1	0	0	0	44	47	31	23	18	31
Whitey Ford	2	4	1.64	7	7	2	1	0	44	40	11	8	9	21
Hal Reniff	0	2	4.28	24	0	0	0	0	40	40	22	19	14	24
Cecil Perkins	0	1	9.00	2	1	0	0	0	5	6	5	5	2	1
Dale Roberts	0	0	9.00	2	0	0	0	0	2	3	2	2	2	0

1967 New York Yankee Hitting Statistics

PLAYER	AB	R	H	2B	3B	HR	RBI	BB	SO	SB	OBP	SLG	AVG
Horace Clarke	588	74	160	17	0	3	29	42	64	21	.321	.316	.272
Joe Pepitone	501	45	126	18	3	13	64	34	62	1	.301	.377	.251
Tom Tresh	448	45	98	23	3	14	53	50	86	1	.301	.377	.219
Steve Whitaker	441	37	107	12	3	11	50	23	89	2	.283	.358	.243
Mickey Mantle	440	63	108	17	0	22	55	107	113	1	.391	.434	.245
Charley Smith	425	38	95	15	3	9	38	32	110	0	.278	.336	.224
Ruben Amaro	417	31	93	12	0	1	17	43	49	3	.297	.259	.223
Jake Gibbs	374	33	87	7	1	4	25	28	57	7	.291	.289	.233
Bill Robinson	342	31	67	6	1	7	29	28	56	2	.259	.281	.196
Roy White	214	22	48	8	0	2	18	19	25	10	.287	.290	.224
Elston Howard	199	13	39	6	0	3	17	12	36	0	.247	.271	.196
John Kennedy	179	22	35	4	0	1	17	17	35	2	.265	.235	.196
Dick Howser	149	18	40	6	0	0	10	25	15	1	.381	.309	.268
Mike Hegan	118	12	16	4	1	1	3	20	40	7	.266	.212	.136
Mel Stottlemyre	82	5	8	0	0	0	5	2	38	0	.119	.098	.098
Al Downing	66	5	8	1	0	1	2	5	29	0	.183	.182	.121
Bob Tillman	63	5	16	1	0	2	9	7	17	0	.324	.365	.254
Jerry Kenney	58	4	18	2	0	1	5	10	8	2	.412	.397	.310
Fritz Peterson	48	2	7	1	0	0	1	5	19	0	.226	.167	.146
Fred Talbot	38	3	6	0	1	1	2	6	13	0	.289	.289	.158
Bill Monbouquette	32	1	5	0	0	0	0	1	8	0	.182	.156	.156
Steve Barber	29	2	5	1	1	0	4	1	17	0	.200	.276	.172
Frank Fernandez	28	1	6	2	0	1	4	2	7	1	.281	.393	.214
Tom Shopay	27	2	8	1	0	2	6	1	5	2	.310	.556	.296
Ray Barker	26	2	2	0	0	0	0	3	5	0	.172	.077	.077
Joe Verbanic	18	1	2	1	0	0	2	0	7	0	.111	.167	.111
Thad Tillotson	16	1	1	0	0	0	0	1	12	0	.167	.063	.063
Dooley Womack	14	1	4	0	0	0	3	0	1	0	.286	.286	.286
Whitey Ford	13	0	2	0	0	0	0	0	4	0	.154	.154	.154
Billy Bryan	12	1	2	0	0	1	2	5	3	0	.412	.417	.167

PLAYER	AB	R	H	2B	3B	HR	RBI	BB	SO	SB	OBP	SLG	AVG
Steve Hamilton	9	0	1	0	0	0	0	0	1	0	.111	.111	.111
Ross Moschitto	9	1	1	0	0	0	0	1	2	0	.200	.111	.111
Jim Bouton	7	0	0	0	0	0	0	0	5	0	.125	.000	.000
Frank Tepedino	5	0	2	0	0	0	0	1	1	0	.500	.400	.400
Lou Clinton	4	1	2	1	0	0	2	1	1	0	.600	.750	.500

SIX

1968: The Year of the Pitcher

The Yankees' 72–90 record and ninth place finish in 1967 marked only the third time in franchise history that the team had finished below the .500 mark and in the American League's second division for three consecutive years, with the last time having been from 1912 to 1915. The front office knew that much work needed to be done if the team was going to be restored to prominence.

The offense was weak, with only second baseman Horace Clarke having a decent year in 1967. Joe Pepitone and Tom Tresh were talented players, but both were coming off sub-par seasons. The deals for third baseman Charley Smith and outfielder Bill Robinson had not panned out, and shortstop Ruben Amaro and catcher Jake Gibbs added virtually nothing to the offense. Outfield prospects Roy White and Steve Whitaker had yet to show that they could produce consistently at the major league level, and there was speculation that 1968 could be Mickey Mantle's last year.

The plight of the pitching staff was somewhat less ominous, but even that was not without its flaws. While Al Downing and Mel Stottlemyre had both performed admirably in 1967, second-year left-hander Fritz Peterson had struggled for much of the season, finishing with just an 8–14 record. In addition, the team was still searching for a reliable fourth starter to fill the void left by the retired Whitey Ford, since neither Fred Talbot nor Steve Barber had proven that they were capable of handling the responsibility. The bullpen was adequate, with Dooley Womack, Bill Monbouquette, Joe Verbanic, and Steve Hamilton providing decent support for the starters. However, it lacked that one man who could enter a game in the late innings with the team in front and practically guarantee victory.

While the front office was well aware of the team's shortcomings, it decided to adopt a somewhat different approach than it had the previous off-season, when it had gone on a trading spree, dealing away, among others, Roger Maris and Clete Boyer. This time, the philosophy instead was to promote from within and to see if any of the younger players already on the roster, or coming up from the minor leagues, could inject the team with some new life. The only deals that were made during this off-season were three relatively minor ones.

First, New York purchased 29 year-old switch-hitting shortstop Gene Michael from the Los Angeles Dodgers. Michael was a career minor leaguer who had come up through the Pittsburgh Pirates' organization. While he was smooth and graceful in the field, he had never been much of a hitter and, therefore, had languished in the minor leagues for several years. Finally, after a brief trial with the Pirates in 1966, he had been dealt to the Dodgers prior to the 1967 season. In 223 at-bats with Los Angeles, he batted only .202, with no home runs and 7 runs batted in. He was expected to compete with Ruben Amaro for the Yankees' starting shortstop job.

Then, the team traded back-up catcher Bob Tillman and pitcher Dale Roberts to the Braves for third baseman Bobby Cox. Cox had originally signed with the Dodgers, in 1959, for a $40,000 bonus. After spending seven mostly unproductive years in the Dodgers' farm system, the right-handed hitting Cox was traded to the Braves late in 1966. There, he spent the entire 1967 season in Richmond, since Atlanta had acquired Clete Boyer from the Yankees to play third base for them. Cox was not a particularly good hitter and did not have a great deal of range in the field, but he was a hard-nosed, scrappy kind of player who got the most out of his extremely limited natural ability. He would soon become a fan favorite with his aggressive style of play, and would wind up beating out incumbent Charley Smith for the third base job in New York.

The other deal involved 26 year-old right-handed hitting outfielder Andy Kosco, who was obtained from the Minnesota Twins. Kosco had never been given much of an opportunity to play in Minnesota due to the Twins' crowded outfield situation. With Bob Allison in left, Jimmie Hall in center, and perennial All-Star Tony Oliva in right, Kosco had been used sparingly the previous three seasons, never coming to the plate more than 158 times in any one season, and shuttling back and forth between the big league club and its top minor league affiliate much of the time. While, at 6'3" and over 200 pounds, Kosco was not particularly fleet afoot, he did have some pop in his bat, and the Yankees hoped that he would be able to provide them with some much-needed power, either in an outfield platoon situation, or off the bench.

Most of the other improvements to the team were expected to come from within the organization. First, it was hoped that Joe Pepitone and Tom Tresh would have better years than they did in 1967. After leading the team in both home runs and runs batted in 1966, Pepitone had slumped to just 13 homers and 64 RBIs the following year. Tresh, after being one of the best all-around players in the league in 1965, had seen his batting average dip, first to .233 in 1966, then, to .219 in 1967, and his productivity drop along with it. The Yankees needed both of them to return to their earlier form if they were going to show any marked improvement.

The team was also looking for an increase in productivity from its catchers. The previous year, in 374 at-bats as the primary backstop, Jake Gibbs had hit only 4 home runs, driven in just 25 runs, and batted only .233. New York was hoping that a platoon of the left-handed hitting Gibbs and right-handed batting Frank Fernandez would bring greater results. The rookie Fernandez had always had a difficult time making contact in the minor leagues, and had shown the same propensity in his brief trial with the Yankees in 1967, striking out 7 times in 28 at-bats. But he was big and strong, hit the ball a long way when he connected, and the Yankees hoped that he would add some power to their offense.

In the outfield, in addition to counting on a return to top form by both Tresh and Pepitone, the team was hoping that Bill Robinson would be able to live up to his potential and justify the trade that had brought him here just one year earlier. He appeared to have all the physical tools; it seemed to be more a matter of him gaining enough self-confidence for him to perform at the major league level. If he was unable to produce, perhaps either Roy White or Andy Kosco would finally be given an opportunity to show what they could do in the big leagues on an everyday basis.

On the pitching staff, the Yankees were hoping that Fritz Peterson would return to his 1966 form, when he tied for the team lead in victories. They were also hoping that rookie right-hander Stan Bahnsen would be able to break into the starting rotation, and, along with an improved Peterson, and an already solid Downing and Stottlemyre, give the team four dependable starters. Bahnsen had done very well on his way up through the Yankees' minor league system, and, with the possible exception of Downing, threw as hard as anyone on the staff. The team was looking for big things from him.

New York also hoped that Steve Barber would find his control and, once again, pitch the way he had just a few seasons earlier, in Baltimore. Fred Talbot, Bill Monbouquette, and Joe Verbanic would be the swingmen, available for starting assignments in case either Bahnsen or Barber faltered, or later in the season, when doubleheaders started to pile up. The staff would be completed by relievers Dooley Womack and Steve Hamilton.

Rather conspicuous by his absence from the Yankees' plans, however, was Jim Bouton, who continued to struggle with arm problems. The team was no longer counting on his return to the starting rotation, since he had failed in attempts in each of the past three seasons.

The Yankees' plans received their first serious blow, however, when Al Downing developed soreness in his pitching shoulder during spring training. The team's most effective starter in 1967 would be forced to miss most of spring training and almost two-thirds of the regular season.

New York attempted to compensate for the loss of Downing by giving both Talbot and Monbouquette a shot at the fifth starter's job, and by acquiring left-handed reliever John Wyatt from the Boston Red Sox early in the season. Earlier in his career, Wyatt had been quite effective in his role as closer for both the Athletics and Red Sox. As the ace of the A's bullpen from 1962 to 1965, he had saved 70 games and had led the American League with a then major league record 81 appearances in his All-Star year of 1964. After being traded to Boston in mid-1966, he had another fine year as the Red Sox' closer in their pennant-winning 1967 season, finishing 10–7, with 20 saves.

The team got off to a good start in the regular season winning their first game against the Angels, 1–0, on a four-hit shutout by Mel Stottlemyre. Making things even sweeter, the only run of the game was scored on a Frank Fernandez home run. The Yankees lost their next four games, however, before winning five out of their next six, to leave their record at 6–5. This sort of inconsistent play was typical of the team's performance during the first month of the season, when they continued to follow every short winning streak with a set of losses. On May 11, after 28 games, New York's record stood at 13–15. Then, the Yankees went on to lose their next six games, placing the team's record at 13–21, and leaving them in seventh place, 8 games out of first.

There were many factors that contributed to the team's erratic performance in the early-going. For one thing, they lost center-fielder Joe Pepitone for almost two months in just the third game of the season with a fractured left elbow.

Then, there was Horace Clarke, who had been the team's most consistent offensive performer the previous year. This season, however, would turn out to be a different story as Clarke would struggle for much of the campaign. He ended up batting only .230, 42 points below his 1967 average.

In spite of his Opening Day heroics, catcher Frank Fernandez would prove to be incapable of making consistent contact at the plate. Although he went on to hit 7 home runs and knock in 30 runs in just 135 at-bats, he also struck out 50 times and batted just .170. Regular catcher Jake Gibbs hit only 3 home runs, drove in just 29 runs, and batted only .213 in 423 plate appearances. So, once again, the Yankees failed to get much in the way of offensive support from their catchers.

In addition, the team wasn't getting much production from third baseman Bobby Cox, outfielders Bill Robinson and Tom Tresh, and shortstop Gene Michael.

Finally, about one month into the season, Manager Ralph Houk decided to make a rather bold move by taking the struggling Michael out of the lineup and replacing him at shortstop with Tresh, who had played the position earlier in his career. While the latter's offensive decline continued, he offered far more productivity than Michael and seemed to light a fire under his teammates. Even though he hit only 11 home runs, knocked in just 52 runs, and batted only .195 on the season, the move paid big dividends. In spite of his 31 errors at shortstop, Tresh made many outstanding plays in the field and provided leadership to the infield. The team also wound up finishing among the league leaders in double-plays, and Tresh, in spite of his .195 batting average, provided much more offense than Michael. With his 76 walks, Tresh's on-base percentage was a respectable .304 (almost 100 points higher than Michael's .218), and his 52 runs batted in and 60 runs scored were decent numbers, for a shortstop. Meanwhile, Michael, in 116 at-bats, drove in just 8 runs, and scored 8 others.

More importantly, however, the move gave more playing time in the outfield to Roy White and Andy Kosco, who were the team's most consistent offensive performers during the first half of the season. Kosco was a primary source of power, as he led the team in both home runs and runs batted in for the first few months. Although he slumped during the season's second half, he finished tied for third on the team, with 15 home runs, and second in runs batted in, with 59.

With Pepitone out of the lineup for two months and Tresh playing shortstop, White finally got his chance to play everyday, and he made the most of it. During the first month, with Tresh still the regular left-fielder, White was used all over the outfield, playing some centerfield, and even seeing some action in right. However, with the shifting of Tresh to shortstop, White settled in beautifully in left, making several spectacular catches, and providing consistent offense in the middle of the lineup after being moved to the cleanup spot by Manager Houk during the season's second half.

The results were a five-game winning streak that brought the Yankees' record to within two games of .500, at 21–23, and an overall improvement in the team's play. However, that would be as close as they would come to the .500 mark during the first half of the year, as the offense continued to struggle.

While Bobby Cox added a spark to the team with his aggressive style of play, and was even named to the Topps Rookie All-Star team at the end of the season, he brought little to the offense. In 437 at-bats, he hit 7 home runs, drove in 41 runs, and batted .229. Yet he was able to supplant Charley Smith as the starting third baseman. Smith, who just one year earlier had been acquired for Roger Maris, was relegated to pinch-hitting duty. In 70 at-bats, he hit 1 home run, drove in 7 runs, and batted .229.

Other reserves who struggled at the plate included Ruben Amaro, Steve Whitaker, and Dick Howser. Amaro, who had been the starting shortstop the previous year, came to the plate only 41 times on the season, and batted .122, with no home runs and no runs batted in. Whitaker, who had once been looked upon as a potential power-hitter, had only 60 at-bats, batted just .117, and had no homers and 3 runs batted in. Both players were released before the end of the year. Howser, in his role as utility infielder, came to the plate 150 times and batted just .153.

Another player who failed to impress in the limited playing time he received during the season was third base prospect Mike Ferraro, who was brought up to the big club during the year. Ferraro, who had been voted the top Yankee farmhand in 1966, came to the plate 87 times and batted .161, with no home runs and 1 run batted in.

Also making his first appearance in a Yankee uniform was a young first baseman named Tony Solaita. Solaita was a left-handed power hitter, who was called up at the end of the season after hitting 49 home runs and batting .302 for High Point-Thomasville of the Class-A Carolina League. He struck out in his only plate appearance.

Another reason for the team's struggling offense was the lack of production provided by Joe Pepitone once he returned to the lineup after recovering from his fractured elbow. In 380 at-bats on the season, he ended up hitting 15 home runs, knocking in 56 runs, and batting just .245.

In all fairness, though, the Yankees were not the only team having a difficult time scoring runs in 1968. In this *Year of the Pitcher*, offensive productivity was down throughout all of baseball. In the American League alone, by the end of the season, 460 fewer runs would be scored than in 1967, almost 100 fewer home runs would be hit, and the league batting average would drop from .236 to .230. While New York's team ERA of 2.79 would be a 45–point improvement over their previous season's mark, it would only be good enough for fifth best in the league. Led by Cleveland Indian right-hander Luis Tiant, who went on to compile a 1.60 ERA, no fewer than five starting pitchers would allow less than 2 earned runs a game by season's end. Detroit Tiger hurler Denny McLain would go on to win 31 games, while, in the National League, Cardinal great Bob Gibson would go on to compile a 1.12 ERA — the lowest by a starting pitcher since the dead ball era — and the Dodgers' Don Drysdale would establish a new record for consecutive scoreless innings pitched.

Yet, the Yankees' offense may very well have been the worst in baseball. While New York finished a respectable fourth in the league in home runs (109) and sixth in runs scored (536), their .214 team batting average was the lowest in the American League, 16 points below the league average of .230.

To add some much needed punch to the offense, on June 15 the Yankees signed outfielder Rocky Colavito, who had recently been released by the Dodgers. To make room for him on the roster, they sold John Wyatt to the Tigers.

Colavito had once been one of the most feared sluggers in the game. The Bronx native had originally come up with the Cleveland Indians in 1955. The following year, he began a string of 11 consecutive seasons with at least 20 home runs, averaging 32 a year during that stretch. He had his finest seasons in Cleveland in 1958 and 1959, hitting 41 homers, knocking in 113 runs, and batting .303 in the first of those years, and tying Harmon Killebrew for the league lead in home runs the following year, with 42. After being traded to the Detroit Tigers in 1960, he had his greatest season the following year. With the Tigers in 1961, he hit 45 home runs, drove in 140 runs, and batted .290. After four seasons in Detroit, Colavito was dealt to Kansas City, where he spent one season before being reacquired by Cleveland in 1965. That year, Colavito led the league with 108 runs batted in and played 162 errorless games in the outfield. He was also known for having one of the strongest throwing arms in baseball.

However, by the time the Yankees acquired him, Colavito's best days were clearly behind him, and he could do little to help their staggering offense. He went on to hit 5 home runs, drive in 13 runs, and hit .220 for New York, in 91 at-bats.

After losing 8 of their last 13 games, on July 7, at the All-Star break, the Yankees' record stood at 36–43, and they were 17 games behind the first-place Detroit Tigers.

New York had two representatives on the American League All-Star team — Mel Stottlemyre and Mickey Mantle. Stottlemyre's selection was well-deserved, while Mantle's was a sentimental one. At the break, the Yankee right-hander's record stood at 11–5, and he appeared to be on his way to his second 20–win season. It was known throughout all of baseball that this was, quite possibly, going to be Mantle's last year. As a result, the thought of leaving him off the All-Star team seemed sacrilegious, and he was chosen in spite of the fact that he, statistically, did not belong. Mantle finished the season with 18 home runs, 54 runs batted in, and a .237 batting average, although he did manage to finish second in the league, with 106 walks, and third in on-base percentage, with a mark of .367.

Shortly after the All-Star break, the Yankees acquired reliever Lindy McDaniel from the San Francisco Giants for Bill Monbouquette. That deal would turn out to be the biggest one the team would make all year, as McDaniel would prove to be invaluable during the second half of the season, stabilizing the bullpen, and giving the team the closer it had been looking for the last couple of years.

After playing .500 ball the previous month, New York's record stood at 51–60 on August 11. However, the team's play began to improve, and, after a four-game sweep of the eventual world champion Detroit Tigers at Yankee Stadium at the end of August, the Yankees' reached the .500 mark, at 63–63, for the first time since April 28. The team's record continued to hover around .500 until mid-September, when they put together their longest winning streak of the season. After winning their tenth consecutive game on September 15, the Yankees' record stood at 80–70. Although they subsequently lost their next six games, New York recovered and finished the season with an 83–79 record, topping the .500 mark for the first time since their last pennant-winning season of 1964. They finished in fifth place, also making it into the first division for the first time since 1964. However, they finished 20 games behind the first-place Detroit Tigers.

There were several contributors to the team's second-half turnaround and improved performance in 1968. As was mentioned earlier, Lindy McDaniel had a major impact on the team's fortunes. With Dooley Womack faltering somewhat after his fine 1967 season, McDaniel picked up the slack and gave the Yankees the kind of relief pitching they had not had since Pedro Ramos had been so effective three years earlier. In 24 appearances, he compiled a 4–1 record, with 10 saves, and a 1.75 ERA. In fact, at one point, he tied a league record by retiring 32 consecutive batters over four appearances.

After missing much of the season, Al Downing returned in the second half to give the team a fourth reliable starter. Although he finished only 3–3, with a 3.52 ERA in his 12 starts, he gave the team quality starts and much-needed innings, something neither Fred Talbot nor Bill Monbouquette had been able to do in his absence. In his 29 appearances, 11 of them starts, Talbot compiled a 1–9 record. Before his trade to San Francisco for McDaniel, Monbouquette appeared in 17 games, starting 11, and compiled a 5–7 record and a 4.43 ERA.

Another plus was the return of Fritz Peterson to his 1966 form. Peterson finished the season with a record of 12–11 and an ERA of 2.63 in his 212 innings of work.

After struggling to keep his batting average above the .200 mark during the first half of the season, Bill Robinson batted .280 during the second half to finish the year at .240. In addition, he provided excellent defense in the outfield and finally started to show some signs of fulfilling the promise that New York had seen in him when they traded Clete Boyer for him following the 1966 season.

Most of all, though, three men were responsible for the team's improvement in 1968. The first of these was Roy White, who was the Yankees' one consistent offensive player all year. In spite of the lack of support he received from the rest of the lineup, White performed admirably, leading the team in virtually every offensive category, and even batting fourth for much of the season — a spot he truly was not suited for. While Mantle led in home runs, with 18, White was right behind him, with 17. He led in runs batted in (62), batting average (.267), runs scored (89), base hits (154), and tied Horace Clarke for the team lead in stolen bases (20). While it may not seem like a lot, White's 89 runs scored was the third highest total in the American League that year. In addition, he provided excellent defense in left-field and, along with Clarke, was the team's best base-runner. At season's end, he finished twelfth in the league MVP voting.

Next was rookie right-hander Stan Bahnsen, who gave the team another fine starting pitcher and picked up much of the slack when Al Downing was lost for a good portion of the season. Bahnsen finished the year with a 17–12 record, led the staff with a 2.06 ERA and 162 strikeouts, and allowed just 216 hits in 267 innings of work. He was awarded for his fine performance by being voted the American League's Rookie of the Year.

However, the most outstanding Yankee in 1968 was the ace of the pitching staff, right-hander Mel Stottlemyre. In *The Year of the Pitcher*, he was one of the very best in the game. Stottlemyre finished the season with a record of 21–12, tying him for the third most wins in the American League. He also compiled a 2.45 ERA, finished third in the league with 278 innings pitched, and tied for second with 19 complete games and 6 shutouts. Had Stottlemyre pitched for a better team, he, quite possibly, would have won as many as 24 or 25 games. As it is, his record was impressive enough to earn him a tenth place finish in the league MVP voting.

In spite of the team's improved performance during the season, Yankee fans were saddened by the fact that they would never again have the opportunity to see Mickey Mantle play for their team. During the off-season, on March 1, 1969, he officially announced his retirement from baseball. Ironically, another man who would always be linked to Mantle because of the things he said about him in his book also played his last game for the Yankees in 1968. During the season, the team released Jim Bouton, who finished the year pitching for the Seattle Angels of the Pacific Coast League.

Jim Bouton was one of the new breed of ballplayers that started to enter the game during the 1960s. He was not as hardened or as rough around the edges as many of the players who had come before him had been. His pursuits were more intellectual. Rather than spending much of his free time hunting or chasing women, Bouton was more interested in discussing politics or journalism. In fact, he had quite a good relationship with many members of the press—a fact that annoyed many of his Yankee teammates. However, they were far more hesitant to express this displeasure in Bouton's early years with the team, when he was winning and was one of the American League's top pitchers.

Bouton first came up to the Yankees in 1962, compiling a 7–7 record in his rookie season. He became a star in his first full season with the team the following year, finishing 21–7, with a 2.53 ERA in 249 innings of work, and ranking among the league leaders in several pitching categories. That year, his 21 wins were the second highest total in the American League, his 2.53 ERA was fourth best, his 6 shutouts were second best, and he made the All-Star team for the only time in his career. He also suffered a tough loss in the World Series that year, losing Game Three to the Dodgers and Don Drysdale. In the 1–0 loss, Bouton surrendered the only run of the game in the first inning on a walk, a wild pitch, and a single.

Bouton had another outstanding season in 1964, compiling a record of 18–13, with a 3.02 ERA, throwing 271 innings, and leading the league with 37 starts. He also won two games in the World Series against the Cardinals that year, winning Game Three, 2–1, on a complete-game six-hitter, and capturing Game Six, 8–3.

However, Bouton's ferocious style of pitching eventually proved to be his downfall. He was tenacious on the mound, and fiercely competitive, frequently losing his cap as he hurled both the ball and his body toward the plate. For his energetic and competitive style, he was nicknamed *The Bulldog*. Unfortunately, his style of pitching took its toll on him as he blew out his arm early in 1965. Although he doggedly pitched through pain for the next two seasons, he was never again the same pitcher. In addition, the Yankee offense often failed to give him any support. As a result,

After winning a total of 39 games for the Yankees in 1963 and 1964, plus another two in the World Series, Jim Bouton would never again be an effective major league pitcher (National Baseball Hall of Fame Library, Cooperstown, N.Y.).

his record in 1965 was a poor 4–15, while he finished just 3–8 the following year, even though his ERA was a solid 2.69.

Having lost his fastball, Bouton became more of a *junk* pitcher, and even began experimenting with the knuckleball after he moved to the bullpen in 1968. After being released by the Yankees during the season, he spent the rest of the year pitching in the minor leagues before resurfacing with the expansion Seattle Pilots the following year. He split 1969 between the Pilots and Houston Astros before ending his career with the Astros the following year.

However, Bouton is best remembered for his book *Ball Four,* which was a combination of his diary of the 1969 season and his recollections of his Yankee career. The book was a true ground-breaker in that it broke baseball taboos by revealing the personal lives of his teammates, past and present. Up until that time, the whole of baseball journalism had concealed from the public the private affairs of the players and their sometimes raucous behavior. In particular, the book painted a somewhat negative picture of baseball hero and icon Mickey Mantle, disclosing his drinking habits and womanizing, and portraying him as a somewhat self-absorbed, immature, and adolescent jock. Needless to say, the book was not well-received by the baseball world, with then-Commissioner Bowie Kuhn calling it "detrimental to baseball." Nevertheless, it made an even bigger star out of Bouton, as the book quickly soared to the top of the best-seller list and even opened the door to him for a brief career as a television sports reporter.

A successful minor league comeback in 1975 didn't lead to any offers, but he tried again in 1977 and was given a chance by the owner of the Braves, Ted Turner, in 1978. After going 1–3 in five starts, he retired for the final time and wrote about his attempted comeback in an update of his first book called *Ball Five.* Since his retirement, he has gone into various baseball-related businesses and was one of the inventors of *Big League Chew,* bubble-gum shredded to resemble tobacco.

Yankee fans who first started following the team during this particular period in Yankee history undoubtedly regret not having seen Mickey Mantle when he was at his peak. For, in his prime, Mantle was perhaps the most naturally gifted ballplayer who ever lived, and one of the greatest players of all time.

Mantle first came up to the Yankees in 1951, in Joe DiMaggio's final season. Manager Casey Stengel, whose relationship with the *Yankee Clipper* had been a tenuous one from the beginning, further antagonized the aging superstar by building Mantle up as the next truly great player, saying he would eventually become Babe Ruth, Lou Gehrig, and Joe DiMaggio, all rolled into one. The proud and self-absorbed DiMaggio took the remark personally and treated the rookie with a distinct aloofness that would always exist between the two men in the future, whenever they were in each other's company. More than anything, though, the prediction put an undue amount of pressure on the shy and insecure youngster.

Mantle struggled in his first big league season, even being sent down

Although just a shell of his former self, when able to play, Mickey Mantle was still the most dangerous hitter in the Yankees lineup from 1965 to 1968.

to the minors at one point, before returning later in the year to finish the season with decent numbers. However, in the World Series that year, he experienced the first of what would become a long list of crippling injuries that severely limited his playing time and robbed him of his blinding speed. Playing right-field in Yankee Stadium, he moved towards right-center to catch a fly ball hit by Willie Mays. However, with Mantle all set to catch the ball, center-fielder DiMaggio called him off at the last moment because he wanted to make sure he could make the play and look good at the same time. Mantle was forced to make an abrupt stop to avoid a collision, and, in the process, caught his right foot in an outfield drainage ditch. The incident seriously injured his right leg and prevented him from ever again playing at 100 percent capacity.

Yet, even at less than 100 percent, Mantle may still have had, in his youth, the greatest combination of speed and power ever seen on any baseball player. Although only about 5'10" tall, he was thick throughout his muscular body and had amazing natural strength that allowed him to hit a ball more than 500 feet from either side of the plate. He also had tremendous running speed, being timed once in a record 3.1 seconds going from home to first base.

It was this immense natural talent, and the greatness predicted for him at such an early stage in his career, that made his first few big league seasons so difficult. While he showed signs of greatness his first five years, occasionally hitting mammoth home runs, driving in close to 100 runs, batting around .300, and making the All-Star team in all but his rookie season, he failed to live up to his tremendous potential. He struck out frequently, and when he failed to perform at the lofty level that had been predicted for him, the New York fans treated him with disdain, failing to acknowledge that he was the best player on the team.

Finally, in 1956, Mantle had the kind of season that it was always thought he was capable of having — one of the greatest seasons any player has ever had. That year, he won the American League triple crown, leading not just the A.L., but the *Major Leagues,* in home runs (52), runs batted in (130), and batting average (.353), being named the league's Most Valuable Player for the first of three times, and being awarded the Hickock Belt as the top professional athlete of the year. Mantle had another great season in 1957, hitting 34 home runs, knocking in 94 runs, batting .365, and winning his second consecutive MVP Award. However, when he was merely "good" the next couple of years, the fans, once again, took to booing Mantle every chance they had.

All that began to change in 1960, though, at the expense of Roger Maris. With Mantle and Maris involved in the first of two consecutive home run races they would wage against one another, the fans chose sides. With the newcomer Maris challenging the "home-gown" Yankee for both team and league leadership, suddenly Mantle became the fan favorite. The rivalry, and the fans' feelings, intensified the following year when the two players simultaneously strove to break Babe Ruth's single-season home run record of 60. Most of the fans, and even the Yankee players, felt that the record had been set by a Yankee, and that, if it was going to be broken, it should be broken by a "true Yankee." Maris was cast as the inter-

Unfortunately, Mantle was unable to perform much of the time during this period. Here, in all-too-familiar scene at Yankee Stadium, Mickey lies face down, writhing in pain, after injuring his leg.

loper, while Mantle was cheered wildly every time he came to the plate. Even the press, much fonder of the now more gregarious Mantle than the shy and, at times, uncooperative Maris, chose sides. They began to write stories of how courageous Mantle was, and how much pain he had to constantly play in. From that point on, Mantle became as much of a folk hero as he was an athlete, and he experienced the kind of popularity that very few players ever have.

The stories of the pain that Mantle had to endure every time he went on to the ball field were, in fact, not exaggerated in the least. Following the wrenching of his right knee in the 1951 World Series, there was a string of injuries that ensued. Perhaps the most serious of these occurred in Baltimore, in 1963, when Mantle ran into a wire fence in the outfield, breaking his left foot and tearing the cartilage in his left (good) knee. When the season was over, he immediately underwent surgery to remove cartilage from it.

By 1964, Mantle could not swing the bat from either side of the plate, chase after a ball in the outfield, or run the bases without experiencing some kind of pain. He had very little cartilage left in his right knee, and he already knew that he would limp in some manner for the rest of his life, and that the limp would be accompanied by pain.

This is the Mickey Mantle that the fans of my generation remember, not the one who could run like the wind and swing a bat without experiencing any discomfort. This Mickey Mantle hobbled every time he chased a fly ball. He limped running down to first base, or going from first to third on a base hit. If he swung at a pitch and missed, or if he tried to check his swing, his leg buckled. Even when he hit a home run, he hobbled around the bases.

Opposing players, as well as Mantle's teammates, had a tremendous amount of respect for him because they knew the effort he had to go through late in his career just to be able to take the field to start a game. They also respected him because he had a keen sense of fair play and refused to ever try to embarrass the opposition. Early in his career, the Yankee front office suggested to Mickey that, when he hit a home run, he should do something colorful to draw attention to himself, like tip his cap to the fans. However, Mantle refused, insisting on always circling the bases with his head down for fear of embarrassing the opposing team's pitcher. It was this sort of gesture, and this kind of humility that made him so popular with his teammates, and with opposing players.

In his book *Few And Chosen,* former teammate and close friend Whitey Ford refers to Mantle as: "… a superstar who never acted like one. He was a humble man who was kind and friendly to all his teammates, even the rawest rookie. He was idolized by all the other players."

Ford also says, "Often he played hurt, his knees aching so much he could hardly walk. But he never complained, and he would somehow manage to drag himself onto the field, ignore the pain, and do something spectacular."

Roy White, who only saw Mickey in the latter stages of his career, talked about the inspiration he was to him: "I was really impressed with the way he played the game, how hard he played the game, and the way he hustled, especially with the bad legs he had. I have a vivid memory of him in DC Stadium, after a doubleheader on a Sunday. It was something like 120 (degrees) down on the floor of the DC Stadium, in July. Looking at him afterwards wrapping the tape off his legs … just sitting there totally exhausted. He had played both games. Mickey would hit a one-hopper over to second base, and he would run all-out to first base. How could you give any less watching a guy like that play the game?"[36]

Another former teammate of Mantle's, Clete Boyer, once expressed his admiration for Mickey by saying, "He is the only baseball player I know who is a bigger hero to his teammates than he is to the fans."[37]

Although the Mickey Mantle that played during this particular period was merely a shell of his former self, it is perhaps worthwhile to take a look at some of his accomplishments to realize what a great player he had been earlier in his career.

Mantle led the American League in home runs four times, topping the 50–mark twice. He led the league in runs batted in once, batting average once, triples once, on-base percentage three times, slugging percentage four times, total bases three times, runs scored six times, and bases on balls five times. He scored more than 100 runs nine consecutive seasons, from 1953 to 1961. He batted over .300 ten times, was selected to the All-Star team in 16 of his 18 seasons, won a Gold Glove Award, won three MVP Awards, finished in the top 10 in the MVP voting a total of nine times, and won a triple crown. When he retired at the end of the 1968 season, Mantle's 536 career home runs were third on the all-time list, behind only Babe Ruth and Willie Mays. Imagine what he might have done if he had been able to go through his career without enduring so many debilitating injuries.

Season Highlights, Outstanding Performances, and Memorable Moments:

April 10   On Opening Day at Yankee Stadium, New York gets only three hits off Angels' starter George Brunet, but one of them is a solo home run by catcher Frank Fernandez. Yankee starter Mel Stottlemyre makes the run stand up by allowing only four hits and no runs in winning the opener, 1–0.

April 26   At Yankee Stadium, New York defeats Detroit, 5–0, as Mel Stottlemyre allows just three hits in going the distance. The big blow of the game is a two-run homer off the bat of Mickey Mantle.

May 11   Only one month into the season, Mel Stottlemyre throws his third shutout and wins his second 1–0 game by topping Jose Santiago and the Boston Red Sox at Yankee Stadium.

May 19   At Boston's Fenway Park, New York scores four runs in the first inning, and another four in the second en route to an 11–3 victory over the Red Sox. Andy Kosco completes the Yankee scoring with a three-run homer in the sixth inning. Stan Bahnsen is the recipient of the offensive outburst.

May 30   The Yankees and Washington Senators split a doubleheader at Yankee Stadium, with New York winning the first game, 13–4, and Washington taking the nightcap, 6–2. In the opener, Mickey Mantle goes 5–for–5, with two home runs and five

RBIs. The 5-for-5 effort is his first such performance since May 24, 1956.

August 1   At Fenway Park, the Yankees defeat the Red Sox, 1–0, on a three-hit shutout by Stan Bahnsen. Bill Robinson collects two hits and drives in the only run of the game with a base hit in the seventh inning.

August 7   In the first game of a doubleheader split with the Athletics at Yankee Stadium, Mel Stottlemyre tops Oakland's Jim Nash, 3–0. Joe Pepitone's two-run homer in the fourth inning gives Stottlemyre all the runs he needs. The shutout is the Yankee right-hander's fifth of the year.

August 20   At Minnesota's Metropolitan Stadium, Mel Stottlemyre throws his sixth and final shutout of the year, topping the Twins, 5–0, and allowing just four hits.

August 22   At Metropolitan Stadium, the Yankees lose to the Twins, 3–1, with the lone New York run coming in the ninth inning on a pinch-hit home run by Mickey Mantle. The homer is the 534th of Mantle's career, tying him with Jimmie Foxx for third on the all-time list, behind only Babe Ruth and Willie Mays.

August 23   At Yankee Stadium, in the first game of a doubleheader against the league-leading Detroit Tigers, Yankee right-hander Stan Bahnsen out-duels Earl Wilson to give New York a 2–1 win over Detroit. In the nightcap, the two teams battle for 19 innings before the game is suspended by curfew with the score 3–3. In the long tie, Yankee reliever Lindy McDaniel retires 21 consecutive Tiger batters, six on strikeouts. In his last three relief appearances, he has retired 30 batters in a row.

August 24   The Yankees defeat the Tigers again, 2–1, with Mel Stottlemyre getting the best of Detroit ace right-hander Denny McLain, who has already won 25 games. McLain will go on to win 31 for the season, becoming the first pitcher to top 30 wins in 34 years. The win is Stottlemyre's 17th of the year. The only New York runs are scored on a first-inning two-run homer by Yankee cleanup hitter Roy White.

August 25   The Yankees complete a four-game sweep of the eventual world champions by taking both ends of a doubleheader, 6–5 and 5–4. In the first game, New York falls behind 5–0 early in the game, but rallies behind successive home runs by Bill Robinson and Bobby Cox. The game is highlighted by a relief appearance by Rocky Colavito, who comes out of the Yankee bullpen with two Tigers on base and only one man out in the fourth inning. The slugger retires Al Kaline and Willie Horton, goes on to toss 2⅔ innings of scoreless relief to earn the victory, and eventually scores the winning run himself. In the eighth inning, Yankee reliever Lindy McDaniel ties the American League record for consecutive batters retired by setting down the first Tiger he faces, giving him 32 straight batters retired over four appearances. Colavito homers in New York's 5–4 second-game victory.

Sept. 7   In a twi-light doubleheader at Yankee Stadium, New York defeats the Senators by a combined margin of 26–2, winning the first game, 16–2, and taking the nightcap, 10–0. In the opener, the Yankees collect 19 hits, including home runs by Jake Gibbs, Joe Pepitone, and Roy White, to help Mel Stottlemyre to his 19th victory. Rocky Colavito and Frank Fernandez homer in the second game to support the two-hit pitching of Fritz Peterson.

Sept. 13   At Washington's RFK Stadium, the Yankees sweep the Senators in a doubleheader, winning the first game, 4–2, and the second, 2–1. The victory in the opener is Mel Stottlemyre's 20th of the season, while Stan Bahnsen wins his 16th in the nightcap.

Sept. 15   The Yankees complete a four-game sweep of Washington, defeating the Senators, 3–2, behind Fritz Peterson. The victory is New York's 10th in a row — the team's longest winning streak of the year.

Sept. 19   At Tiger Stadium, the Yankees lose to Detroit and Denny McLain, 6–2. The victory is the Tiger right-hander's 31st of the year. The game, however, is highlighted by Mickey Mantle's 535th career home run, which is a gift from McLain. With Detroit comfortably in the lead, the Tiger pitcher calls his catcher, Jim Price, out to the mound and tells him to inform Mantle that he will be throwing him nothing but fastballs. After failing to connect with the first couple of pitches, Mantle hits one out and tips his cap to McLain as he rounds third base. The home run puts the Yankee slugger in sole possession of third place on the all-time home run list. He will hit one more before he retires at the end of the season.

Sept. 24   In a doubleheader split with the Indians at Yankee Stadium, Mel Stottlemyre tops Cleveland strikeout artist Sam McDowell in the first game, 5–1, for his 21st and final win of the year.

Sept. 25   In Mickey Mantle's last appearance at Yankee Stadium, he slices a two-out first inning single off Cleveland's Luis Tiant for the only hit for the Yankees. Tiant tosses his ninth shutout of the year, tops in the American League, to win, 3–0, and lower his league-leading ERA to 1.60.

1968 American League Final Team Standings and Offensive Statistics

TEAM	G	W	L	PCT	GB	R	H	2B	3B	HR	BB	SO	SB	AVG	OBP	SLG
DET	162	103	59	.636	—	671	1292	190	39	185	521	964	26	.235	.309	.385
BAL	162	91	71	.562	12	579	1187	215	28	133	570	1019	78	.225	.306	.352
CLE	161	86	75	.534	16.5	516	1266	210	36	75	427	858	115	.234	.294	.327
BOSTON	162	86	76	.531	17	614	1253	207	17	125	582	974	76	.236	.316	.352
NY	162	83	79	.512	20	536	1137	154	34	109	566	958	90	.214	.293	.318
OAK	162	82	80	.506	21	569	1300	192	40	94	472	1022	147	.240	.306	.343
MINN	162	79	83	.488	24	562	1274	207	41	105	445	966	98	.237	.301	.350
CAL	162	67	95	.414	36	498	1209	170	33	83	447	1080	62	.227	.293	.318
CHI	162	67	95	.414	36	463	1233	169	33	71	397	840	90	.228	.286	.311
WASH	161	65	96	.404	37.5	524	1208	160	37	124	454	960	29	.224	.289	.336
TOTAL						5532	12359	1874	338	1104	4881	9641	811	.230	.299	.339

Team Pitching and Fielding Statistics

TEAM	CG	SH	SV	IP	H	HR	BB	SO	ERA	FA	E	DP
DET	59	19	29	1489	1180	129	486	1115	2.71	.983	105	133
BAL	53	16	31	1451	1111	101	502	1044	2.66	.981	120	131
CLE	48	23	32	1464	1087	98	540	1157	2.66	.979	127	130
BOSTON	55	17	31	1447	1303	115	523	972	3.33	.979	128	147
NY	45	14	27	1467	1308	99	424	831	2.79	.979	139	142
OAK	45	18	29	1455	1220	124	505	997	2.94	.977	145	136
MINN	46	14	29	1433	1224	92	414	996	2.89	.973	170	117
CAL	29	11	31	1437	1234	131	519	869	3.43	.977	140	156
CHI	20	11	40	1468	1290	97	451	834	2.75	.977	151	152
WASH	26	11	28	1439	1402	118	517	826	3.64	.976	148	144
TOTAL	426	154	307	14553					2.98	.978	1373	1388

1968 New York Yankee Pitching Statistics

PLAYER	W	L	ERA	G	GS	CG	SHO	SV	IP	H	R	ER	BB	SO
Mel Stottlemyre	21	12	2.45	36	36	19	6	0	278	243	86	76	65	140
Stan Bahnsen	17	12	2.05	37	34	10	1	0	267	216	72	61	68	162
Fritz Peterson	12	11	2.63	36	27	6	2	0	212	187	72	62	29	115
Steve Barber	6	5	3.23	20	19	3	1	0	128	127	63	46	64	87
Fred Talbot	1	9	3.36	29	11	1	0	0	99	89	47	37	42	67
Joe Verbanic	6	7	3.15	40	11	2	1	4	97	104	36	34	41	40
Bill Monbouquette	5	7	4.43	17	11	2	0	0	89	92	47	44	13	32
Dooley Womack	3	7	3.21	45	0	0	0	2	61	53	23	22	29	27
Al Downing	3	3	3.52	15	12	1	0	0	61	54	24	24	20	40
Lindy McDaniel	4	1	1.75	24	0	0	0	10	51	30	10	10	12	43

PLAYER	W	L	ERA	G	GS	CG	SHO	SV	IP	H	R	ER	BB	SO
Steve Hamilton	2	2	2.13	40	0	0	0	11	50	37	13	12	13	42
Jim Bouton	1	1	3.68	12	3	1	0	0	44	49	20	18	9	24
Thad Tillotson	1	0	4.35	7	0	0	0	0	10	11	6	5	7	1
John Wyatt	0	2	2.16	7	0	0	0	0	8	7	3	2	9	6
Rocky Colavito	1	0	0.00	1	0	0	0	0	2	1	0	0	2	1
John Cumberland	0	0	9.00	1	0	0	0	0	2	3	4	2	1	1

1968 New York Yankee Hitting Statistics

PLAYER	AB	R	H	2B	3B	HR	RBI	BB	SO	SB	OBP	SLG	AVG
Horace Clarke	579	52	133	6	1	2	26	23	46	20	.258	.254	.230
Roy White	577	89	154	20	7	17	62	73	50	20	.350	.414	.267
Tom Tresh	507	60	99	18	3	11	52	76	97	10	.304	.308	.195
Andy Kosco	466	47	112	19	1	15	59	16	71	2	.268	.382	.240
Bobby Cox	437	33	100	15	1	7	41	41	85	3	.300	.316	.229
Mickey Mantle	435	57	103	14	1	18	54	106	97	6	.385	.398	.237
Jake Gibbs	423	31	90	12	3	3	29	27	68	9	.270	.277	.213
Joe Pepitone	380	41	93	9	3	15	56	37	45	8	.311	.403	.245
Bill Robinson	342	34	82	16	7	6	40	26	54	7	.294	.380	.240
Dick Howser	150	24	23	2	1	0	3	35	17	0	.321	.180	.153
Frank Fernandez	135	15	23	6	1	7	30	35	50	1	.341	.385	.170
Gene Michael	116	8	23	3	0	1	8	2	23	3	.218	.250	.198
Rocky Colavito	91	13	20	2	2	5	13	14	17	0	.330	.451	.220
Mel Stottlemyre	91	4	13	3	0	0	5	8	33	0	.210	.176	.143
Mike Ferraro	87	5	14	0	1	0	1	2	17	0	.180	.184	.161
Stan Bahnsen	81	4	4	0	0	0	3	6	49	0	.114	.049	.049
Charley Smith	70	2	16	4	1	1	7	5	18	0	.280	.357	.229
Fritz Peterson	63	2	5	1	1	0	4	1	24	0	.106	.127	.079
Steve Whitaker	60	3	7	2	0	0	3	8	18	0	.221	.150	.117
Ruben Amaro	41	3	5	1	0	0	0	9	6	0	.280	.146	.122
Steve Barber	39	1	2	0	0	0	0	6	23	0	.178	.051	.051
Bill Monbouquette	26	2	3	1	0	0	2	2	6	0	.179	.154	.115
Joe Verbanic	25	1	2	0	0	0	0	1	5	0	.115	.080	.080
Ellie Rodriguez	24	1	5	0	0	0	1	3	3	0	.296	.208	.208
Al Downing	17	1	3	0	0	0	1	1	10	0	.222	.176	.176
Fred Talbot	17	2	2	0	0	1	1	1	7	0	.167	.294	.118
Lindy McDaniel	13	1	0	0	0	0	0	0	10	0	.000	.000	.000
Jim Bouton	7	0	0	0	0	0	0	1	4	0	.125	.000	.000
Dooley Womack	5	0	1	0	0	0	0	0	1	1	.200	.200	.200
Steve Hamilton	3	0	0	0	0	0	0	1	1	0	.250	.000	.000
Tony Solaita	1	0	0	0	0	0	0	0	1	0	.000	.000	.000

SEVEN

1969: A Year of Change

The 1969 season ushered in many changes throughout all of major league baseball. In 1968, pitchers in both leagues had combined to produce an overall ERA of 2.98, which was the lowest earned run mark in nearly forty years. Since 1963, when the strike zone had been expanded to aid pitchers, offensive production and batting averages had both been on a steady decline. In 1962, 14,461 total runs were scored in both leagues, and the combined batting average of all major league players was .258. The following year, those numbers dropped to 12,780 and .246, respectively. In 1968, the figures had bottomed out at 11,109 and .237. In addition, Carl Yastrzemski had won the American League batting title with an average of just .301, making him the only player in the league to surpass the .300 mark. In an attempt to bring more offense back into the game, during the off-season the rules committee had voted to narrow the strike zone and lower the pitching mound for the 1969 season. However, those were only two of the changes that were set in place for the subsequent season.

In 1968, major league owners had voted to add two teams to each league, thus increasing the 1969 major league membership to twenty-four teams. The four new franchises would be the Montreal Expos and San Diego Padres in the National League, and the Kansas City Royals and Seattle Pilots in the American League. In addition, each league was to be realigned into two six-team divisions, one representing the East and the other the West. The 162–game seasonal schedule was to be retained, but instead of playing every other team in the league 18 times, as had been done under the ten-team format, each team would play its intra-divisional opponents 18 times while playing teams from the other division 12 times. At the end of the regular season, the new format called for the two divisional winners in each league to meet in a best-of-five playoff series to determine the league champions. Afterward, the two league champions would meet in the traditional World Series competition to determine the ultimate winner. The logic behind creating two divisions in each league was to promote fan interest by doubling the number of pennant races and, thereby, increasing the number of teams that remained hopeful of making it into the post-season deep into the season.

The new alignment had the Montreal Expos joining the Mets, Cardinals, Phillies, Pirates, and Cubs in the N.L. East, and the San Diego Padres joining the Giants, Dodgers, Braves, Reds, and Astros in the West. In the American League, both new teams would join the Western Division, as the Royals and Pilots were to be grouped with the Athletics, White Sox, Twins, and Angels, leaving the Eastern Division comprised of the Yankees, Orioles, Tigers, Red Sox, Indians, and Senators. Therefore, New York had been placed in perhaps the most competitive division in baseball, since, among those teams, only the Senators had finished out of the first division the previous season. In addition, in Baltimore, Boston, and Detroit, the division featured the last three American League champions.

Those were not the only changes that surrounded the Yankees as they went to spring training prior to the start of the 1969 season, however. For the first time in 19 years, they went into a season knowing that their great star, Mickey Mantle, would not be a part of their plans. In Mantle's retirement announcement made during the off-season, he had said that he knew it was time to leave the game because he just couldn't do the things anymore that he needed to be able to do to help the team win. He could no longer hit with any regularity or take the extra base when he needed to, so he knew it was time to get out.

Mantle's departure left Joe Pepitone and Tom Tresh as the regular players with the greatest amount of seniority on the team. They would both be looked to for leadership, and it was hoped that both men would be able to perform better than they had the past few seasons. After leading New York in both home runs and runs batted in during the 1966 season, Pepitone had been injured for parts of the last two seasons, and had performed erratically when he was in the lineup. In Mantle's absence, he would be returning to his natural position of first base, where he had previously won two Gold Gloves. Pepitone seemed to know that the Yankees would be looking to him for leadership as he arrived at spring training feeling very confident and optimistic about the upcoming season, and appearing ready to shoulder the added responsibility that was expected of him.

Tresh's situation was a slightly different one. After performing at a very high level in 1965, he had slumped the following three seasons, with his offensive productivity declining each year. The two-time All-Star had seen his batting average drop from .279 in 1965, to .233, .219, and .195 the next three seasons, and his home run and RBI totals drop along with it.

It wasn't clear what was causing his steady decline, but it was quite apparent that he needed to improve his performance if he was going to be able to provide any kind of leadership and remain the everyday shortstop.

The remainder of the lineup was, for the most part, young and inexperienced. None of the other players had proven yet that they could perform consistently at the major league level. Horace Clarke would be returning at second base, but, after his solid 1967 season that had seen him bat .272 and lead the team in several offensive categories, he had slumped to just .230 in 1968. The Yankees hoped he would be able to bounce back.

Bobby Cox was expected to be relegated to back-up duties at third base as one of the team's hopes for the future, Bobby Murcer, was returning after two years of military service. Murcer had made brief appearances at the ends of both the 1965 and 1966 seasons, first coming up as a skinny 19 year-old shortstop. However, his two years in the military had helped him mature physically, and he now possessed a more solid 5'11", 175 pound frame. The Yankees hoped that he would be able to add some much-needed power to the lineup, and also hoped that he would be able to make the switch to third base. At shortstop, Murcer had shown neither the hands nor the arm-accuracy to play the position on a regular basis. Therefore, he had been moved to third, where it was hoped that his great offensive potential would eventually be able to compensate for any shortcomings he might have in the field.

Gene Michael would be the back-up at shortstop, after his failed attempt the previous season at winning the starting job. The primary back-up at first base and second would be Len Boehmer, a 28 year-old rookie who had been a career minor-leaguer with several different organizations. Boehmer was a right-handed hitter whose only other major league experience had come two seasons earlier, with the Cincinnati Reds. In his three at-bats with Cincinnati, he had failed to get a hit.

Behind the plate, the Yankees would once again go with a platoon of the left-handed hitting Jake Gibbs and the right-handed batting Frank Fernandez. The duo had combined for a total of just 10 home runs and 59 runs batted in the previous year, with neither man batting any higher than .213. The team was looking for increased productivity from their catchers.

Many question marks also surrounded the Yankee outfield going into the season. Left-fielder Roy White had been the team's best everyday player in 1968, leading the team in most offensive categories. However, that was his first year as a regular player in the major leagues. Would he be able to repeat, or even improve upon his performance, or was he a one-year wonder?

Right-fielder Bill Robinson had batted only .240 in 1968. Yet his average over the second half of the season had been a solid .280, and he seemed to gain confidence in his ability to hit major league pitching as the season progressed. Would his maturation as a hitter continue, and his performance continue to improve, or would he regress and continue to be the disappointment he had been since the Yankees acquired him from the Braves?

In centerfield would be youngster Jerry Kenney who had not played at all in 1968 due to his military commitments. While Kenney had come up through the minor league system as an infielder, the Yankees had converted him to an outfielder because of his excellent running speed. It was thought he could cover Yankee Stadium's vast centerfield expanse and, batting in the number two spot, along with Clarke, Murcer and White, give the team four consecutive men at the top of the lineup with good running ability.

Veterans Dick Simpson and Billy Cowan would be the outfield reserves. Simpson was 6'4" and had great speed, but in parts of six seasons had never shown that he was capable of hitting major league pitching. A reserve throughout his entire career, Simpson originally came up in 1962 with the Dodgers. From Los Angeles, he went to California, Cincinnati, St. Louis and Houston before coming to New York. Splitting 1968 between the Cardinals and Astros, Simpson hit just .197 in 233 at-bats, with 6 home runs and 19 runs batted in.

Cowan experienced a moderate amount of success in his one season as a regular with the Chicago Cubs in 1964. That year, he hit 19 home runs and drove in 50 runs. However, he batted only .241 and finished second in the National League with 128 strikeouts. After that, he played for the Mets, Braves, and Phillies, failing to bat over .200 in any of his other big league seasons.

The pitching staff, which had been the strength of the team in 1968, appeared to be solid once more. In Mel Stottlemyre, Stan Bahnsen, Fritz Peterson, and Al Downing the Yankees had four strong starters. The fifth spot in the rotation would go to either right-hander Bill Burbach or lefty Mike Kekich.

Burbach was a 6'4" hard-throwing right-hander who ended up being named the outstanding Yankee rookie of training camp. Just 21 years old, the team was counting on him to be a cornerstone of their rebuilding plans.

Kekich was the Yankees' most notable off-season acquisition, as they acquired him in a deal with the Dodgers for outfielder Andy Kosco. Like Burbach, Kekich also had an excellent fastball, and had an assortment of pitches that, it was felt, could eventually make him a big-winner. He had originally come up as a 20 year-old with the Dodgers in 1965, where, in 10 innings of work, he struck out 9 and walked 13. After failing to make the Dodger roster in either of the following two seasons, he had another trial with the team in 1968, going 2–10 with a 3.91 ERA, and striking out 84 batters while walking 46 in 115 innings. Kekich's two main problems had always been his lack of control and his inability to earn a regular spot in his team's pitching rotation. Quite possibly, if he pitched more regularly, his control would improve. But, first, he had to prove that he was worthy of a regular spot in the rotation, and that was something he had yet to do.

Lindy McDaniel, the previous season's key acquisition, would head the bullpen. He would be joined by left-handed specialist Steve Hamilton, long-man Fred Talbot, veteran right-hander Don Nottebart, who had been acquired from Cincinnati during the off-season, and the loser of the Burbach-Kekich competition.

Unfortunately, as had been the case in 1968, Al Downing developed soreness in his pitching shoulder during spring training and was lost to the team for much of the first half of the season. As a result, Burbach moved into the fourth spot in the rotation, while Kekich was awarded the fifth spot.

The regular season opened on a positive note on April 7 in Washington's RFK Stadium, with the Yankees defeating the Senators 8–4. However, Washington took the next two games before New York took two out of three from the Tigers in Detroit, evening their record at 3–3.

The Yankees played solid ball throughout most of April, compiling a record of 10–6 by April 26. The keys to their early-season success were the superb pitching of Mel Stottlemyre, the hot hitting of Bobby Murcer, and a shrewd deal pulled off by the front office. Stottlemyre got off to his best start ever, winning his first five games. Murcer led the team in home runs and runs batted in through the first month, even though he struggled mightily at third base. Early in the season, the Yankees made a deal to acquire reliever Jack Aker from the expansion Seattle Pilots. That would turn out to be the best move the team would make all year as Aker would go on to solidify the bullpen and supplant Lindy McDaniel as the Yankee closer.

The right-handed Aker was a side-arming sinker-baller who was nicknamed "Chief" for his Potowatomie Indian ancestry and fierce mound-presence. He had been A.L. Fireman of the Year with the 1966 A's, going 8–4 with a 1.99 ERA and 32 saves—a major league record until 1970. In August 1967, the Kansas City players, with Aker as their representative, became embroiled in a feud with owner Charlie Finley. Having enraged

Finley, Aker found himself pitching less and less, until he was finally left unprotected in the expansion draft and was selected by the Pilots.

The Yankees also acquired another veteran right arm for the bullpen early in the season, picking up Ken Johnson from the Braves. Johnson had first come up to the big leagues with the A's in 1958 as a starter. However, he first gained notoriety as a member of the Cincinnati Reds' pitching staff. After being acquired by the Reds in July of 1961, he went 6–2 for them in their second-half drive to the pennant. As a member of the Astros in 1964, he pitched a no-hitter against the Reds, but lost 1–0 on two walks and two errors. He had his first winning season in 1965 as a member of the Braves, finishing the year with a record of 16–10 and an ERA of 3.42. He followed that up with records of 14–8 and 13–9 in 1966 and 1967, respectively, before falling to 5–8 in 1968.

Despite their fast start, however, New York started to slump in late April. After losing their seventh consecutive game on May 4, the Yankees' record stood at 11–15, and they were in fifth place, eight full games behind the first-place Baltimore Orioles. The slide continued well into the month of May as the team had another six game losing streak that left their record at 12–21, putting them in fifth place, 9½ games out of first.

The Yankees were able to reverse things before the end of the month, compiling an eight-game winning streak that improved their record to 20–21, moving them into fourth place, nine games out of first. That would be the closest New York would come to first place the rest of the season, however, since Baltimore was putting together a tremendous year. By season's end, the Orioles would compile a record of 109–53 and finish 19 games ahead of the second-place Tigers in the A.L. East.

Meanwhile, by mid-May, the Yankees decided to scrap the idea of playing Bobby Murcer at third base. In his 31 games there, he had committed 14 errors, and his fielding woes seemed to be affecting his hitting as well. While he had started the season off as the team's hottest hitter, Murcer's bat had cooled off quite a bit during the month of May, and it appeared that he was starting to press at the plate. To improve the team's defense, and to take some of the pressure off Murcer, Manager Ralph Houk decided to move Bobby to centerfield, switching Jerry Kenney to third base. The move paid off as Murcer proved to be much more comfortable in the outfield, while Kenney did a very respectable job at third, committing only 7 errors in 83 games there.

The Yankees played reasonably well through the first week of June, finally reaching the .500–mark on June 8, after a doubleheader sweep of the White Sox on *Mickey Mantle Day* at Yankee Stadium. At that point, their record stood at 28–28.

As had been the case the previous year, the Yankees' pitching was forced to carry the team, since it received little in the way of run-support from the offense. Roy White, Horace Clarke, Bobby Murcer, and Joe Pepitone provided what little offense there was, but none of the other starters contributed very much.

Shortstop Tom Tresh's funk continued as he batted only .182, with 1 home run and 9 runs batted in over his first 45 games. Finally, on June 14, the Yankees gave up on him, sending him to the Detroit Tigers for outfielder Ron Woods. While Tresh's offensive productivity had declined considerably over the last few seasons, his departure was a sad one since he had been such a fine player just a few years earlier, and since he represented one of the last vestiges of what had once been a great dynasty.

Woods was an excellent defensive outfielder but offered little in the way of offense. Slight of build, he had little power, and was used mostly in platoon situations throughout his career. He finished the season with a .175 batting average, with 1 home run and 7 runs batted in, in his 171 at-bats with the Yankees.

After a fast start, Jerry Kenney cooled off as the season progressed. Although he stole 25 bases, he could manage only two home runs, 34 runs batted in, and a .257 batting average in his 447 at-bats. Ironically, his two home runs came on the first and last days of the season.

Once again, Yankee catchers failed to provide much in the way of offense. In his 219 at-bats during the season, Jake Gibbs failed to hit a homer, drove in only 18 runs, and batted just .224. Frank Fernandez was more productive, hitting 12 home runs and knocking in 29 runs in 229 at-bats. He also walked 65 times, allowing him to compile the highest on-base percentage on the team (.399). However, he batted only .223 and struck out 68 times.

Another disappointment was Bill Robinson who, unfortunately, reverted to his 1967 form. In 222 at-bats, he hit only 3 home runs, knocked in just 21 runs, and batted only .171. By season's end, he was sitting on the bench, finishing out his last season with the team that had once projected him to be "the next Mickey Mantle." Although he would resurface several years later in the National League and have some fine seasons with both the Phillies and Pirates, the deal that brought him to New York for Clete Boyer turned out to be a poor one.

Due to their offensive failures, the Yankees continued to play mediocre ball through the first half of the season. On July 20, at the All-Star break, their record stood at 46–52, they were in fifth place, 20 games out of first, and were effectively eliminated from playoff contention.

The team did, however, field two representatives on the All-Star team.

Pitcher Mel Stottlemyre was having another fine season, and was selected for the fourth time, while outfielder Roy White was proving that he was one player the Yankees could definitely build their future around. He was selected to the team for the first time in his career.

With the Yankee offense continuing to struggle during the season's second half, several moves were made in an attempt to improve the lineup. First, Jimmie Hall was acquired from the Cleveland Indians. Hall had made the All-Star team twice as a member of the Minnesota Twins during the mid-sixties. Their center-fielder by default, since he really didn't cover enough ground to play the position, he had finished fourth in the league in home runs, with 33, in his rookie season of 1963. He had perhaps his finest all-around year with the team two years later, though, when he established career highs in batting average (.285), runs batted in (86), steals (14), and doubles (25), while making the All-Star team for the second consecutive time. However, following a beaning during the 1966 season, Hall lost much of his effectiveness and never again was able to perform at an All-Star level. He spent 1967 and part of 1968 with the Angels before being dealt to Cleveland. By the time the Yankees got him, he was more of a platoon player, although he ended up playing fairly regularly for New York during the second half of the year. In 212 at-bats, he hit 3 home runs, drove in 26 runs, and batted .236.

Then, there were several minor league call-ups. Two of these were outfielders Tom Shopay and Jim Lyttle. Shopay had experienced a moderate amount of success as a late-season call-up two years earlier. However, this time, he failed to make any sort of impression, batting just .083 in 48 at-bats. Lyttle was a speedy, solid defensive outfielder who was not as effective at the plate. In 83 at-bats, he hit just .181.

Also called up were outfielder/first baseman Frank Tepedino and first baseman Dave McDonald. Tepedino had been with the team briefly once before, and was still considered to be a good-hitting prospect. In his 39 at-bats, he batted .231 with 4 runs batted in. McDonald was brought up by the big club for the first time. In his 23 at-bats, he batted .217 with 2 runs batted in.

Also making their first appearances in a Yankee uniform were three players the team had high hopes for in the near future—catchers Thurman Munson and John Ellis, and outfielder Ron Blomberg. Both Munson and Ellis were called up at the beginning of September and made favorable impressions. In his 86 at-bats, Munson batted .256, with 1 home run and 9 runs batted in. Ellis hit an inside-the-park home run, drove in 8 runs, and batted .290 in his 62 at-bats. Blomberg came to the plate only 6 times, but got 3 hits for an average of .500.

Nothing seemed to help the offense, though, as the Yankees finished the season next to last in the league in runs scored (562) and home runs (94), and tenth in batting average (.235).

To compound matters, just as the team was starting to play better ball during the second half, finally topping the .500 mark with a record of 58–57 on August 12, one of the team's more productive offensive players, Joe Pepitone, entered into a phase that would make his last two months of the season resemble a soap opera. First, on August 12, citing "personal problems," he went AWOL. The following day, he returned to the team. Then, on August 29, he quit the team after being fined $500 for leaving the bench during a game. Finally, on September 2, he was reinstated. Pepitone finished the season with 27 home runs, 70 runs batted in, and a .242 batting average, and was awarded the third Gold Glove of his career. However, he left the team little choice. At the end of the season, he would be traded away.

The Yankees spent the better part of the last two months of the season flirting with the .500 mark, finally finishing at 80–81, in fifth place in the A.L. East, 28½ games behind the Orioles. In head-to-head competition with Baltimore, New York won 7 of 18 contests. In fact, with the exception of the Senators, the Yankees had a sub-.500 record against every team in the A.L. East. They fared much better against the Western division, feasting on both the Angels and White Sox, winning 9 of 12 meetings against both. However, the division winners in the West, the Minnesota Twins, dominated their season series with New York, winning 10 of 12 meetings. Of course, the Twins featured the league's MVP in 1969, slugger Harmon Killebrew, who beat out Baltimore's Boog Powell for the award. Killebrew led the league in home runs (49), runs batted in (140), bases on balls (145), and on-base percentage (.430).

In spite of New York's difficulties in scoring runs, there were a few players who had productive seasons. Roy White led the team in batting with an average of .290. He also finished second on the team in runs batted in, with 74, third in stolen bases, with 18, and compiled the highest on-base percentage (.392) among the regulars. White had clearly established himself as the Yankees' most consistent offensive performer, and was considered to be one of the league's better players.

In his first full major league season, Bobby Murcer showed promise. His 26 home runs were second on the team to Pepitone's 27, and he led in runs batted in (82), runs scored (82), and slugging percentage (.454). While his .259 batting average was somewhat disappointing, he was only 23 years old, and there was plenty of time for him to improve upon that figure. In addition, he had done a fine job defensively after being shifted to centerfield during the season.

Horace Clarke had a fine season at second base, leading the team with 183 base hits and 33 stolen bases, tying Murcer for the team lead in runs scored, with 82, and finishing second in batting, with a mark of .285. His 183 hits were the second highest total in the league, and his 7 triples tied him for second in the A.L.

In addition, after taking over the shortstop job from Tom Tresh, Gene Michael surprised everyone by batting .272.

However, once again, it was the pitching staff that carried the team. The Yankees' team ERA of 3.23 was the second lowest in the league, and their 53 complete games were the second highest total.

Mel Stottlemyre had another outstanding season, finishing with a record of 20–14 and an ERA of 2.82, while leading the team with 3 shutouts, 303 innings pitched, and 24 complete games. In fact, his 24 complete games led the American League. He also finished third in the league in wins and second in innings pitched.

Fritz Peterson's 17 victories (against 16 losses) were the second highest total on the team, and he led in ERA (2.55) and strikeouts (150).

Jack Aker had a tremendous year in the bullpen, finishing the season with a record of 8–4, an ERA of 2.06, and 11 saves. In fact, at one point during the season he was able to string together 33 consecutive scoreless innings of relief.

However, somewhat disappointing were Bill Burbach and Mike Kekich. In his rookie season, Burbach finished with a record of only 6–8, while compiling a 3.65 ERA. Kekich, in a dual role as both a starter and a reliever, won 4 games while losing 6, and finished the season with a 4.54 ERA.

Even more disappointing was 1968's Rookie of the Year, Stan Bahnsen. After pitching so effectively the previous year, Bahnsen lost his first six decisions and ended up only 9–16, with an ERA of 3.83. Perhaps because he depended more on his fastball, which he generally threw high in the strike zone, Bahnsen seemed to be more affected by the smaller strike zone and lower pitching mound than any other Yankee pitcher. While his performance improved somewhat during the season's second half, he plainly was not the pitcher he had been in 1968.

With regards to the rules changes that were implemented in 1969 to bring more offense into the game, they clearly had their desired effect. Looking at just the American League, hitters in 1968 had combined for an average of .230. In 1969, that figure rose to .246. The prior season, A.L. teams had averaged 553 runs scored. In 1969, the average was 663, or .7 more runs a game. The prior year, league pitchers had combined for a 2.98 ERA. In 1969, that figure rose to 3.62. While some of the discrepancy was

undoubtedly due to expansion and the presence of more mediocre pitchers on major league rosters, the primary factors were the smaller strike zone
and lower pitching mound.

After he returned to the team during the season, Al Downing pitched
effectively, both as a starter and out of the bullpen, compiling a record of
7–5 and an ERA of 3.37. However, the Yankee front office had become
frustrated with his constant arm problems, and had grown impatient waiting for him to fulfill his great promise. Finally, during the off-season,
Downing was traded away from the only major league organization he had
ever been associated with.

While Downing was leaving, Ralph Houk was staying. On September 2, he signed a new 3–year contract to manage the Yankees at $65,000
a season, the highest managerial salary in either league.

The season had been one of great change, both in and out of the Yankee organization. Unfortunately, the changes were even more extensive for
three players who had been an important part of the last Yankee pennant-
winning team in 1964, since Tom Tresh, Joe Pepitone, and Al Downing
each played their last game with the team in 1969.

Early in the career of Tom Tresh, it appeared that the switch-hitter
had a bright future and a lengthy career ahead of him as the next star of
the Yankees. He could hit from both sides of the plate, hit for power, run
well, field, and throw. It was difficult to imagine that the talented youngster's career would last only eight seasons, and that he would be a quality
player in only three or four of those.

Tresh was the son of former major league catcher Mike Tresh, who
had played for the Chicago White Sox from 1938 to 1948. Originally
brought up by the Yankees for a brief look at the end of the 1961 season,
Tresh took over as the regular shortstop the following year with Tony
Kubek missing all but 45 games due to his military commitments. Playing 111 games at short and another 43 in the outfield, Tresh had a fine season, hitting 20 home runs, knocking in a career-high 93 runs, scoring
another 94, batting a career-best .286, and collecting 178 hits and 26 doubles. At the end of the season, he was named American League Rookie of
the Year, was selected to *The Sporting News* All-Star team, and finished
twelfth in the American League MVP voting.

Upon Kubek's return to the team in 1963, Tresh was shifted to the
outfield where he had another productive season, being named to the

Injuries helped to limit the effectiveness and shorten the once-promising career of Yankee outfielder-shortstop Tom Tresh.

American League All-Star team for the second time in as many seasons and finishing eleventh in the league MVP voting. That year, Tresh hit 25 home runs, knocked in 71 runs, batted .269, and led the team in runs scored (91) and doubles (28). On September 1 of that year, he became only the eighth player in major league history to homer from each side of the plate in the same game, joining teammate Mickey Mantle as one of only four American League players to accomplish the feat. In fact, at that particular point in Tresh's career, he was being compared, in some ways, to the great Yankee slugger. While he didn't possess Mantle's tremendous power or the great running speed Mickey had earlier in his career, Tresh was, like Mantle, a switch-hitter who could hit, and hit with power, from either side of the plate. He also had good speed and a strong throwing arm, and was an excellent defensive outfielder.

Tresh's performance dropped off somewhat in 1964, as he hit only 16 home runs and batted just .246. However, he had probably his finest all-around season the following year, as he led New York in virtually every offensive category. Tresh led the team in home runs (26), runs batted in

(74), batting average (.279), runs scored (94), hits (168), doubles (29), and triples (6). He finished third in the league in runs scored, fourth in base hits, fourth in doubles, fifth in home runs, second in total bases, and tenth in batting average. He also won the only Gold Glove of his career for his outstanding play in left field, and finished ninth in the league MVP voting, in spite of the fact that the Yankees finished sixth in the standings, a full 25 games out of first place. On June 6, 1965, Tresh had the greatest day of his career, hitting four home runs in a doubleheader, including three in the nightcap. In that second game, he also hit home runs from both sides of the plate for the third and last time in his career.

Tresh remained productive in 1966, hitting a career-high 27 home runs, despite batting just .233. However, after injuring his knee during the 1967 campaign, his batting average continued to drop over the next two seasons, reaching a low of .195 in 1968. Finally, with Tresh hitting only .182 in his first 143 at-bats in 1969, the Yankees knew it was time to part ways with their former standout. On June 14, they traded him to Detroit for spare outfielder Ron Woods. Tresh finished his career with the Tigers that year, batting just .224 in his final 331 at-bats.

While Tresh's regular season performance proved to be somewhat erratic over the years, he was consistently productive for the Yankees in post-season play. In three World Series with New York, he hit 4 home runs, drove in 13 runs, and batted .277 in 65 at-bats. Tresh won Game Five of the 1962 Series against the Giants with a 3–run 8th inning homer off Jack Sanford to give the Yankees and Ralph Terry a 5–3 win, and his team a 3–2 lead in the series. In Game Five of the 1964 World Series against the Cardinals, it was Tresh's 9th inning 2–run homer off Bob Gibson that tied the score at 2–2, sending the game into extra innings, where St. Louis eventually won on a Tim McCarver 3–run homer.

Nevertheless, the Yankees and Tresh had to be somewhat disappointed in the way his career turned out. It seemed that he was destined for bigger and better things, and that he would be around for longer than he was.

Roy White, who replaced Tresh in left-field after the latter was moved to shortstop during the 1968 campaign, cited two factors as the primary reasons for his predecessor's decline: "I think the injuries were part of it. Then, I think Mickey getting older, and Roger and all those guys leaving the ballclub made him kind of a marked man. He really didn't have anybody to hit behind him, or protect him, so the pitchers could throw him something off-speed on a 3–2 count. He really didn't get good pitches to hit. I think the injuries hurt him more than anything else, though. He really had bad knees."[38]

Yet Tresh feels fortunate in many ways. In particular, he is happy that he had the opportunity to play on the same team as his childhood hero, Mickey Mantle.

"Mantle was my idol as a kid," said Tresh. "He was the greatest player to ever play the game, in my opinion. I named my only son Mickey, so that should be a testament to my admiration for the man."[39]

He also doesn't feel cheated, watching the huge salaries being bandied about these days.

"Sure, I might make millions today," Tresh said, "but you really can't have any regrets when you played for one of the greatest teams in history. I'll always cherish the experience."[40]

Perhaps no other player who ever wore the Yankee pinstripes wasted his God-given natural ability as much as Joe Pepitone did. Pepitone was blessed with great physical skills, but, unfortunately, never possessed the focus and commitment needed to take full advantage of them.

Born on October 9, 1940 in Brooklyn, New York, the fun-loving and carefree Pepitone spent his $20,000 signing bonus with the Yankees on a fancy car and a motorboat. He first appeared in a Yankee uniform in 1962, splitting his time between first base and the outfield. Possessing soft hands, good speed, and a strong throwing arm, Pepitone did a fine job at both positions. However, first base came more naturally to him and was where he felt most comfortable. Standing in his way, though, was Moose Skowron, who had been with the team since 1954. As a rookie, the bold and brazen Pepitone frequently told Skowron to watch out because he was going to take his job. On May 23 of that year, Pepitone became only the sixth player in American League history to hit two home runs in one inning. In 138 at-bats as a rookie, he hit 7 home runs, knocked in 17 runs, and batted .239. The combination of his power numbers and Pepitone's compact, but powerful swing convinced the Yankee brass that he was ready to take over the first base job. So, in November of 1962, Pepitone's prediction came to fruition when the Yankees traded Skowron to the Dodgers. After the deal was consummated, Pepitone sent Skowron a cable saying: "Dear Moose: Told you so. Joe Pep."[41]

It seemed that the Yankee front office had made the correct decision when, in his first full season, Pepitone hit 27 home runs, knocked in 89 runs, batted .271, and was selected to both the American League and *The Sporting News* All-Star teams. Although his batting average dropped to .251 in 1964, his 28 home runs and 100 runs batted in both placed him in the league's top ten and earned him his second All-Star game selection.

Those two years were fun for Pepitone. He was performing well and he had the opportunity to play alongside his idol, Mickey Mantle, who he also loved. In fact, he adored Mantle so much that he derived great pleasure out of his hero nicknaming him *"Pepinose,"* in honor of his prominent proboscis. He was absolutely thrilled when, prior to the start of the 1963 season, Mantle told a sportswriter that Pepitone would be the key to the Yankees' success that year. "I figure we'll win by a nose," Mantle said.[42]

Pepitone was one of the more colorful and flamboyant players of his time. He enjoyed wearing his hair long and his uniform and street clothes form-fitting, and was the first Yankee to bring a hair dryer into the clubhouse.

None of his quirks seemed to bother Yankee management very much until his on-field performance started to slip in 1965. Although he was selected to the A.L. All-Star team for the third and final time in his career, he hit only 18 home runs, drove in just 62 runs, and batted only .247. However, he rebounded in 1966 to hit 31 home runs, knock in 83 runs, bat .255, and win his second consecutive Gold Glove Award at first base.

With Mantle's legs bothering him too much to play the outfield anymore, the two men switched positions in 1967, with Mickey moving to first and Joe moving to centerfield.

Over the next two seasons, though, Pepitone's productivity slipped, due in part to injuries he sustained, and in part to off the field distractions. Although, after returning to first base in 1969 following Mantle's retirement, he led the team with 27 home runs, Pepitone's outside affairs and "personal problems" began to overwhelm him. After leaving the team twice, being suspended once, and being fined another time, he was finally traded at the end of the season to the Houston Astros.

Pepitone's stay in Houston didn't last very long as his carefree personality clashed with that of conservative manager Harry Walker. Midway through the season, he was dealt to the Chicago Cubs, for whom he had one of his best seasons in 1971. Although he hit only 16 home runs and knocked in just 61 runs in 427 at-bats, Pepitone topped the .300–mark for the only time in his career, batting .307.

After two more years in Chicago, Pepitone decided to move to Japan, where he played ball for three more years. However, the regimented Japanese had a difficult time understanding the free-spirited Pepitone, who was unhappy away from home. He ended up jumping the Yakult Sparrows, while batting just .163, and becoming a one-man international incident.

While back in the States during the 1980s, Pepitone was arrested on gun and drug charges while associating with the wrong people. He served a small amount of time in prison before getting out on a work-release pro-

Although he was selected to three American League All-Star teams and won three Gold Glove awards while with the Yankees, Joe Pepitone never lived up to the great potential he exhibited early in his career (National Baseball Hall of Fame Library, Cooperstown, N.Y.).

gram and eventually being given a job by George Steinbrenner in the Yankee front office.

Looking back, it seems sad that a player with the natural gifts of Pepitone did not amount to more. The quick, compact swing that emanated from his 6'2", 200–pound frame was the source of great power. It also allowed him to make good contact with the ball, as he never struck out more than 63 times in any single season.

Roy White remembers the swing of Pepitone very well, saying, "I really tried to pattern my swing after Joe Pepitone's because I was so impressed with the bat speed he had — a very short, compact stroke. I remember the first Yankee spring camp that I went to in Fort Lauderdale. There was a strong wind that blew in from right, across to left, so, in order to hit the ball out through a 25 or 30 mile per hour wind, you really had to hit it. The first day, Maris got up and hit one ball out. Mantle got up and hit three. Then, Joe Pepitone got up and hit about seven in a row right through the wind ... just screaming line drives that were hit so low and hard that the wind didn't even affect them. That left a lasting impression on me. Also, he held his hands kind of low, so that's where I got that from

—from watching Joe. I thought he had the quickest bat that I had seen in major league baseball ... and, to this day, I still say that. He had the most compact swing I have ever seen."[43]

Defensively, Pepitone was as good a first baseman as you will find. Yet, while his three All-Star appearances and three Gold Gloves would make many players happy, with his skills, Pepitone should have been able to accomplish much more.

In his book *Few And Chosen*, Whitey Ford says, "The only Yankee first baseman I've ever seen who even came close to Don Mattingly defensively was Joe Pepitone, who could have been one of the greatest Yankees ever if he paid a little more attention to playing."

Ford adds, "Pepitone had so much ability, but he let his off-field behavior get in his way."

As strange as it may seem, Al Downing's tremendous natural ability may have retarded his development as a complete pitcher, for he was so talented that, early in his professional career, he never had to learn how to outthink batters—he could simply overpower them.

Downing was first signed for the Yankees in 1960 by former Negro Leaguer Bill Yancey. Although only 19 at the time, Downing had the skills that made Yancey certain he would eventually be able to become the first black starting pitcher for New York. However, first the young left-hander needed to mature, both as a pitcher and as a man.

Born in Trenton, New Jersey, Downing had never before been exposed to the kind of racial segregation that still existed in the South. Once his minor league career began, though, he experienced it first-hand. When he first arrived at the Yankee minor-league center at Bartow, Florida, he was shocked to learn that he would not be allowed to stay in the same hotel as his white teammates. Instead, he and a few of the other players had to stay with a black family in another section of town. That was his first lesson.

Then, there was the matter of Downing learning to become a complete pitcher. Pitching for the first time with the Yankee minor-league affiliate in Double A Binghamton, Downing fared extremely well. Although a bit on the wild side, he averaged about one strikeout per inning, simply overpowering the weaker competition. In mid-July, with his record 9–1, he was called up to the major-league club.

That turned out to be a huge mistake, though, because, never even having pitched at the Triple A level, Downing was simply not ready to pitch in the big leagues. In the minors, whenever he got into trouble, he would merely rear back and throw harder. More often than not, he had the ability to throw the ball by minor league hitters. However, that was

Joe Pepitone congratulating Al Downing after the pitcher connected for one of his rare home runs.

not the case in the majors. Major league batters could see that Downing had not yet learned how to change speeds, or to go to different pitches, so they simply waited for his fastball. Unable to consistently overpower hitters at the major-league level, Downing attempted to throw even harder. When he tried, his control failed him, and he wound up falling behind in the count and walking an inordinate amount of batters. Banished to the bullpen, he lost all of his confidence and was soon returned to the minors.

Although it took some time, Downing eventually regained his confidence. Pitching at Triple A Richmond in 1962, he finished the season strong and felt that he was ready to return to the major leagues. The Yankees agreed and brought him up for the 1963 season.

As a rookie, Downing showed flashes of brilliance, finishing the season with a record of 13–5, an ERA of 2.56, and 171 strikeouts in just 175 innings of work, while allowing just 5.84 hits per nine innings. However, he also walked 80 men, occasionally lapsing into serious bouts with his control. Downing followed that up in 1964 with a record of 13–8, an ERA of 3.47, and a league-leading 217 strikeouts and 120 bases on balls.

Downing posted losing records in each of the next two seasons, often being plagued by inconsistency and control problems. However, in 1967, he became a complete pitcher, cutting down on his strikeouts, mastering a changeup, and mixing up his pitches. He finished 14–10, with a 2.63 ERA and made the All-Star team for the only time in his major league career.

With Downing being bothered by arm problems in each of the next two seasons, the Yankees finally grew tired of waiting for him to develop into the dominating pitcher they felt he had the ability to be. At the end of the 1969 season, he was dealt to Oakland as part of the deal that brought Danny Cater to New York. After splitting 1970 between the A's and Brewers, Downing was traded to the Dodgers, for whom he had his best year in 1971. That season, Downing compiled a record of 20–9, an ERA of 2.68, and threw a league-leading 5 shutouts. He finished second in the N.L. in wins, third in the Cy Young voting, and tenth in the league MVP voting. He spent six more seasons in Los Angeles, failing to win more than nine games in any of those. However, Downing is probably best-remembered for giving up Hank Aaron's record-breaking 715th home run.

While it could be said that Downing's legacy was one of unfulfilled potential, he was a very good pitcher for four seasons, and was among the staff's two or three best throughout most of his Yankee career.

Former teammate Roy White, who played with Downing for five seasons, had only nice things to say about the left-hander: "I still see Al every once in awhile. Al is a real quiet, very nice guy; a real gentleman ... very soft-spoken. He threw so easy, you really didn't know how hard he threw,

Recurring arm problems and inconsistency plagued Al Downing during much of his time in New York and prevented the Yankee pitcher from ever fulfilling the great promise he displayed in his first two seasons in pinstripes.

but he really had a great fastball and a great changeup. It's too bad he couldn't have stayed a Yankee."[44]

Season Highlights, Outstanding Performances, and Memorable Moments:

April 7   On Opening Day at Washington's RFK Stadium, 45,000 fans, including President Richard Nixon, look on as Ted Williams makes his managerial debut for the Senators. The Yankees spoil it, though, winning 8–4, as Jerry Kenney and Bobby Murcer hit back-to-back home runs in the third inning against Washington starter Camilo Pascual. Mel Stottlemyre gets his third consecutive complete game victory on Opening Day, despite giving up 14 hits, including a two-run homer to Frank Howard.

April 12   At Tiger Stadium in Detroit, Mel Stottlemyre throws a one-hitter against the Tigers, beating Denny McLain, 4–0. Horace Clarke collects three hits for New York, and the only Detroit hit comes on an opposite-field double by Jim Northrup.

April 15   In New York's home opener, Bobby Murcer goes 3–for–4, with a home run and four runs batted in, as the Yankees defeat the Senators, 8–2. Joe Pepitone adds a homer, and Fritz Peterson is the recipient of the Yankee offensive outburst, gaining his first victory of the young season.

April 20   In the second game of a doubleheader split with Detroit at Yankee Stadium, Yankee rookie right-hander Bill Burbach gains his first major league victory, topping the Tigers and Denny McLain, 2–0.

April 24   At Cleveland's Municipal Stadium, the Yankees defeat the Indians, 11–3, as Bobby Murcer goes 3–for–5, with two homers and 4 runs batted in.

April 25   At Baltimore's Memorial Stadium, Mel Stottlemyre wins his fifth game of the season, without a loss, as the Yankees defeat the Orioles, 7–2.

April 28   At Yankee Stadium, Fritz Peterson shuts out the Red Sox, 1–0, stopping Boston's consecutive game homer streak at 11, and a record 27 home runs.

May 16   Trailing the Angels 1–0, the Yankees score two runs in the bottom of the ninth inning to win the game, 2–1. Bobby Murcer breaks out of a horrendous slump with a game-winning two-out, two-run double off losing pitcher Rudy May. Fritz Peterson gets the victory.

May 23   At Yankee Stadium, the Yankees extend their winning streak to eight games by defeating the Twins, 3–1. Mel Stottlemyre gains his seventh victory of the year. The winning streak will turn out to be the longest of the season for New York.

June 8   On *Mickey Mantle Day* at Yankee Stadium, the team retires Mickey's number 7 and presents him with a plaque that will hang on the centerfield wall, alongside that of Joe DiMaggio, who Mickey presents with a plaque. In front of 60,096 fans, the Yankees win both ends of a doubleheader from Chicago, winning the first game, 3–1, on a three-hitter by Mel Stottlemyre, and taking the nightcap, 11–2, behind Bill Burbach. The two victories complete a four-game sweep of the White Sox and even the Yankees' season record at 28–28.

July 26   At Anaheim Stadium, Mel Stottlemyre gains his sixth victory in his last seven decisions by out-pitching the Angels' Jim McGlothlin, 3–1. The victory is the Yankee right-hander's 15th of the year, against only 7 losses.

August 12   At Yankee Stadium, the Yankees win their fourth consecutive game, defeating the Twins, 10–3. Horace Clarke goes 3–for–4, with two runs scored and two runs batted in. The victory puts New York's record at 58–57 on the season, making it the first time since April 30, when they were 11–10, that their record is above the .500 mark.

Sept. 28   At Yankee Stadium, Mel Stottlemyre wins his 20th game of the season in his final start, defeating the Baltimore Orioles, 3–2. It will turn out to be the last 20–win season of Stottlemyre's career.

October 1   The Yankees conclude their season with a five-game winning streak, defeating the Cleveland Indians, 4–3, at Yankee Stadium. The victory is the fourth of the year for Yankee left-hander Mike Kekich, against six defeats. Cleveland starter Luis Tiant loses his 20th game of the year. The win leaves the Yankees' final won-lost record for the season at 80–81.

1969 American League Final Team Standings and Offensive Statistics

TEAM	G	W	L	PCT	GB	R	H	2B	3B	HR	BB	SO	SB	AVG	OBP	SLG
EAST																
BAL	162	109	53	.673	—	779	1465	234	29	175	634	806	82	.265	.346	.414
DET	162	90	72	.556	19	701	1316	188	29	182	578	922	35	.242	.318	.387
BOSTON	162	87	75	.537	22	743	1381	234	37	197	658	923	41	.251	.335	.415
WASH	162	86	76	.531	23	694	1365	171	40	148	630	900	52	.251	.332	.378
NY	161	80	81	.497	28.5	562	1247	210	44	94	565	840	119	.235	.310	.344
CLE	161	62	99	.385	46.5	573	1272	173	24	119	535	906	85	.237	.309	.345
WEST																
MINN	162	97	65	.599	—	790	1520	246	32	163	599	906	115	.268	.342	.408
OAK	162	88	74	.543	9	740	1400	210	28	148	617	953	100	.249	.330	.376
CAL	162	71	91	.438	26	528	1221	151	29	88	516	929	54	.230	.302	.319
KC	162	69	93	.426	28	586	1311	179	32	98	522	901	129	.240	.311	.338
CHI	162	68	94	.420	29	625	1346	210	27	112	552	844	54	.247	.322	.357
SEA	162	64	98	.395	33	639	1276	179	27	125	626	1015	167	.234	.317	.346
TOTAL						7960	16120	2385	378	1649	7032	10845	1033	.246	.323	.369

Team Pitching and Fielding Statistics

TEAM	CG	SH	SV	IP	H	HR	BB	SO	ERA	FA	E	DP
EAST												
BAL	50	20	36	1473	1194	117	498	897	2.83	.984	101	145
DET	55	20	28	1455	1250	128	586	1032	3.31	.979	130	130
BOSTON	30	7	41	1466	1423	155	685	935	3.92	.975	157	178
WASH	28	10	41	1447	1310	135	656	835	3.49	.978	140	159
NY	53	13	20	1440	1258	118	522	801	3.23	.979	131	158
CLE	35	7	22	1437	1330	134	681	1000	3.94	.976	145	153
WEST												
MINN	41	8	43	1497	1388	119	524	906	3.24	.977	150	177
OAK	42	14	36	1480	1356	163	586	887	3.71	.979	136	162
CAL	25	9	39	1438	1294	126	517	885	3.54	.978	136	164
KC	42	10	25	1464	1357	136	560	894	3.72	.975	157	114
CHI	29	10	25	1437	1470	146	564	810	4.21	.981	122	163
SEA	21	6	33	1463	1490	172	653	963	4.35	.974	167	149
TOTAL	451	134	389	17503					3.62	.978	1672	1852

1969 New York Yankee Pitching Statistics

PLAYER	W	L	ERA	G	GS	CG	SHO	SV	IP	H	R	ER	BB	SO
Mel Stottlemyre	20	14	2.82	39	39	24	3	0	303	267	105	95	97	113
Fritz Peterson	17	16	2.55	37	37	16	4	0	272	228	95	77	43	150
Stan Bahnsen	9	16	3.83	40	33	5	2	1	220	222	102	94	90	130
Bill Burbach	6	8	3.65	31	24	2	1	0	140	112	68	57	102	82
Al Downing	7	5	3.37	30	15	5	1	0	130	117	57	49	49	85
Mike Kekich	4	6	4.54	28	13	1	0	1	105	91	58	53	49	66
Lindy McDaniel	5	6	3.55	51	0	0	0	5	83	84	37	33	23	60
Jack Aker	8	4	2.06	38	0	0	0	11	65	51	17	15	22	40
Steve Hamilton	3	4	3.32	38	0	0	0	2	57	39	22	21	21	39
Ken Johnson	1	2	3.46	12	0	0	0	0	26	19	11	10	11	21
Ron Klimkowski	0	0	0.64	3	1	0	0	0	14	6	1	1	5	3
Fred Talbot	0	0	5.11	8	0	0	0	0	12	13	9	7	6	7
Don Nottebart	0	0	4.50	4	0	0	0	0	6	6	3	3	0	5
John Cumberland	0	0	4.50	2	0	0	0	0	4	3	2	2	4	0

1969 New York Yankee Hitting Statistics

PLAYER	AB	R	H	2B	3B	HR	RBI	BB	SO	SB	OBP	SLG	AVG
Horace Clarke	641	82	183	26	7	4	48	53	41	33	.339	.367	.285
Bobby Murcer	564	82	146	24	4	26	82	50	103	7	.319	.454	.259
Joe Pepitone	513	49	124	16	3	27	70	30	42	8	.284	.442	.242
Roy White	448	55	130	30	5	7	74	81	51	18	.392	.426	.290
Jerry Kenney	447	49	115	14	2	2	34	48	36	25	.328	.311	.257
Gene Michael	412	41	112	24	4	2	31	43	56	7	.341	.364	.272
Frank Fernandez	229	34	51	6	1	12	29	65	68	1	.399	.415	.233
Bill Robinson	222	23	38	11	2	3	21	16	39	3	.226	.279	.171
Jake Gibbs	219	18	49	9	2	0	18	23	30	3	.294	.283	.224
Jimmie Hall	212	21	50	8	5	3	26	19	34	8	.296	.363	.236

PLAYER	AB	R	H	2B	3B	HR	RBI	BB	SO	SB	OBP	SLG	AVG
Bobby Cox	191	17	41	7	1	2	17	34	41	0	.332	.293	.215
Ron Woods	171	18	30	5	2	1	7	22	29	2	.273	.246	.175
Tom Tresh	143	13	26	5	2	1	9	17	23	2	.269	.266	.182
Len Boehmer	108	5	19	4	0	0	7	8	10	0	.233	.213	.176
Mel Stottlemyre	101	9	18	2	1	1	4	9	41	0	.250	.248	.178
Thurman Munson	86	6	22	1	2	1	9	10	10	0	.330	.349	.256
Jim Lyttle	83	7	15	4	0	0	4	4	19	1	.218	.229	.181
Fritz Peterson	80	8	9	3	0	0	2	8	22	0	.193	.150	.113
John Ellis	62	2	18	4	0	1	8	1	11	0	.308	.403	.290
Stan Bahnsen	60	1	5	1	0	0	1	2	33	0	.113	.100	.083
Billy Cowan	48	5	8	0	0	1	3	3	9	0	.216	.229	.167
Tom Shopay	48	2	4	0	1	0	0	2	10	0	.120	.125	.083
Al Downing	44	2	6	1	0	0	5	2	17	0	.174	.159	.136
Bill Burbach	40	4	4	1	0	0	0	3	22	0	.163	.125	.100
Frank Tepedino	39	6	9	0	0	0	4	4	4	1	.302	.231	.231
Mike Kekich	27	0	3	1	0	0	1	0	10	0	.111	.111	.111
Dave McDonald	23	0	5	1	0	0	2	2	5	0	.280	.261	.217
Dick Simpson	11	2	3	2	0	0	4	3	6	0	.429	.455	.273
Jack Aker	9	0	1	0	0	0	0	0	5	0	.111	.111	.111
Lindy McDaniel	8	1	0	0	0	0	0	1	7	0	.111	.000	.000
Ron Blomberg	6	0	3	0	0	0	0	1	0	0	.571	.500	.500
Steve Hamilton	5	0	0	0	0	0	0	0	2	0	.000	.000	.000
Ken Johnson	3	0	0	0	0	0	1	1	2	0	.250	.000	.000
Ron Klimkowski	3	0	0	0	0	0	0	0	2	0	.000	.000	.000

EIGHT

1970: *Them Damn Birds*

The Yankees' disappointing fifth-place finish in 1969 was a clear indication to the front office that several changes needed to be made if the team was going to improve their standing in the highly competitive American League East. For the third consecutive season, New York had finished near the bottom of the league rankings in several offensive categories. In 1969, the Yankees' totals of 562 runs scored and 94 home runs were both next to last in the A.L., and their .235 team batting average was tenth best.

Horace Clarke had done a solid job at second base, batting .285 and leading the team with 183 base hits and 33 stolen bases, while tying for the team lead with 82 runs scored and providing steady, if unspectacular, defense in the field. Gene Michael had a surprisingly good year at the plate, hitting .272 and giving the team solid defense at shortstop after taking over for the departed Tom Tresh. Left-fielder Roy White had, once again, been the team's most consistent player, leading New York with a .290 batting average and .392 on-base percentage, finishing second in runs batted in (74) and third in stolen bases (18), and committing only 3 errors in the field. Bobby Murcer, although somewhat inconsistent at the plate, had shown outstanding potential, leading the team with 82 runs batted in, tying for the team lead in runs scored (82), and finishing second in home runs (26) in his first full big league season. He had also made tremendous progress as an outfielder after being shifted from third base to centerfield during the season's first half. These four positions appeared to be strengths going into 1970. However, every other position needed to be upgraded.

Once again, New York had gotten little in the way of production from their catchers. Between them, Jake Gibbs and Frank Fernandez had hit 12 home runs, driven in 47 runs, and batted .223 in 1969. There was help on the way, though, as the Yankees planned to give rookie receiver Thurman Munson a shot at the everyday job. Although Munson had played in fewer than 100 minor league games, he had hit at every level, was quick as a cat behind the plate, and possessed a tremendous amount of self-confidence that seemed to indicate he was ready to play at the major league level.

Right-field had been a disaster in 1969, as whoever the Yankees had put out there had failed miserably. Whether it was Bill Robinson, who had since been banished to the minor leagues, Jimmie Hall, Ron Woods, or Jim Lyttle, none of the players that the team had tried at the position had added much to the offense. That was one position that clearly needed to be improved upon.

Jerry Kenney had provided adequate defense at third base after switching positions with Bobby Murcer early in the season. He had also had a decent season offensively, batting .257 and stealing 25 bases. However, his 2 home runs, 34 runs batted in, and 49 runs scored were not nearly productive enough for a third baseman. It was imperative that the Yankees upgrade that position as well.

Then, there was first base. While Joe Pepitone had led the team in 1969 with 27 home runs, had knocked in 70 runs, and had been awarded his third Gold Glove at season's end, his erratic behavior had proved to be a major distraction over the last two months. He had forced the Yankees' hand, and they clearly needed to dispose of their talented, but enigmatic, slugger. After rumors abounded for two months about what his eventual destination might be, one of which even involved a possible trade with the Phillies for their troubled superstar, Richie Allen, on December 4 the Yankees finally settled on a deal with the Houston Astros for first baseman/outfielder Curt Blefary.

The Brooklyn-born Blefary had originally signed with the Yankees, but had been sold to the Baltimore Orioles while he was still in the minors. With Baltimore in 1965, Blefary had been named the American League's Rookie of the Year for hitting 22 home runs, while knocking in 70 runs and batting .260. After playing the outfield exclusively in his rookie year, Blefary, due to his lack of speed and poor glove, was subsequently tried at first base and catcher by the Orioles in an attempt to keep his bat in the lineup. However, he proved to be deficient at each of those positions, and his offensive numbers gradually started to decline as well. Blefary blamed the constant defensive shuffling for his offensive decline. Finally, after hitting 15 home runs, knocking in just 39 runs, and batting only .200 for the Orioles in 1968, he was traded to Houston as part of the deal that brought Mike Cuellar to Baltimore.

With the Astros, Blefary experienced philosophical differences in hitting styles with Houston Manager Harry Walker, who wanted the pull-hitting Blefary to become more of a spray hitter. With the Astros in 1969, Blefary hit 12 home runs, drove in 67 runs, and batted .253. However, the

Walker-Blefary relationship was not working out, and, at season's end, Blefary was put on the trading block. So, the Pepitone-for-Blefary deal was really one that both sides felt was necessary. However, it seemed that, perhaps, the Yankees had gotten less than equal value for their talented first baseman. Only time would tell if that was the case, though.

On the same day the Yankees made the deal to acquire Blefary, they also made another trade. In that one, they sent veteran left-hander Al Downing and catcher Frank Fernandez to Oakland for first baseman/third baseman Danny Cater. New York had grown increasingly impatient waiting for Downing to develop into the star they had always felt he had the ability to be. In addition, they had high hopes for both Bill Burbach and Mike Kekich as starting pitchers, so Downing had become somewhat expendable. Fernandez' value to the team had also diminished with the arrival of rookie receiver Thurman Munson, and New York had a glaring need for another consistent bat in the lineup, so the deal made sense from their perspective.

Cater had originally signed as a shortstop with the Phillies, but had played first base, third base, and the outfield in his six previous major league seasons. After spending his first season with Philadelphia in 1964, hitting .296 in 152 at-bats, he had subsequently been dealt first to the White Sox and then to the Athletics. A solid right-handed hitter throughout his career, Cater had finished second to Boston's Carl Yastrzemski in the 1968 A.L. batting race, hitting .290 as Oakland's regular first baseman. He had an unusual batting stance, with his feet close together, and a smooth, lazy-looking swing that made him a predominantly opposite field hitter, with the majority of his hits going to right and right-center field.

With the acquisitions of Blefary and Cater the Yankees planned to play the former in right-field, where, hopefully, his lack of speed would not be as much of a factor. With Cater, they envisioned setting up a platoon, playing Cater at first and the left-handed hitting Jerry Kenney at third against right-handed pitchers, while employing Cater at third and rookie John Ellis at first against left-handers.

The 6'2", 225 pound Ellis was a powerfully-built and extremely intense youngster who had played mostly catcher during his minor league career. However, with Munson considered to be the team's catcher of the future, the Yankees decided to convert Ellis into a first baseman in order to take advantage of his great power. While not very graceful in the field, Ellis did a reasonably good job in making the transition to first during spring training.

Having addressed the needs of the starting lineup, the Yankees turned their attention towards improving their bench. Two weeks after acquiring Blefary and Cater, they sent minor league pitcher Mickey Scott and cash to the Chicago White Sox for former American League Rookie of the Year Pete Ward.

After making his major league debut with Baltimore in 1962, Ward was included in the blockbuster deal that sent shortstop Luis Aparicio and third baseman Al Smith to the Orioles for Ron Hansen, Dave Nicholson, Hoyt Wilhelm, and Ward. Placed at third base by the White Sox to replace Smith, Ward showed good range but led A.L. third basemen with 38 errors in 1963. However, he also finished fifth in the league with a batting average of .295, hit 22 home runs, drove in 84 runs, scored another 80, and finished second in the league in total bases (289), hits (177), and doubles (34). At season's end, he was selected as *The Sporting News* Rookie of the Year and finished ninth in the league MVP voting. After another fine season in 1964 in which he established career highs in home runs (23) and runs batted in (94), while batting .282 and cutting his error total in half, to 19, he finished sixth in the league MVP voting. However, during the off-season, he was involved in a minor auto accident that caused him to be bothered by muscle spasms in his neck throughout the 1965 season. As a result, his productivity slipped to 10 home runs, 57 runs batted in, and a .247 batting average. A back injury in 1966 permitted him to appear in only 84 games, bat just .219, and forced him to move to the outfield. Although he rebounded somewhat in 1967, his playing time diminished in each of the subsequent two seasons, and, by the time the Yankees obtained him, he was viewed essentially as a solid left-handed bat off the bench.

Another player New York obtained during the off-season to strengthen their bench was veteran infielder Ron Hansen, who also had first come up with the Baltimore Orioles. After winning American League Rookie of the Year honors as a shortstop for the Orioles in 1960 by hitting 22 home runs and driving in 80 runs, he led league shortstops in double plays the following season. However, while spending six months of 1962 in the Marines due to the Cuban Missile Crises, he injured his back and was subsequently traded to the White Sox in the January, 1963 deal that brought Luis Aparicio to the Orioles. With Chicago, Hansen led the league twice more in double plays and four times in assists, even turning the majors' first unassisted triple play in 41 years in a 1968 game. However, due to recurring back problems, Hansen's playing time and productivity had both been on the decline since 1966, and by the time the Yankees picked him up, he, too, was seen more as a utility player.

Other reserves would be Jake Gibbs behind the plate, and Ron Woods and Jim Lyttle in the outfield.

The pitching staff, which had been the team's strength once again in

1969, was not tinkered with nearly as much. Mel Stottlemyre was coming off his third 20–win season, and Fritz Peterson had been solid in 1969 as well. Third starter, Stan Bahnsen, had slumped the previous year, but was expected to bounce back and pitch more like he had in 1968, when he had been named American League Rookie of the Year. With Al Downing gone, Bill Burbach, whose rookie season had been a somewhat disappointing one, was expected to assume the role of fourth starter, while Mike Kekich was expected to move into the fifth spot in the rotation.

Lindy McDaniel and Jack Aker, the bullpen closers in 1968 and 1969, respectively, were back, and Steve Hamilton was returning as well. The only new additions to the pitching staff were two youngsters— right-hander Ron Klimkowski and lefty John Cumberland.

Klimkowski had led the International League with 15 wins and a 2.18 ERA in 1969, primarily as a starter. Although he was not a particularly hard thrower, he had a wide variety of off-speed pitches that usually allowed him to keep opposing batters off balance. Cumberland had brief trials with the team in each of the previous two seasons and finally earned a roster spot as the second left-hander in the bullpen. Both Klimkowski and Cumberland were expected to pitch mostly in middle and long relief.

The regular season began with a 4–3 Opening Day loss at Yankee Stadium to the Red Sox, with Mel Stottlemyre suffering his first Opening Day defeat. After Fritz Peterson evened the score with a 4–3 victory in the next game, the Yankees struggled in the early-going, losing 10 of their first 15 games. Particularly ineffective over that stretch were Mel Stottlemyre, Thurman Munson, and Curt Blefary. Stottlemyre won only one of his first four decisions, almost a complete reversal of the prior year, when he had won his first five. Munson had only 1 hit in his first 31 at-bats, providing an early test to the rookie's self- confidence. Blefary also struggled at the plate, failing to hit his first home run until well into the season's first month.

However, Stottlemyre's pitching improved, Munson started to hit, and New York won 8 of their next 10 contests to leave their record at 13–12. It was during this period, though, that it was discovered that Bill Burbach was suffering from mononucleosis. After making just four starts, he would be lost for the remainder of the season, forcing New York to look elsewhere for another starting pitcher.

Over the next month, both John Cumberland and Ron Klimkowski were given opportunities to break into the rotation. However, it soon became apparent that neither was particularly well-suited for that role. Cumberland did a decent job in his eight starts, but he was clearly not the answer. Klimkowski started just three games and also did a creditable job, but he was much more effective coming out of the bullpen.

For much of that month, the Yankees stayed right around the .500–mark, finishing the month of May with an overall record of 26–23, in second place, 7½ games behind Baltimore.

However, the team soon took off, winning 12 of their next 14 games, compiling winning streaks of 5 and 6 games in the process. After 63 games, their record stood at 38–25, they were in second place, and they had closed to within 1½ games of Baltimore.

Right around this time, the Yankees picked up veteran right-hander Gary Waslewski from the Montreal Expos to compete for the fifth starter's spot. Waslewski was a journeyman pitcher who had a brief moment of glory as a rookie in the 1967 World Series as a member of the Red Sox. As the Game Six starter, he gave Boston five-plus solid innings as they went on to beat the Cardinals, 8–4. However, with the Yankees, he would end up pitching mostly in relief, making only five starts and compiling a 2–2 record, with a 3.11 ERA.

Having particularly good seasons at this juncture were Fritz Peterson and Roy White.

Peterson, after starting off the season 1–3, had put together an eight game winning streak at one point, and had a 10–5 record after the team's first 63 games. White was having his finest season, and, for quite some time, was among the league leaders in batting. They were also receiving a great deal of support from Danny Cater, Thurman Munson, and the Yankee bench. Cater, from the beginning of the season to the end, was the team's most consistent hitter. After starting off the season so terribly, Munson was now tearing the cover off the ball, moving his average up steadily. Reserves Ron Hansen and Pete Ward were providing the kind of play off the bench that the team had not seen in years, both supplying several big pinch-hits, and Hansen filling in admirably at both second and short.

Nevertheless, New York went into a tailspin, losing 14 of their next 22 games. So, on July 12, at the All-Star break, the Yankees' record stood at 46–39, they had fallen to third place in the standings, behind Baltimore and Detroit, and they were a full 7 games out of first.

The Yankees had three representatives on the American League All-Star team — pitchers Fritz Peterson and Mel Stottlemyre, and outfielder Roy White. Peterson was having his finest season in the big leagues and was clearly deserving. White had slumped badly during the last three weeks, but he was still having his best year and was batting well over .300. Stottlemyre's first half was not a particularly good one, but he was still one of the better pitchers in the league. Nevertheless, his selection to the team was probably based largely on past performance.

Following the All-Star break, the Yankees played .500 ball over the next two weeks before getting hot again and compiling a six-game winning streak that put their record on August 1 at 57–46, leaving them in second place, 7½ games behind Baltimore.

New York had not yet given up trying to find a capable fifth starter, though. Late in July, they acquired veteran left-hander Mike McCormick from the San Francisco Giants.

McCormick had originally signed with the Giants as a 17–year-old flame-thrower in 1956. After leading the National League with a 2.70 ERA in 1960, while compiling a record of 15–12, he began to experience arm problems in 1962. Traded to Baltimore prior to the start of the 1963 season, he continued to have problems with his arm, as well as his control. He was eventually returned to the minors before resurfacing with the Washington Senators. After two mediocre seasons in Washington, McCormick was reacquired by the Giants in December of 1966. Although he had lost his blazing fastball by then, he had mastered his breaking pitches and developed a screwball. McCormick had a career year in 1967, going 22–10 for the Giants, leading the league in wins, compiling a 2.85 ERA, and winning both the Cy Young and Comeback Player of the Year awards. However, over the next two-plus seasons, he had gone only 26–27, and was clearly past his prime by the time he joined the Yankees. He ended up appearing in 9 games with New York, 4 of them starts, and compiling a 2–0 record and a 6.10 ERA.

Finally, the Yankees settled on young right-hander Steve Kline, who had been brought up from the minors a few weeks earlier, as their fifth starter. In 15 starts, Kline finished 6–6, with a 3.41 ERA.

New York remained hot throughout most of August, compiling a 19–12 record during the month. However, no matter how well they played, they were unable to make up any ground on the Orioles, who were putting together another fabulous season. By the end of the year, Baltimore would compile a record of 108–54 and would go on to sweep the Minnesota Twins in the ALCS, and defeat the Cincinnati Reds in the World Series in 5 games. In spite of their outstanding August record, the Yankees actually *lost* 4½ games in the standings to Baltimore and trailed them by a full 12 games at the start of September.

From that point on, it was merely a matter of playing for second place in the standings, something the Yankees were able to accomplish. By winning 19 of their final 29 contests during the month of September, New York was able to finish the season with an outstanding record of 93–69, in second place, six games ahead of the third place Red Sox. However, they also finished a full 15 games behind the Orioles. In head-to-head competition with the eventual world champions, the Yankees won only 7 of 18 contests. Boston, with a record of 10–8, was the only other team in the league that held an advantage over New York in their season series. The Yankees were particularly hard on Kansas City, Minnesota, and Milwaukee. Against the Royals, they won 11 of 12 contests, while they took 9 of 12 from both the Twins and the Brewers.

There were many reasons for the Yankees' 1970 turnaround. First, there was a tremendous amount of improvement in the offense. The team batting average of .251 was 16 points higher than it had been in 1969 and tied them for fifth best in the league. Their 680 runs scored were the fourth highest total in the league and were 118 more than they had scored the previous year. With 111, they also hit 17 more home runs than they had in 1969. Though not possessing any dominant-type hitters, New York's lineup featured many solid line-drive hitters and seemed to come up with many timely hits all season. Roy White, Danny Cater, and Thurman Munson were particularly effective.

White had his most productive season, finishing second on the team with 22 home runs, third in batting, with an average of .296, and leading in runs batted in (94), base hits (180), runs scored (109), and stolen bases (24). He finished third in the league in runs scored and fifth in hits, played in all 162 games, committed only two errors, and finished 15th in the league MVP voting.

Cater provided the team with consistency and stability in the middle of the lineup all season, never experiencing any lengthy slumps, and keeping his average around the .300–mark for much of the year. Playing both first base and third, Cater finished the season with only 6 home runs, but finished third on the team with 76 runs batted in, second in hits, with 175, and second in batting, with an average of .301.

After starting off the season so slowly, Munson proved to be everything the Yankees thought he could be. He led the team with an average of .302, provided tremendous leadership behind the plate, especially for a rookie, and established himself as a cornerstone around which the team could build their future. At season's end, he received 23 of a possible 24 votes in being named the American League's Rookie of the Year.

Both Ron Hansen and Pete Ward excelled as role players. Filling in for Gene Michael at shortstop and Horace Clarke at second, and also coming off the bench as a right-handed pinch-hitter, Hansen, in 91 at-bats, hit 4 home runs, knocked in 14 runs, and batted .297. Ward, in 77 at-bats, mostly as a pinch-hitter, hit only 1 home run, but drove in 18 runs and batted .260.

Jake Gibbs also thrived in his reduced role as Munson's back-up. In just 153 at-bats, he hit 8 home runs, knocked in 26 runs, and batted .301.

However, the offense did have its fair share of disappointments.

Although he led the team with 23 home runs and finished second to Roy White in both runs batted in, with 78, and runs scored, with 95, Bobby Murcer did not make the kind of progress the Yankees were hoping he would. He batted only .251, struck out 100 times, and was prone to lengthy slumps at times. Yet he did play a solid centerfield, making only 3 errors and collecting 15 assists.

The double play combination of Horace Clarke and Gene Michael did not perform as well as they had in 1969. Although he finished second on the team in stolen bases (23) and third in hits (172), Clarke batted just .251, 34 points below his average the previous season, and committed 18 errors in the field. Michael batted just .214 and made 28 errors.

John Ellis and Jerry Kenney did not fare particularly well in their first base/third base platoon situation with Danny Cater. Ellis, who the Yankees had hoped would eventually become the full-time first baseman, only occasionally provided glimpses of the great power he possessed. In 226 at-bats, he hit just 7 home runs, knocked in only 29 runs, and batted .248. Kenney's offensive performance was downright anemic. In 404 at-bats, he hit 4 home runs, drove in 35 runs, and batted just .193.

However, the biggest disappointment was undoubtedly Curt Blefary, who ended up platooning in right field for much of the season with Ron Woods. In his 269 at-bats, Blefary hit just 9 home runs, knocked in just 37 runs, and batted only .212. The Yankees had clearly accepted less-than-equal-value when they traded Joe Pepitone to acquire him.

The pitching staff had, once again, performed admirably. The Yankees' team ERA of 3.24 was the third lowest in the league, their 36 complete games was the third highest total, and their 49 saves tied them for second most.

Fritz Peterson had his finest season and was the team's best starter. He finished the year with a record of 20–11, led the team with a 2.90 ERA, tied Stan Bahnsen for the team lead in shutouts, with 2, led in strikeouts, with 127, and finished second to Mel Stottlemyre with 260 innings pitched. He finished fifth in the league in wins and fourth in earned run average.

Mel Stottlemyre had a somewhat disappointing season, finishing only 15–13. Nevertheless, he finished second on the team with a 3.09 ERA, and led in innings pitched (271) and complete games (14).

Stan Bahnsen had a far better year than he had in 1969, finishing the season with a record of 14–11 and an ERA of 3.33.

Ron Klimkowski did a good job in middle relief, finishing with a 6–7 record and a 2.65 ERA.

The combination of Lindy McDaniel and Jack Aker proved to be as formidable a bullpen duo as there was in the major leagues. In his 62 relief appearances and 111 innings of work, McDaniel compiled a record of 9–5, with an ERA of 2.01, and 29 saves, good enough for second in the American League. In 41 relief appearances, Aker's record was 4–2, his ERA was 2.06, and he saved 16 games.

While the Yankees still needed to improve in certain areas, and while the Baltimore Orioles provided a huge obstacle to their ultimate goal of winning the division, the Yankees had apparently turned the corner in 1970. For the first time in several seasons, the team and their fans were able to approach the off-season with a feeling of optimism.

Season Highlights, Outstanding Performances, and Memorable Moments:

May 3   At Yankee Stadium, the Yankees win both ends of a double-header from the Brewers, taking the first game, 8–7, and the nightcap, 4–2. The big blows in the first game are a home run into the right-center field bleachers by Bobby Murcer and a two-run triple by Thurman Munson. The victories give New York a five-game winning streak and leave their record at 13–12, putting them over the .500–mark for the first time all season.

May 7   At Oakland-Alameda County Stadium, the Yankees defeat the Athletics, 7–3. Fritz Peterson gets the win and Roy White homers from both sides of the plate.

May 18   At Yankee Stadium, the Yankees defeat the first-place Orioles, 10–4, to move to within five games of first-place Baltimore. Fritz Peterson gets the win, and also hits a home run.

May 21   In a 2–0 victory over the Washington Senators at Yankee Stadium, Mel Stottlemyre walks 11 batters over 8⅓ innings. Steve Hamilton gets the final two outs to preserve the win, made possible by a two-run homer in the fifth inning by Danny Cater.

May 24   Despite three home runs by Cleveland first baseman Tony Horton, the Yankees sweep a doubleheader from the Indians at Cleveland's Municipal Stadium, winning the first game, 6–5, and taking the nightcap, 8–7.

June 4   At Yankee Stadium, after being no-hit for eight innings by Kansas City's Jim Rooker, the Yankees rally for two runs in the bottom of the ninth to win the game, 2–1. Horace Clarke breaks up the no-hitter, leading off the inning with a single, then comes around to score on Bobby Murcer's game-winning double. Stan Bahnsen gets the victory. Meanwhile, Clarke will break up two other no-hit bids later this month with ninth-inning hits.

June 16   At Comiskey Park in Chicago, the Yankees win their sixth consecutive game, and eleventh in their last twelve, defeating the White Sox, 6–2. Mel Stottlemyre out-pitches Tommy John, leaving the Yankees' season record at 37–24.

June 24   In a doubleheader split with the Indians at Yankee Stadium, Bobby Murcer hits four consecutive home runs. Murcer connects in his final at-bat against Sam McDowell in the Yankees' first-game 7–2 loss. He then hits three more in New York's second-game 5–4 victory, connecting twice against Cleveland starter Mike Paul and once against reliever Fred Lasher.

August 29 At Yankee Stadium, New York loses to Minnesota, 3–1, but Mickey Mantle returns to the team as first base coach.

Sept. 20   At Boston's Fenway Park, the Yankees defeat the Red Sox, 4–3, in the final game of the season for Fritz Peterson's 20th victory. The Yankees finish the year with a record of 93–69, their best mark since their last pennant-winning season of 1964.

1970 American League Final Team Standings and Offensive Statistics

TEAM	G	W	L	PCT	GB	R	H	2B	3B	HR	BB	SO	SB	AVG	OBP	SLG
EAST																
BAL	162	108	54	.667	—	792	1424	213	25	179	717	952	84	.257	.346	.401
NY	162	93	69	.574	15	680	1381	208	41	111	588	808	105	.251	.327	.365
BOSTON	162	87	75	.537	21	786	1450	252	28	203	594	855	50	.262	.338	.428
DET	162	79	83	.488	29	666	1282	207	38	148	656	825	29	.238	.325	.374
CLE	162	76	86	.469	32	649	1358	197	23	183	503	909	25	.249	.316	.394
WASH	162	70	92	.432	38	626	1302	184	28	138	635	989	72	.238	.323	.358
WEST																
MINN	162	98	64	.605	—	744	1438	230	41	153	501	905	57	.262	.329	.403
OAK	162	89	73	.549	9	678	1338	208	24	171	584	977	131	.249	.327	.392
CAL	162	86	76	.531	12	631	1391	197	40	114	447	922	69	.251	.311	.363
MIL	162	65	97	.401	33	613	1305	202	24	126	592	985	91	.242	.321	.358
KC	162	65	97	.401	33	611	1341	202	41	97	514	958	97	.244	.311	.348
CHI	162	56	106	.346	42	633	1394	192	20	123	477	872	53	.253	.317	.362
TOTAL						8109	16404	2492	373	1746	6808	10957	863	.250	.324	.379

Team Pitching and Fielding Statistics

TEAM	CG	SH	SV	IP	H	HR	BB	SO	ERA	FA	E	DP
EAST												
BAL	50	12	31	1478	1317	139	469	941	3.15	.981	117	148
NY	55	6	49	1471	1386	130	451	777	3.24	.980	130	146

TEAM	CG	SH	SV	IP	H	HR	BB	SO	ERA	FA	E	DP
EAST												
BOSTON	30	8	44	1446	1391	156	594	1003	3.87	.974	156	131
DET	28	9	39	1447	1443	153	623	1045	4.09	.978	133	142
CLE	53	8	35	1451	1333	163	689	1076	3.91	.979	133	168
WASH	35	11	40	1457	1375	139	611	823	3.80	.982	116	173
WEST												
MINN	41	12	58	1448	1329	130	486	940	3.23	.980	123	130
OAK	42	15	40	1442	1253	134	542	858	3.30	.977	141	152
CAL	25	10	49	1462	1280	154	559	922	3.48	.980	127	169
MIL	42	2	27	1446	1397	146	587	895	4.21	.978	136	142
KC	29	11	25	1463	1346	138	641	915	3.78	.976	152	162
CHI	21	6	30	1430	1554	164	556	762	4.54	.975	165	187
TOTAL	382	110	467	17447					3.71	.978	1629	1850

1970 New York Yankee Pitching Statistics

PLAYER	W	L	ERA	G	GS	CG	SHO	SV	IP	H	R	ER	BB	SO
Mel Stottlemyre	15	13	3.09	37	37	14	0	0	271	262	110	93	84	126
Fritz Peterson	20	11	2.90	39	37	8	2	0	260	247	102	84	40	127
Stan Bahnsen	14	11	3.33	36	35	6	2	0	232	227	100	86	75	116
Lindy McDaniel	9	5	2.01	62	0	0	0	29	111	88	29	25	23	81
Steve Kline	6	6	3.41	16	15	5	0	0	100	99	42	38	24	49
Mike Kekich	6	3	4.83	26	14	1	0	0	98	103	59	53	55	63
Ron Klimkowski	6	7	2.65	45	3	1	1	1	98	80	36	29	33	40
Jack Aker	4	2	2.06	41	0	0	0	16	70	57	19	16	20	36
John Cumberland	3	4	3.94	15	8	1	0	0	64	62	31	28	15	38
Gary Waslewski	2	2	3.11	26	5	0	0	0	55	42	20	19	27	27
Steve Hamilton	4	3	2.78	35	0	0	0	3	45	36	16	14	16	33
Mike McCormick	2	0	6.10	9	4	0	0	0	20	26	15	14	13	12
Bill Burbach	0	2	10.26	4	4	0	0	0	16	23	19	19	9	10
Joe Verbanic	1	0	4.60	7	0	0	0	0	15	20	9	8	12	8
Rob Gardner	1	0	4.91	1	1	0	0	0	7	8	4	4	4	6
Loyd Colson	0	0	4.50	1	0	0	0	0	2	3	1	1	0	3
Gary Jones	0	0	0.00	2	0	0	0	0	2	3	0	0	1	2

1970 New York Yankee Hitting Statistics

PLAYER	AB	R	H	2B	3B	HR	RBI	BB	SO	SB	OBP	SLG	AVG
Horace Clarke	686	81	172	24	2	4	46	35	35	23	.286	.309	.251
Roy White	609	109	180	30	6	22	94	95	66	24	.387	.473	.296
Danny Cater	582	64	175	26	5	6	76	34	44	4	.340	.393	.301
Bobby Murcer	581	95	146	23	3	23	78	87	100	15	.348	.420	.251
Thurman Munson	453	59	137	25	4	6	53	57	56	5	.386	.415	.302
Gene Michael	435	42	93	10	1	2	38	50	93	3	.292	.255	.214
Jerry Kenney	404	46	78	10	7	4	35	52	44	20	.284	.282	.193
Curt Blefary	269	34	57	6	0	9	37	43	37	1	.324	.335	.212
John Ellis	226	24	56	12	1	7	29	18	47	0	.305	.403	.248
Ron Woods	225	30	51	5	3	8	27	33	35	4	.324	.382	.227
Jake Gibbs	153	23	46	9	2	8	26	7	14	2	.331	.542	.301
Jim Lyttle	126	20	39	7	1	3	14	10	26	3	.355	.452	.310

PLAYER	AB	R	H	2B	3B	HR	RBI	BB	SO	SB	OBP	SLG	AVG
Frank Baker	117	6	27	4	1	0	11	14	26	1	.323	.282	.231
Ron Hansen	91	13	27	4	0	4	14	19	9	0	.420	.473	.297
Fritz Peterson	90	7	20	3	0	2	7	0	24	0	.228	.322	.222
Mel Stottlemyre	85	8	16	2	2	2	7	14	25	0	.303	.329	.188
Pete Ward	77	5	20	2	2	1	18	9	17	0	.333	.377	.260
Stan Bahnsen	74	3	11	0	1	0	1	2	34	0	.171	.176	.149
Mike Kekich	32	2	3	0	0	0	2	2	7	0	.147	.094	.094
Steve Kline	28	3	5	0	0	0	2	4	10	0	.303	.179	.179
Lindy McDaniel	24	2	4	1	0	0	2	0	7	0	.167	.208	.167
Bobby Mitchell	22	1	5	2	0	0	4	2	3	0	.320	.318	.227
Ron Klimkowski	19	0	1	0	0	0	0	0	9	0	.053	.053	.053
Frank Tepedino	19	2	6	2	0	0	2	1	2	0	.350	.421	.316
John Cumberland	17	0	1	0	0	0	2	0	12	0	.059	.059	.059
Jack Aker	16	0	1	0	0	0	1	0	6	0	.063	.063	.063
Gary Waslewski	10	0	1	0	0	0	1	0	9	0	.100	.100	.100
Steve Hamilton	6	0	0	0	0	0	0	0	2	0	.000	.000	.000
Bill Burbach	5	0	0	0	0	0	0	0	4	0	.000	.000	.000
Mike McCormick	5	1	1	0	0	0	0	0	3	0	.200	.200	.200
Rob Gardner	3	0	1	1	0	0	0	0	1	0	.333	.667	.333
Joe Verbanic	3	0	1	0	0	0	0	0	1	0	.333	.333	.333

NINE

1971: The Team Regresses but a Star Is Born

The Yankees had high hopes going into spring training prior to the start of the 1971 season. The prior year, they had finished second in their division to the eventual world champion Baltimore Orioles, they had improved their record by 12½ games over what it had been in 1969, and their offense had improved dramatically. In 1970, they had scored 118 more runs (or .73 more per game) than they had the previous season, their team batting average had risen 16 points, and they had been one of only two American League teams to steal as many as 100 bases (the Oakland Athletics were the other). The everyday lineup featured young and talented players such as Roy White, Bobby Murcer, and Thurman Munson, while the steady Danny Cater added a veteran presence.

The pitching staff had also performed admirably, once again finishing among the league leaders in various team pitching categories. In 1970, Yankee pitchers had combined for the third lowest ERA in the league, the third most complete games, and the second most saves. The team had three quality starters in Mel Stottlemyre, Fritz Peterson, and Stan Bahnsen, and appeared to have finally settled on young right-hander Steve Kline as the fourth man in the rotation. The bullpen was one of the strongest in baseball, led by dual-closers Lindy McDaniel and Jack Aker. For the first time in more than half a decade, the outlook going into spring training was not an ominous one.

Yet, if the team had any hopes of providing serious competition to the Orioles for the division title in 1971, certain weaknesses still needed to be addressed. Danny Cater had provided consistency to the middle of the lineup, while shifting back and forth between first and third base in 1970. However, John Ellis and Jerry Kenney had added little to the offense in their first base/third base platoon. The Yankees still hoped that Ellis would develop into the first baseman of the future, but he would have to improve upon the 7 home runs, 29 runs batted in, and .248 batting average he compiled in his 226 at-bats the prior year. Meanwhile, Kenney would have to do a lot better than the .193 he had batted if he expected to garner any kind of meaningful playing time.

Horace Clarke had not performed nearly as well in 1970 as he had the prior year, but he was still a decent leadoff hitter and an adequate second baseman. However, his double play partner, Gene Michael, had batted only .214 — 58 points below his 1969 average — and had committed 28 errors in the field. As a result, the Yankees intended to give youngster Frank Baker a full shot at the shortstop job in the spring. Baker was a left-handed hitter who, in 117 at-bats with New York the prior year, had batted .231, with no home runs and 11 runs batted in. He was a smooth fielder, though, who, at 24, was eight years younger than the 32–year-old Michael. However, Baker failed to impress and Michael, once again, started the season at shortstop.

The other glaring weakness was in right-field, where Curt Blefary had failed so miserably the prior year. In his 269 at-bats, the former American League Rookie of the Year had hit only 9 home runs, driven in just 37 runs, and batted only .212. His platoon-mate, Ron Woods, in 225 at-bats, had hit 8 homers, knocked in 27 runs, and batted .227. New York clearly needed to get more production from that position.

The bench, which had performed so well in 1970, received a blow when left-handed pinch-hitting specialist Pete Ward retired during the off-season due to lingering back and neck problems. The Yankees needed to find a replacement for him. However, Ron Hansen was returning as a backup infielder and right-handed pinch-hitter, Jake Gibbs, coming off his finest season, would, once again, spell Thurman Munson behind the plate, and Jim Lyttle and Ron Woods would provide depth in the outfield.

The starting rotation appeared to be set with Stottlemyre, Peterson, Bahnsen, Kline, and Kekich. Bill Burbach had not recovered from his bout with mononucleosis, so he was no longer being counted on. The first four spots in the bullpen were also taken, with McDaniel, Aker, Ron Klimkowski, and Gary Waslewski having spots reserved for them. However, towards the end of the 1970 season, the team had dealt veteran left-handed relief specialist Steve Hamilton to the Chicago White Sox, leaving them without a left-hander in the bullpen. That spot would be vied for by youngsters Gary Jones, Terry Ley, and Alan Closter, and veteran Rob Gardner. Jones, Ley, and Closter had practically no major league experience, while Gardner had pitched previously with the Mets, Cubs, Indians, and, briefly, with the Yankees the prior year. He had seen his most extensive duty with the Mets in 1966, starting 17 games, appearing in 24 others, and compiling a record of 4–8, with a 5.12 ERA. He ended up winning the last spot on the staff in spring training.

The regular season opened on April 6 with a 3–1 loss to the Red Sox at Fenway Park. With Mel Stottlemyre troubled by a slight stiffness in his shoulder, Stan Bahnsen got the Opening Day assignment and pitched well, allowing just two runs over seven innings. However, Boston's Ray Culp was even better, giving up just one run and five hits in going the distance. After losing their second game as well, the Yankees got their first win of the season as Stottlemyre returned to the mound by shutting out the Senators in Washington, 6–0.

Right at this time, though, on April 9, the Yankees addressed their need for another bat in the lineup by making a deal with the Oakland A's. The trade brought New York veteran outfielder Felipe Alou for pitchers Rob Gardner and Ron Klimkowski. Felipe was the oldest of the three Alou brothers who played in the major leagues, having debuted with the Giants in 1958. The only Alou who hit for power, the right-handed hitting Felipe hit more than 20 homers four times in his career, once hitting as many as 31. He was a three-time National League All-Star who also finished in the top ten in the league MVP voting twice. His best season for San Francisco came in 1962, when he hit 25 home runs, drove in 98 runs, scored 96 others, and batted .316. After being traded to the Braves prior to the start of the 1964 season, Alou had his finest year in 1966 when he established career-highs in home runs (31) and batting average (.327), while leading the league in runs scored (122) and base hits (218). After three more successful seasons with the Braves, Alou was traded to the A's, for whom he batted .271 in 1970. However, with young outfielders such as Reggie Jackson and Joe Rudi on the Oakland roster, the 36–year-old Alou was expendable, so they dealt him to New York for bullpen help. Alou quickly became the Yankees' regular right-fielder, also seeing some action at first base.

However, even with the addition of Alou, New York struggled throughout much of April and early May, failing to win more than two consecutive games at any time. Finally, after putting together a five-game winning streak, on May 13 the Yankees' record stood at 15–14, making it the first time since the season's first week that they were over the .500–mark. Unfortunately, the team then lost seven of their next eight games, dropping their record to 16–21.

This sort of inconsistent play was characteristic of the Yankees' performance over the first half of the season. Every short winning streak was followed by a losing streak, making it virtually impossible for the team to gain any kind of serious momentum. As a result, they spent virtually the entire first half playing below-.500 ball, prompting them to make several moves in an attempt to find the right mix of players that would allow them to stay competitive within the division.

On May 26, they traded Curt Blefary to Oakland for pitchers Darrell Osteen and Rob Gardner, who they had sent to the A's earlier in the year for Felipe Alou.

On June 7, they acquired outfielder Danny Walton from the Brewers for outfield prospects Bobby Mitchell and Frank Tepedino. Just one year earlier, Walton had hit 17 home runs for Milwaukee, but he was batting only .203 for the Brewers in 1971, and was having a very difficult time making contact with the ball. After striking out 7 times in his 14 at-bats with the Yankees, he was sent down to the minor leagues.

Less than three weeks later, the Yankees sent Ron Woods to the Expos for outfielder Ron Swoboda, who had been a New York baseball hero of sorts earlier in his career with the Mets. As a 20–year-old rookie with the Mets in 1965, Swoboda hit a career-high 19 home runs. However, he also batted only .228 that year, struck out 102 times in just 399 at-bats, and was a horrific outfielder. In his next few seasons with the Mets, Swoboda continued to show occasional signs of power, strike out a lot, and hit for a low batting average (although he did hit a career-high .281 in 1967). One thing that did improve, though, was his defense, as Swoboda worked very hard on that particular aspect of his game and, eventually, turned himself into a pretty good outfielder. In fact, his miraculous catch in Game Four of the 1969 World Series against the Orioles still has to rank among the greatest ever. By the time the Yankees acquired him, Swoboda still had a propensity for striking out fairly frequently, but had cut down on his swing somewhat, was hitting a little less for power but for a slightly higher batting average, and was a competent outfielder. In 138 at-bats with the Yankees, he hit 2 home runs, knocked in 20 runs, batted .261, and struck out 35 times.

Right around the same time New York acquired Swoboda, they also brought up top minor league prospect Ron Blomberg. The powerfully built Atlanta, Georgia native had been selected by the Yankees as the nation's first draft pick in the amateur draft of 1967. The left-handed hitting Blomberg had the perfect swing for Yankee Stadium, and, when he connected, the ball seemed to jump off his bat. His combination of power and speed, as well as the enthusiasm he brought to the park with him everyday, definitely added something to the team that they had previously been lacking. There were, however, two things that prevented him from becoming an immediate impact player. The first was his inability to hit left-handed pitching. While he posed a serious threat to right-handers, Blomberg, who had frequently been platooned even in the minors, seemed lost against left-handers. In addition, he came up to the big club as an outfielder—a position he was clearly not comfortable in. While he had very good running speed and a strong throwing arm, Blomberg possessed neither the instincts nor the judgment needed to be a successful major league outfielder. Still, it was difficult to keep his bat out of the lineup against right-handed pitching. In 199 at-bats, he ended up hitting 7 home runs, driving in 31 runs, and batting .322.

Another player the Yankees called up from the minors was right-handed reliever Roger Hambright, who did a respectable job working strictly out of the bullpen. In 18 relief appearances, Hambright worked 26 innings, compiling a 3–1 record and a 4.39 ERA.

A final addition was right-handed pitcher Jim Hardin, who the Yankees acquired on waivers from Baltimore. Hardin had once been a big winner for the Orioles, compiling a record of 18–13 and an ERA of 2.51 in 1968. However, he had won only six games in each of the last two seasons, working both as a starter and in relief, and was ineffective in New York. In 12 appearances, three as a starter, he finished 0–2, with a 5.08 ERA.

In spite of all their maneuvering, the Yankees' erratic play continued throughout the first half of the season. On July 11, at the All-Star break, New York's record was just 41–47, and they were in fourth place, 14½ games behind the division-leading Baltimore Orioles. Nevertheless, the team placed two men on the league All-Star team—centerfielder Bobby Murcer and catcher Thurman Munson. Murcer, having a superb season, was named as a starter, while Munson was selected as a reserve

Finally, after losing their first game following the break, the Yankees were able to put together a stretch of games during which they sustained a fairly high level of play. Winning 10 of 13 games, New York improved their record to 51–51 on July 25, reaching the .500–mark for the first time since May 17. However, the success was short-lived, and the team continued to hover around the .500–mark for much of the remainder of the season. It was not until they were able to string together four consecutive victories in mid-September, leaving their record at 79–74, that they succeeded in putting a little breathing room between themselves and .500. However, they won only three of their last nine games to finish the season with a record of only 82–80, in fourth place in the American League East, 22 games behind the first-place Orioles, against whom the Yankees posted a record of 7–11 in head-to-head competition.

There were several reasons for the Yankees' disappointing performance in 1971. Danny Cater, who had been, quite possibly, the team's most consistent hitter the previous season, did not have a particularly bad year, batting .276. However, he was not nearly as much of a factor as he had been in 1970. Once again splitting his time between first and third base, he hit only 4 home runs, knocked in just 50 runs, and scored only 39 runs in 428 at-bats.

John Ellis, who the team had such high hopes for, failed to distinguish himself at all in his limited amount of playing time at first base. In 238 at-bats, he hit just 3 home runs, drove in only 34 runs, and batted just .244.

Horace Clarke had another decent year at second base, batting .250, leading the team with 17 stolen bases, and finishing second on the team with 156 base hits. However, once again, he failed to reach the level of play he had performed at two seasons earlier when he finished second on the team with a .285 batting average.

Shortstop Gene Michael cut his error total down from 28 to 20, but batted just .224, knocked in only 35 runs, scored just 36, and added little to the offense.

Yankee catchers were not nearly as productive as they had been in 1970. Thurman Munson, who just one year earlier had batted .302 and been selected as the league's Rookie of the Year, hit just .251 and knocked in only 42 runs. A large part of Munson's problem appeared to be that he had gone away somewhat from what had made him so successful as a rookie — hitting the ball up the middle and to right-field. In attempting to pull the ball more, Munson's home run total increased from 6 to 10, but his batting average dropped 50 points, he drove in 11 fewer runs, and his number of doubles dropped from 25 to 15. Nevertheless, Munson had a tremendous year behind the plate, committing only one error and doing a fine job in handling the pitching staff.

Munson's backup, Jake Gibbs, who had also batted over .300 in 1970 and had, by far, his most productive season, had a year that was more typical for him. In 206 at-bats, he hit 5 home runs, knocked in 21 runs, and batted just .218. He called it quits at the end of the season.

In addition, other than Ron Blomberg and Ron Swoboda, both of whom did well in their part-time roles, the bench was not nearly as productive as it had been the previous year. Back-up infielder and pinch-hitter Ron Hansen, who had done such a fine job in 1970, batted only .207, with 2 home runs and 20 runs batted in in 145 at-bats. Frank Baker, who the team had given a shot to in spring training to win the shortstop job, batted just .139 in 79 at-bats. Reserve outfielder Jim Lyttle, who had batted .310 in a back-up role one year earlier, hit just .198, with 1 home run and 7 runs batted in in 86 at-bats.

The starting pitching, once again, was solid, as three of the five starters finished with ERAs near, or under, 3.00. In fact, the Yankees' total of 67 complete games was, by a wide margin, the second highest total in the American League (Baltimore was first, with 71). However, the bullpen, so effective in 1970, failed to hold up its end.

Lindy McDaniel, who one year earlier had pitched to a record of 9–5 and an ERA of 2.01 while saving 29 games, finished 5–10, with a 5.04 ERA and just 4 saves. Jack Aker had a decent year, finishing with a record of 4–4 and an ERA of 2.59. However, after saving 16 games in 1970, he saved just 4 games. As a result, New York's total of 49 saves in 1970, which had been the second most in the league, dropped to just 12 in 1971, by far, the lowest total in the American League.

Nevertheless, there were some players who performed well. After coming over from Oakland at the start of the season, Felipe Alou provided a solid bat in the middle of the lineup. Playing 80 games in the outfield and 42 at first base, he came to the plate a total of 461 times, hit 8 home runs, and finished third on the team in both runs batted in (69) and batting average (.289).

Roy White had another fine season in left-field. He finished second on the team in home runs (19), runs batted in (84), batting average (.292), runs scored (86), and stolen bases (14). He also set an American League record with 17 sacrifice flies and went through the entire season (314 total chances) without committing a single error in the outfield.

The true star of the team, though, was Bobby Murcer. After showing glimpses of the talent that had prompted the Yankee front office to promote him as the next great Yankee in each of his first two seasons, Murcer developed into a full-fledged star in 1971. After attempting to reach Yankee Stadium's short right-field porch by pulling the ball much of the time in his first two seasons, Murcer became more of a complete hitter. Learning to take what the pitcher was willing to give him and hit the ball the other way, he reduced his strikeout total from 100 in 1970 to just 60. He also raised his batting average 80 points to .331, finishing a close second to Tony Oliva in the American League batting race. Murcer's offensive productivity also increased as he led the team in home runs (25), runs batted in (94), runs scored (94), and base hits (175), while tying for second in stolen bases (14). He finished fourth in the league in runs batted in, third in runs scored, third in total bases, tied for fourth in hits and walks (91), and finished second in slugging percentage (.543) and first in on-base percentage (.429). In 1971, Murcer was arguably the best all-around player in the American League. At season's end, he finished seventh in the league MVP voting and was selected to *The Sporting News* All-Star team.

While the team ERA was up from 3.24 in 1970 to 3.43 in 1971, only seventh best in the league, the sole culprit was the bullpen. The Yankee starters were extremely effective.

Mel Stottlemyre's 16–12 record was somewhat deceiving because he received very little in the way of run support. In 18 of his 35 starts, New York failed to score more than 3 runs, and 11 times they failed to score more than 2. Stottlemyre's 16 victories led the team, as did his 2.87 ERA, 19 complete games, and 7 shutouts, while he finished second on the team with 269 innings pitched. His 7 shutouts tied him for second among the league-leaders.

Fritz Peterson also did not receive very much run support, as the team failed to score more than 3 runs in 19 of his 35 starts, and more than 2 in 12 of those. As a result, his 15–13 record was also deceiving. Peterson's 3.05 ERA was third lowest on the team, while he led in strikeouts (139) and innings pitched (274), and finished second in shutouts (4) and complete games (16).

Steve Kline established himself as the team's fourth starter, finishing with just a 12–13 record, but an ERA of 2.96 and 15 complete games.

Meanwhile, Stan Bahnsen finished his last season in pinstripes with a 14–12 record, a 3.35 ERA, and 14 complete games. During the off-season, he would be dealt away in what would turn out to be a poor trade for New York.

The major league career of Stan Bahnsen began in spectacular fashion when he debuted as a 21–year-old on September 9, 1966 by striking out the side in a 2–1 Yankee victory over the Red Sox at Fenway Park. Pitching in relief, Bahnsen fanned Boston sluggers Carl Yastrzemski and Tony Conigliaro in the process.

After returning to the minors in 1967 for another year of seasoning, Bahnsen came up to the big club for good in 1968. In the *Year of the Pitcher*, he was one of the better ones in the American League, compiling a record of 17–12 and an ERA of 2.05 in 267 innings of work, and being named Rookie of the Year. His 2.05 ERA was the sixth lowest in the league.

Apparently bothered by the lowering of the pitching mound and the shrinking of the strike zone in 1969, the right-hander faltered somewhat, finishing the year with a record of 9–16 and an ERA of 3.83. However, Bahnsen bounced back, winning 14 games for New York in each of the next two seasons and being one of the team's most dependable starters.

Unfortunately, the Yankees were desperate for help at third base and

After winning the American League Rookie of the Year award in 1968, Stan Bahnsen was a solid starter for the Yankees in subsequent seasons. Unfortunately, at the end of the 1971 campaign, New York made one of its more infamous deals by trading Bahnsen to the Chicago White Sox for third baseman Rich McKinney.

dealt Bahnsen to the Chicago White Sox for unproven infielder/outfielder Rich McKinney following the 1971 season in a deal they would later regret having made. McKinney floundered in New York, while Bahnsen went on to win 21 games for the White Sox in 1972 (against 16 losses), although he did set a since-broken major league record in the process by failing to complete 36 of his 41 starts. The following year, Bahnsen won 18 games for Chicago, but also led the American League with 21 losses. After posting a 12–15 record for the White Sox in 1974, he was traded to Oakland during the 1975 campaign. Bahnsen spent the remainder of his career, mostly as a spot-starter/reliever with the A's, Expos, Angels, and Phillies, never winning more than 10 games again and finishing his career with a record of 146–149.

While Bahnsen never fully lived up to the great potential he showed early in his career as a flame-throwing youngster with the Yankees, he had several good years and was one of New York's top pitchers in three of his four seasons there.

Roy White has fond memories of his former teammate: "I have some great memories of Stan because I saw him break into Double-A. I don't know if he had just signed or if he had come up from B ball, or something like that, but he came up to Columbus, Georgia in 1965 to join our club. Here's a guy who looked like a Norman Rockwell type of country bumpkin. I mean, he had the uniform on ... it looked like it was on backwards. He showed up with the straw suitcase ... country guy, you know. We're kind of looking at him saying, 'Who the hell is this guy?' Then he got on the mound and started throwing 90 mph fastballs and a curve that broke right off the table. He just had a great arm. Stan was really fast when he first came up. He was probably throwing a 95 or 96 mph fastball.

Stan had the great arm and became a pretty good pitcher in the American League. Even after he hurt his arm he learned how to pitch and was a very good pitcher."[45]

Season Highlights, Outstanding Performances, and Memorable Moments:

April 10   After dropping their first two contests, the Yankees win their first game of the year, defeating the Senators, 6–0, at Washington's RFK Stadium. Mel Stottlemyre throws the shutout.

May 13   At Milwaukee's County Stadium, the Yankees defeat the Brewers, 4–3, for their fifth straight victory. The win leaves New York's record at 15–14, making it the first time since the season's opening week that they are over the .500–mark.

July 11   At Yankee Stadium, the Yankees complete a three-game sweep of the archrival Red Sox with a 3–2 victory behind Fritz Peterson. The win leaves New York's record at 41–47 at the All-Star break.

July 18   At Yankee Stadium, the Yankees sweep a doubleheader from the White Sox, winning the opener, 3–2, and taking the nightcap, 6–1. New York overcomes a 2–1 deficit against eventual 22-game winner Wilbur Wood in the bottom of the 9th inning of the first game, as Bobby Murcer supplies the game-tying hit and Ron Swoboda gets the game-winner. The sweep gives the Yankees seven wins in their last eight contests.

July 25   At Milwaukee's County Stadium, the Yankees sweep a doubleheader from the Brewers, winning the opener, 6–2, and taking the nightcap, 11–9. The victories give New York a 5–game winning streak and leave their record at 51–51, making it the first time since May 17, when their record stood at 16–16, that they are at .500.

August 6   At Yankee Stadium, the Yankees defeat the Orioles, 12–3, for their fifth straight win. In the process, they knock out Baltimore starter Pat Dobson, ending his 12–game winning streak, his string of nine consecutive complete games, and his consecutive scoreless inning streak of 23.

August 12   At Yankee Stadium, New York takes a pair from the Angels, winning the opener, 3–0, behind Fritz Peterson and taking the nightcap, 2–1, behind Mike Kekich. The sweep leaves the Yankees' record at 60–58, putting them two games over .500 for the first time all season.

August 24   At Oakland-Alameda County Stadium, Mel Stottlemyre throws a two-hit shutout against the A's, beating eventual Cy Young and MVP winner Vida Blue, 1–0.

Sept. 18   At Yankee Stadium, the Yankees defeat the Indians, 9–0, behind Mel Stottlemyre. The shutout is the Yankee right-hander's seventh and last of the year, tying him for second among the league leaders in that category behind only Vida Blue, who will finish the season with eight.

Sept. 19   At Yankee Stadium, New York completes a four-game sweep of Cleveland, defeating the Indians, 3–2, behind Steve Kline. The victory leaves the Yankees' record at 79–74, making it the only time all season they will be as many as five games over .500.

1971 American League Final Team Standings and Offensive Statistics

TEAM	G	W	L	PCT	GB	R	H	2B	3B	HR	BB	SO	SB	AVG	OBP	SLG
EAST																
BAL	158	101	57	.639	—	742	1382	207	25	158	672	844	66	.261	.349	.398
DET	162	91	71	.562	12	701	1399	214	38	179	540	854	35	.254	.327	.405
BOSTON	162	85	77	.525	18	691	1360	246	28	161	552	871	51	.252	.325	.397
NY	162	82	80	.506	21	648	1377	195	43	97	581	717	75	.254	.331	.360
WASH	159	63	96	.396	38.5	537	1219	189	30	86	575	956	68	.230	.309	.326
CLE	162	60	102	.370	43	543	1303	200	20	109	467	868	57	.238	.302	.342
WEST																
OAK	161	101	60	.627	—	691	1383	195	25	160	542	1018	80	.252	.323	.384
KC	161	85	76	.528	16	603	1323	225	40	80	490	819	130	.250	.316	.353
CHI	162	79	83	.488	22.5	617	1346	185	30	138	562	870	83	.250	.327	.373
CAL	162	76	86	.469	25.5	511	1271	213	18	96	441	827	72	.231	.292	.329
MINN	160	74	86	.463	26.5	654	1406	197	31	116	512	846	66	.260	.326	.372
MIL	161	69	92	.429	32	534	1188	160	23	104	543	924	82	.229	.306	.329
TOTAL						7472	15957	2426	351	1484	6477	10414	865	.247	.320	.364

Team Pitching and Fielding Statistics

TEAM	CG	SH	SV	IP	H	HR	BB	SO	ERA	FA	E	DP
EAST												
BAL	71	15	22	1415	1257	125	416	793	2.99	.981	112	148
DET	53	11	32	1468	1355	126	609	1000	3.63	.983	106	156
BOSTON	44	11	35	1443	1424	136	535	871	3.80	.981	116	149
NY	67	15	12	1452	1382	126	423	707	3.43	.981	125	159
WASH	30	10	26	1418	1376	132	554	762	3.70	.977	141	170
CLE	21	7	32	1440	1352	154	770	937	4.28	.981	116	159
WEST												
OAK	57	18	36	1469	1229	131	501	999	3.05	.981	117	157
KC	34	15	44	1420	1301	84	496	775	3.25	.979	132	178
CHI	46	19	32	1450	1348	100	468	976	3.12	.975	160	128
CAL	39	11	32	1481	1246	101	607	904	3.10	.980	131	159
MINN	43	9	25	1416	1384	139	529	895	3.81	.980	118	134
MIL	32	23	32	1416	1303	130	569	795	3.38	.977	138	152
TOTAL	537	164	360	17291					3.46	.980	1512	1849

1971 New York Yankee Pitching Statistics

PLAYER	W	L	ERA	G	GS	CG	SHO	SV	IP	H	R	ER	BB	SO
Fritz Peterson	15	13	3.05	37	37	16	4	1	274	269	106	93	42	139
Mel Stottlemyre	16	12	2.87	39	35	19	7	0	269	234	100	86	69	132
Stan Bahnsen	14	12	3.35	36	36	14	3	0	242	221	99	90	72	110
Steve Kline	12	13	2.96	16	31	15	1	0	222	206	87	73	37	81
Mike Kekich	10	9	4.07	26	37	3	0	0	170	167	89	77	82	93
Lindy McDaniel	5	10	5.04	62	44	0	0	4	69	82	41	39	24	39
Jack Aker	4	4	2.59	41	41	0	0	4	55	48	20	16	26	24
Gary Waslewski	0	1	3.28	26	24	0	0	1	35	28	15	13	16	17
Alan Closter	2	2	5.08	35	14	0	0	0	28	33	22	16	13	22
Jim Hardin	0	2	5.08	9	12	0	0	0	28	35	19	16	9	14
Roger Hambright	3	1	4.39	4	18	0	0	2	26	22	13	13	10	14
Gary Jones	0	0	9.00	7	12	0	0	0	14	19	14	14	7	10
Terry Ley	0	0	5.00	1	6	0	0	0	9	9	9	5	9	7
Bill Burbach	0	1	10.80	1	2	0	0	0	3	6	6	4	5	3
Rob Gardner	0	0	3.00	2	2	0	0	0	3	3	1	1	2	2

1971 New York Yankee Hitting Statistics

PLAYER	AB	R	H	2B	3B	HR	RBI	BB	SO	SB	OBP	SLG	AVG
Horace Clarke	625	76	156	23	7	2	41	64	43	17	.321	.318	.250
Bobby Murcer	529	94	175	25	6	25	94	91	60	14	.427	.543	.331
Roy White	524	86	153	22	7	19	84	86	66	14	.388	.469	.292
Felipe Alou	461	52	133	20	6	8	69	32	24	5	.334	.410	.289
Gene Michael	456	36	102	15	0	3	35	48	64	3	.299	.276	.224
Thurman Munson	451	71	113	15	4	10	42	52	65	6	.335	.368	.251
Danny Cater	428	39	118	16	5	4	50	19	25	0	.308	.364	.276
Jerry Kenney	325	50	85	10	3	0	20	56	38	9	.368	.311	.262
John Ellis	238	16	58	12	1	3	34	23	42	0	.322	.340	.244
Jake Gibbs	206	23	45	9	0	5	21	12	23	2	.270	.335	.218

PLAYER	AB	R	H	2B	3B	HR	RBI	BB	SO	SB	OBP	SLG	AVG
Ron Blomberg	199	30	64	6	2	7	31	14	23	2	.363	.477	.322
Ron Hansen	145	6	30	3	0	2	20	9	27	0	.245	.269	.207
Ron Swoboda	138	17	36	2	1	2	20	27	35	0	.391	.333	.261
Mel Stottlemyre	94	6	16	1	0	1	11	5	29	0	.210	.213	.170
Jim Lyttle	86	7	17	5	0	1	7	8	18	0	.271	.291	.198
Fritz Peterson	85	2	7	1	0	0	8	5	22	0	.132	.094	.082
Stan Bahnsen	79	6	12	2	1	0	3	1	32	0	.163	.203	.152
Frank Baker	79	9	11	2	0	0	2	16	22	3	.281	.165	.139
Steve Kline	66	6	9	1	0	0	1	4	16	0	.186	.152	.136
Mike Kekich	52	2	8	0	0	0	4	2	11	0	.185	.154	.154
Curt Blefary	36	4	7	1	0	1	2	3	5	0	.256	.306	.194
Ron Woods	32	4	8	1	0	1	2	4	2	0	.333	.375	.250
Rusty Torres	26	5	10	3	0	2	3	0	8	0	.385	.731	.385
Danny Walton	14	1	2	0	0	1	2	0	7	0	.143	.357	.143
Lindy McDaniel	9	0	1	0	0	0	0	0	2	0	.111	.111	.111
Alan Closter	6	0	0	0	0	0	0	0	1	0	.000	.000	.000
Frank Tepedino	6	0	0	0	0	0	0	0	0	0	.000	.000	.000
Len Boehmer	5	0	0	0	0	0	0	0	0	0	.000	.000	.000
Jim Hardin	4	0	0	0	0	0	0	0	1	0	.000	.000	.000
Jack Aker	3	0	0	0	0	0	0	0	3	0	.000	.000	.000
Bill Burbach	2	0	0	0	0	0	0	0	1	0	.000	.000	.000
Roger Hambright	2	0	1	0	0	0	1	0	1	0	.500	.500	.500
Gary Jones	1	0	0	0	0	0	0	0	0	0	.000	.000	.000
Gary Waslewski	1	0	0	0	0	0	0	0	1	0	.000	.000	.000

TEN

1972: Parity Comes to the American League East

Following their 93–69 record and second place finish in 1970, the Yankees' performance during the 1971 season had been a disappointing one. Winning 11 fewer games than they had the previous year, New York finished with a record of just 82–80, in fourth place in the American League East. Players such as Danny Cater, Thurman Munson, Fritz Peterson, Lindy McDaniel, and Jack Aker had all performed brilliantly in 1970, helping to conceal the team's shortcomings. However, when each of these men failed to reach the same level of play the following year, those weaknesses were exposed.

Hitting fewer than 100 home runs for the second time in three seasons, New York clearly lacked power in the middle of their lineup. Much of this power shortage emanated from the fact that they received so little help in this area from their first and third basemen. John Ellis had been unable to establish himself as a legitimate power threat at first, and the Yankees had all but given up on him. Jerry Kenney was now being viewed more as a utility player due to his lack of offensive productivity. In their first base/third base platoon, the trio of Ellis, Kenney, and Cater had produced only 7 home runs and 104 runs batted in between them in 1971. Both of those positions needed to be upgraded.

The double play combination of Horace Clarke and Gene Michael was merely adequate, but there were worse pairings in the American League, and there was really no one in the organization who was capable of unseating either man. Therefore, both players' starting roles appeared to be safe, for the time being.

The bench, which had been one of the team's greatest strengths two years earlier, with Ron Hansen, Pete Ward, and Jake Gibbs playing so well in their reserve roles, had not performed nearly as well in 1971. It needed to be improved upon as well.

However, the team's most glaring need was for help in the bullpen. Two seasons earlier, the Yankees had finished second in the American League with 49 saves. In 1971, that total had diminished to just 12, the lowest figure in the league. The primary culprit was Lindy McDaniel, who had gone from 9 wins, 29 saves, and a 2.01 ERA in 1970 to a record of 5–10, with only 4 saves and a 5.04 ERA in 1971. As a result, Manager Ralph Houk had been forced to go with his starters longer than he would have liked to, and the staff ended up finishing a close second in the league to Baltimore, with 67 complete games. If the Yankees were going to pose any kind of serious threat in 1972 they would have to greatly improve their bullpen.

Yet, the team was not without its strengths. While Thurman Munson had not hit as well in his sophomore season as he had as a rookie, he was still among the best catchers in the league, having been selected to his first All-Star team the previous season. He had a great year behind the plate, committing only one error all year and doing an excellent job of handling the pitching staff. The Yankees expected him to progress offensively and viewed him as being one of the cornerstones around which they could build their future.

After being acquired from Oakland at the start of the season, rightfielder Felipe Alou had been one of the team's most consistent hitters, driving in 69 runs and batting .289. The only question surrounding him was his age, since he would be turning 37 in May.

Left-fielder Roy White was, perhaps, New York's most consistent player, once again finishing among the team's leaders in most offensive categories, while doing a fine job defensively.

In centerfield, Bobby Murcer had become a true star, not only establishing himself as the team's best player in 1971, but as one of the best in baseball. The previous season, he had finished among the top five players in the league in eight different offensive categories, and he was rapidly developing into an excellent outfielder.

Yankee starters had also performed admirably in 1971, finishing among the league leaders in total complete games and shutouts. Led by Mel Stottlemyre, Fritz Peterson, and Stan Bahnsen, this group formed one of the league's stronger units. Steve Kline and Mike Kekich had yet to develop into top starters, but they were both young, and Yankee brass had high hopes for both of them.

The Yankee front office began addressing the team's needs during the off-season when, on December 2, it made two deals. First, pitcher Stan Bahnsen was traded to the Chicago White Sox for infielder/outfielder Rich McKinney. The Yankees hoped that the 25–year-old McKinney would become their everyday third baseman. In 369 at-bats with Chicago the previous season, the right-handed hitting McKinney had hit 8 home runs, driven in 46 runs, and batted .271. However, the deal appeared to be somewhat suspect for a number of reasons. To begin with, Bahnsen was a solid pitcher who had won 14 games in each of the last two seasons. In addition, McKinney had never played third base regularly in the major leagues. In parts of two seasons with the White Sox, he had appeared in a total of 157 games, playing just 28 games at the hot corner. The deal was a clear indication of how desperate the Yankee front office was to improve the team's infield play and offensive productivity.

The other trade was a less significant one in which the Yankees acquired utility infielder Bernie Allen from Washington for young left-handers Terry Ley and Gary Jones. The left-handed hitting Allen had originally come up with the Twins, for whom he had his best season as a rookie in 1962. That year, he hit 12 home runs, drove in 64 runs, and batted .269, while committing 13 errors in 158 games at second base. However, he was less productive in subsequent seasons, was dealt to Washington after 1966, and had been a part-time player for the last several years. Playing mostly second base and pinch-hitting in 1971, Allen hit 4 home runs, knocked in 22 runs, and batted .266 in 229 at-bats with the Senators. The Yankees felt he could strengthen their bench by filling in at second and third base and provide another left-handed bat for late-inning situations.

Then, on January 19, the Yankees made another move, acquiring veteran outfielder Johnny Callison from the Chicago Cubs on a conditional basis. New York ended up keeping him and completing the deal by sending reliever Jack Aker to the Cubs on May 17.

The left-handed hitting Callison had once been an outstanding player for the Philadelphia Phillies, possessing a quick and powerful bat, fine running speed, and a tremendous throwing arm. He had originally come up with the White Sox in 1958, but was traded to the Phillies prior to the start of the 1960 season for veteran infielder Gene Freese. After becoming a regular with Philadelphia in 1961, Callison had his first outstanding year in 1962, batting .300 for the only time in his career, while hitting 23 homers, driving in 83 runs, and collecting 24 outfield assists. After having another productive season in 1963, he had his two finest years in 1964 and 1965, hitting more than 30 home runs and driving in more than 100 runs in each of those years, while collecting 19 and 21 assists, respectively. He won the 1964 All-Star game with a home run in the bottom of the ninth inning and finished second to the Cardinals' Ken Boyer in the league MVP voting that year. Twice during his career he hit three home runs in a game, he was a three-time All-Star, and he led the National League in doubles once and in triples twice.

However, with his offensive productivity on the decline, Callison had been traded from the Phillies to the Cubs prior to the start of the 1970 season. With the Cubs in 1971, he hit only 8 home runs, drove in just 38 runs, and batted only .210 in 290 at-bats. Yet, New York hoped the 33–year-old Callison still had something left and planned to give him a shot at the right-field job.

The Yankees made what would turn out to be their biggest move of the off-season by addressing their need for help in the bullpen. On March 22, they traded Danny Cater to the Red Sox for reliever Sparky Lyle. The left-handed Lyle had been an effective closer for Boston in each of the past four seasons, saving as many as 20 games in 1970. However, the Red Sox felt that the right-handed hitting Cater would be a perfect fit for Fenway Park and, to acquire him, they were willing to part with Lyle.

Finally, just before the start of the season, the Yankees picked up utility infielder Hal Lanier from the San Francisco Giants. Lanier had batted .274 with the Giants as a rookie in 1964, but, after a serious beaning in 1965, had failed to bat any higher than .233 since. He was a fine defensive player, though, having led all National League shortstops in putouts and fielding average in 1968.

Having completed their off-season face-lift, the Yankees went into the 1972 season with quite a different look. With Danny Cater gone, the team intended to move Ron Blomberg to first base and platoon him with the right-handed hitting Felipe Alou, who would also be moved in from the outfield. Rich McKinney would take over at third, and the starting infield would be completed by Horace Clarke and Gene Michael. Bernie Allen, Hal Lanier, and Jerry Kenney would come off the bench.

The starting outfield would be comprised of Roy White, Bobby Murcer, and Johnny Callison. Ron Swoboda and young prospect Rusty Torres, who had appeared briefly with the team the prior year, would provide depth in the outfield. Felipe Alou would also see limited action there, when he wasn't playing first base.

Thurman Munson would return behind the plate and, with Jake Gibbs having retired, he would be backed up by John Ellis.

Mel Stottlemyre and Fritz Peterson would, once again, be the top two starters. But, with Stan Bahnsen having been traded, the team would be relying more heavily on Steve Kline and Mike Kekich. Kline had established himself in 1971 as the fourth starter, but he was now expected to move into the third spot. Kekich, after having started sporadically in each of the past three seasons as the team's fifth starter, would now be given an opportunity to pitch every fourth day. The final spot in the rotation would be given to left-hander Rob Gardner.

Sparky Lyle would head the bullpen. He would be joined by Lindy McDaniel, Jack Aker (prior to his being dealt to the Cubs as part of the Johnny Callison deal), and Ron Klimkowski, who had been reacquired from Oakland. Fred Beene and Rich Hinton would battle it out for the last roster spot.

The 29–year-old Beene was a smallish right-hander who had spent eight years in the Baltimore farm system. He had seen very limited action with the Orioles in each season, from 1968 to 1970, pitching a total of only 10 innings and failing to compile either a won-lost record or any saves during his major league career.

Hinton was a 24–year-old left-hander who had been acquired during the off-season from the White Sox for reserve outfielder Jim Lyttle. In 1971 with Chicaco, Hinton had appeared in 18 games, starting 2, and compiled a 3–4 record with no saves and a 4.44 ERA.

The regular season opened with a 3–1 rain-shortened loss to the Orioles at Baltimore's Memorial Stadium. Mel Stottlemyre pitched well, giving up only two earned runs in six innings of work, but winner Pat Dobson pitched even better, giving up just one run in six innings. After being shut out by Baltimore's Dave McNally the following day, the Yankees returned to Yankee Stadium to win their home opener against the Brewers, 2–0, behind Steve Kline. However, the team then lost 11 of their next 16 games, leaving them at 6–13, six games out of first place, after May 10.

While the team struggled as a whole in the early-going, Fritz Peterson and Rich McKinney had a particularly difficult time. The usually steady Peterson failed to earn a win in any of his first six starts. Meanwhile, McKinney was clearly not the answer at third base, as he ended up committing 8 errors in just 33 games there and tying an American League record with four errors in an 11–7 loss to the Red Sox at Fenway Park on April 22. Only one month into the season he was benched in favor of a platoon of Bernie Allen and Hal Lanier. McKinney would finish the year with just 1 home run, 7 runs batted in, and a .215 batting average in 121 at-bats.

The Yankees then went on to win 11 of their next 18 games, to improve their record to 17–20 by the end of May. The surge left them in fourth place, just four games out of first. However, the team then lost 9 of their next 12 games, leaving them at 20–29, in fourth place, seven games out of first after play on June 13.

One of the primary reasons for the team's lackluster play during this period was the failure of both Mel Stottlemyre and Fritz Peterson to pitch as well as they had in previous seasons. Both were having sub-par seasons with records well below the .500–mark at this juncture. Stottlemyre had earned only one victory in his last six starts, while Peterson was pitching better than he had during the season's first month, but still not as well as he was capable of.

The Yankees were fortunate, though, because the division was not nearly as strong as it had been the past few seasons. Having traded away team leader Frank Robinson during the off-season, and, with veterans Boog Powell, Davey Johnson, Brooks Robinson, Paul Blair, Don Buford, and Dave McNally all having off-seasons, the Orioles were no longer a dominant team. As a result, Detroit, Boston, Baltimore, and the Yankees would remain relatively close to each other in the standings for much of the year, producing one of the more hotly-contested pennant-races in recent seasons.

After reeling off six consecutive victories, on June 24, the Yankees' record stood at 26–29, and they were in third place, 5½ games out of first. Right around this time, the team made two deals to acquire veteran help for their bullpen.

First, they picked up left-hander Wade Blasingame from the Houston Astros. A former bonus baby with Milwaukee, Blasingame had his best season with the Braves in 1965, when, at age 21, he compiled a 16–10 record. Possessing an outstanding curveball, he appeared to have a bright future ahead of him. However, after fracturing a finger and developing a sore arm in 1966, he never had another winning season. After going 9–11 in 28 starts with the Astros in 1971, Blasingame was moved to the bullpen in 1972, where he saw very limited action. Prior to the Yankees obtaining him, he had appeared in just 10 games and worked only 8 innings, pitching to an ERA of 8.64. With the Yankees, he would appear in 12 games, all but one in relief, and compile a record of 0–1 and an ERA of 4.24.

New York also acquired left-handed reliever Jim Roland from Oakland. Roland had originally signed as a flame-throwing 19–year-old with Minnesota in 1962. However, after six mostly uneventful seasons with the Twins, he had been dealt to Oakland prior to the start of the 1969 season. Pitching mostly in long relief, he had his best year for the A's in 1969, going 5–1, with a 2.19 ERA. In 1972, though, he had worked only two innings out of Oakland's crowded bullpen before being traded to the Yankees. With New York, he would finish the season with a record of 0–1 and an ERA of 5.04 in 25 innings of work.

The success the Yankees experienced during their six-game winning streak was short-lived as the team followed that up by losing their next five games, leaving them with a record of 26–34, in fifth place, eight games out of first. The team's unpredictable nature surfaced once more when they won their next five games, placing them at 31–34, in third place, 5½ games out of first.

The Yankees finally reached the .500–mark on July 12, when they won for the eleventh time in fourteen tries, evening their record at 37–37. Particularly effective during this surge was Mel Stottlemyre, who won three of four decisions, throwing two consecutive shutouts at one point. The team played close to .500 ball over the next 11 games, going into the All-Star break with a record of 42–43 on July 23.

Despite the fine seasons that Sparky Lyle and Thurman Munson were having, Bobby Murcer was the only Yankee selected to the All-Star team. Murcer was now considered to be the best centerfielder in the league, and was picked for the starting team for the second year in a row.

The Yankees knew that they needed to get improved play from their third basemen if they were going to contend seriously in the season's second half. The Rich McKinney experiment had clearly failed, and his replacements, Bernie Allen and Hal Lanier, were an improvement, defensively, but added little to the offense. In 220 at-bats, Allen finished the season with 9 home runs, 21 runs batted in, and a .227 batting average. Lanier, in 103 at-bats, failed to hit a homer, knocked in 6 runs, and batted .214. So, New York decided to take a chance by turning to the Mexican League for help in the person of Celerino Sanchez.

Sanchez was regarded as one of Mexico's greatest infielders, having batted .448 for Campeche in 1966, and .345 and .368 for the Mexico City Tigers in 1970 and 1971, respectively. Sanchez seemed to add a spark to the team when he joined them following the break. He was flashy with the glove and hit well in the beginning. However, he eventually slumped badly, both in the field and at the plate. Sanchez finished the season with 14 errors in 68 games at third, and failed to hit a home run while knocking in only 22 runs and batting just .248 in 250 at-bats.

The Yankees won three of their first four games after the break to top .500, at 45–44, for the first time all year. After winning 13 of their next 19 games, the Yankees' record stood at 58–50, and they were in second place, just 1½ games out of first.

In the midst of this latest surge, on August 8, the Yankees and New York City reached agreement on a 30–year lease on Yankee Stadium that would keep the team in the Bronx until 2002. The City agreed to spend $24 million on renovations that would begin following the completion of the 1973 season. However, the face-lift would end up costing New York almost $100 million.

With the Yankees closing in on first place, they then proceeded to lose eight of their next eleven contests, to drop to 61–58, in third place, 3½ games out of first. The team got hot once more, however, winning seven of their next eight games to close to within 1 game of the first-place

Tigers, at 68–59. The Yankees could not stand prosperity, though, as they went 10–11 over their next 21 games, to fall three full games out of first place, and into fourth, at 78–70.

With less than two weeks remaining in the regular season and three teams closely bunched just ahead of them, the Yankees needed to play almost perfect baseball down the stretch if they had any hope of winning the division. On September 27, they went to Detroit for a critical two-game series with the Tigers. Behind Steve Kline, the Yankees built a 5–1 lead going into the eighth inning. However, Detroit stormed back with three runs in the eighth and another two in the ninth against Yankee closer Sparky Lyle to all but end New York's title dreams. It was unfortunate that Lyle was victimized in such an important game because he had been such a vital part of the team's success all year. This, however, was one of the few instances in which he failed.

Even though the Yankees defeated the Tigers the next day, 3–2, the earlier loss seemed to take much of the emotion out of New York, and they wound up losing their final five games to finish the season with a record of 79–76, in fourth place, 6½ games behind the first-place Tigers, who finished just a half game ahead of Boston. In head-to-head competition against their Eastern Division rivals, the Yankees finished with records of 9–7 against Detroit, 9–9 against Boston, and 6–7 against Baltimore. They had a very difficult time with the Western Division champion Oakland A's, who would go on to win the World Series, defeating Cincinnati in seven games. In twelve contests with the A's, the Yankees were able to come away with only three victories.

In spite of the fact that their overall team performance in 1972 could be described as inconsistent and mediocre, there were several Yankee players who performed at a level that was either at, or above, what was expected of them prior to the start of the season.

While he hit only 7 home runs, knocked in just 46 runs, and committed 15 errors in the field, Thurman Munson raised his batting average almost 30 points, to .280, and elicited a great deal of confidence from his pitchers.

In just 299 at-bats, Ron Blomberg hit 14 home runs and knocked in 49 runs, while batting .268. Projected over a full season of approximately 500 at-bats, those numbers would come out to about 25 home runs and 85 runs batted in.

After a slow start, Fritz Peterson ended up putting up numbers that were quite comparable to those the team had come to expect from him. He led the team with 17 wins (against 15 losses) and 12 complete games, finished with an ERA of 3.24, and finished second on the team with 250 innings pitched.

Steve Kline was the team's best starting pitcher all year, finishing with a record of 16–9, throwing 236 innings, completing 12 games, and leading the team with an outstanding 2.40 ERA. Kline didn't throw the ball very hard and struck out very few men (just 58 all year), but he had excellent control, having walked only 44 men all season, and was extremely effective when he kept the ball down to opposing batters.

Sparky Lyle had a superb year as the Yankee closer. Appearing in 72 games, a record for a Yankee pitcher at that time, he finished the season with a record of 9–5, an ERA of 1.92, and a league-leading 35 saves. His overall impact on the team can best be seen by the fact that Yankee starters, after finishing second in the league in complete games just one year earlier, completed just 35 games, the second lowest total in the league. Also, after finishing last in the league the previous year, New York's total of 39 saves was the third highest total in the A.L. At season's end, Lyle finished third in the league MVP voting.

Once again, though, the true star of the team was Bobby Murcer, who led the team in virtually every offensive category. He finished first in home runs (33), runs batted in (96), batting average (.292), runs scored (102), and base hits (171). He led the American League in runs scored and total bases (314), finished second in home runs, and finished third in runs batted in, hits, doubles (30), and slugging percentage (.537). At season's end, he won a Gold Glove for his outstanding work in centerfield, was selected to *The Sporting News* All-Star team for the second straight year, and finished fifth in the league MVP voting. With the exception of league MVP Dick Allen, who led the league in home runs (37), and runs batted in (113), while finishing third in batting average (.308) for the White Sox, Murcer was, in all probability, the best player in the American League.

There were, however, several players who did not perform up to expectations. As was noted earlier, Rich McKinney's trial at third base lasted just 33 games. In addition, Roy White was not nearly as productive as he had been the previous two seasons. Although he led the team with 23 stolen bases and finished tied for the league lead in walks, with 99, he hit only 10 home runs, knocked in just 54 runs, batted only .270, and scored just 76 runs.

Horace Clarke batted only .241 and scored just 65 runs. Yet he finished second on the team with 18 stolen bases and committed only 11 errors at second base.

Clarke's double play partner Gene Michael, once again, failed to add much to the offense. In 391 at-bats, he hit 1 home run, drove in 32 runs, scored 29 others, and batted .233.

While he pitched better than his won-lost record would indicate, Mel

Stottlemyre struggled for much of the season, finishing with a record of just 14–18. Yet his earned run average of 3.22 was not particularly bad, and he ended up leading the team in strikeouts (110), shutouts (7), and innings pitched (260). In fact, his 7 shutouts were the third highest total in the American League.

Nevertheless, the Yankees had remained in the pennant race for virtually the entire season and, with Baltimore apparently coming back to the pack, did not appear to be that far away from being a serious contender in the American League East. If a few areas of concern were addressed during the upcoming off-season, there was no reason to believe that the team could not pose a serious threat in 1973.

Season Highlights, Outstanding Performances, and Memorable Moments:

April 18   After losing their first two games in Baltimore, the Yankees earn their first victory of the season, defeating the Brewers, 2–0, in New York's home opener. Steve Kline tosses a three-hit shutout and Horace Clarke collects three hits in three official at-bats.

May 19   After losing his first three starts, Mel Stottlemyre picks up his fourth straight victory, blanking the Red Sox, 6–0, at Yankee Stadium. The shutout is the Yankee right-hander's second straight, and the third in his last four starts. Horace Clarke is the hitting star, as he goes 3–for-4, with one RBI and two runs scored.

May 21   At Yankee Stadium, New York sweeps a doubleheader from Boston, winning the first game, 6–3, and taking the nightcap, 3–2. Roy White goes 3–for-4 in both games, and Felipe Alou adds three hits in the second game.

June 3   At Comiskey Park, the Yankees score eight times in the 13th inning to defeat the White Sox, 18–10. Bobby Murcer and Thurman Munson each hit 3–run homers in New York's big inning, and Murcer scores five runs on four hits.

June 23   In Cleveland, the Yankees defeat the Indians, 4–1, behind Fritz Peterson. The victory is the sixth in a row for New York, completing the longest winning streak the team will have all year.

June 30   At Yankee Stadium, Steve Kline out-duels eventual Cy Young Award winner Gaylord Perry, as the Yankees defeat the Indians, 1–0.

July 8   At Metropolitan Stadium, the Yankees defeat the Twins, 1–0, in 11 innings as Mel Stottlemyre and Bert Blyleven hook up in a classic pitching duel. Both right-handers throw 10 scoreless innings, but Bernie Allen's eleventh inning homer off Minnesota reliever Wayne Granger supplies the margin of victory. Stottlemyre earns his eighth victory of the season, and Sparky Lyle comes on in the 11th to pick up his 18th save.

July 9   The Yankees touch up Twins pitching for 9 runs and 15 hits in their 9–6 victory in Minnesota. Thurman Munson and Gene Michael each collect three hits, and Ron Blomberg drives in four runs on two hits.

July 12   At Anaheim Stadium, Mel Stottlemyre throws his fourth shutout of the year and singles in two runs, as the Yankees defeat the Angels, 5–0. The victory improves New York's record to 37–37, making it the first time since April 19, when their record stood at 2–2, that the team is at the .500–mark.

July 18   At Yankee Stadium, Thurman Munson, Ron Blomberg, and Bobby Murcer each homer to support the six-hit pitching of Steve Kline, as New York defeats Minnesota, 6–0.

July 21   At Yankee Stadium, the Yankees sweep a doubleheader from the Angels, winning the first game, 6–0, and taking the nightcap, 3–0. In the opener, Bobby Murcer homers twice, and both Ron Blomberg and Johnny Callison also homer, as Fritz Peterson throws a four-hit shutout. In the second game, Mel Stottlemyre also pitches a four-hit shutout, and John Ellis supplies the power with a two-run homer.

July 29   At Yankee Stadium, the Yankees defeat the Red Sox, 8–1, behind Mike Kekich. The victory puts New York over the .500–mark for the first time all year, at 45–44.

August 4 At Milwaukee's County Stadium, the Yankees defeat the Brewers, 9–4, with the big blow being Bobby Murcer's seventh-inning grand slam.

August 12 The Yankees defeat the Brewers, 10–6, at Yankee Stadium, behind the hitting of Johnny Callison, who goes 3–for–3, including a home run, three runs scored, and six runs batted in.

August 13 At Yankee Stadium, the Yankees sweep a doubleheader from the Brewers for the second time in a week, winning the opening contest, 5–3, and taking the nightcap, 5–4. The victories improve New York's record to 58–50 and move them to within 1½ games of first place.

August 27   The Yankees sweep a doubleheader from the Royals at Yankee Stadium, winning the opener, 7–6, and taking the nightcap, 9–8, in 16 innings. Johnny Callison and Gene Michael each collect two hits and drive in two runs in the first game, while Bobby Murcer and Celerino Sanchez are the hitting stars of the second game, as they each collect four hits.

August 29   In a doubleheader split with the Rangers at Yankee Stadium, Bobby Murcer becomes the first Yankee to hit for the cycle since Mickey Mantle accomplished the feat in 1957. New York takes the opener, 7–6, but Texas comes back to win the second game, 7–4.

Sept. 1   At Yankee Stadium, Mel Stottlemyre throws a four-hit shutout as the Yankees defeat the White Sox, 4–0. Rookie Charlie Spikes has two hits in his major league debut, drives in a run, and saves another with an outstanding catch in right field. Meanwhile, Thurman Munson goes 3–for–4, with two runs batted in, and Stottlemyre helps his own cause with a triple and a run scored.

Sept. 2   At Yankee Stadium, New York defeats Chicago, 2–1, for their fourth straight victory. The win improves the Yankees' record to 68–59, putting them nine games over .500 for the first time all season. It also moves them into second place, just one-half game out of first.

Sept. 10   At Tiger Stadium, Mel Stottlemyre throws a three-hit shutout and Horace Clarke collects three hits, including his third home run of the year, scores twice, and drives in two runs, as the Yankees defeat Detroit and Mickey Lolich, 5–0. The shutout is Stottlemyre's seventh of the season, which will turn out to be the third highest total in the league, behind only Nolan Ryan's nine and Wilbur Wood's eight.

Sept. 12   At Yankee Stadium, the Yankees defeat the Red Sox, 3–2, behind Fritz Peterson. The win is New York's fourth straight and leaves them, at 74–64, ten games over .500 for the first and only time all year.

Sept. 24   At Cleveland's Municipal Stadium, the Yankees sweep a doubleheader from the Indians, winning the opener, 5–4, and taking the second game, 8–3. In the nightcap, Sparky Lyle sets an American League record and ties the major league mark by collecting his 35th save of the year, while John Ellis collects three hits and drives in three runs and Bobby Murcer adds three hits of his own, including his 30th home run of the year.

1972 American League Final Team Standings and Offensive Statistics

TEAM	G	W	L	PCT	GB	R	H	2B	3B	HR	BB	SO	SB	AVG	OBP	SLG
EAST																
DET	156	86	70	.551	—	558	1206	179	32	122	483	793	17	.237	.306	.356
BOSTON	155	85	70	.548	0.5	640	1289	229	34	124	522	858	66	.248	.320	.376
BAL	154	80	74	.519	5	519	1153	193	29	100	507	935	78	.229	.304	.339
NY	155	79	76	.510	6.5	557	1288	201	24	103	491	689	71	.249	.318	.357
CLE	156	72	84	.462	14	472	1220	187	18	91	420	762	49	.234	.295	.330
MIL	156	65	91	.417	21	493	1204	167	22	88	472	868	64	.235	.303	.328
WEST																
OAK	155	93	62	.600	—	604	1248	195	29	134	463	886	87	.240	.308	.366
CHI	154	87	67	.565	5.5	566	1208	170	28	108	511	991	100	.238	.311	.346
MINN	154	77	77	.500	15.5	537	1277	182	31	93	478	905	53	.244	.311	.344
KC	154	76	78	.494	16.5	580	1317	220	26	78	534	711	85	.255	.329	.353
CAL	155	75	80	.484	18	454	1249	171	26	78	358	850	57	.242	.294	.330
TEX	154	54	100	.351	38.5	461	1092	166	17	56	503	926	126	.217	.292	.290
TOTAL						6441	14751	2260	316	1175	5742	10174	853	.239	.308	.343

Team Pitching and Fielding Statistics

TEAM	CG	SH	SV	IP	H	HR	BB	SO	ERA	FA	E	DP
EAST												
DET	46	11	33	1388	1212	101	465	952	2.96	.984	96	137
BOSTON	48	20	25	1382	1309	101	512	918	3.47	.978	130	141
BAL	62	20	21	1371	1116	85	395	788	2.53	.983	100	150
NY	35	19	39	1373	1306	87	419	625	3.05	.978	134	179
CLE	47	13	24	1410	1232	123	534	846	2.92	.981	116	157
MIL	37	14	32	1391	1289	116	486	740	3.45	.977	139	145
WEST												
OAK	42	23	43	1417	1170	96	418	862	2.58	.979	130	146
CHI	36	14	42	1385	1269	94	431	936	3.12	.977	135	136
MINN	37	17	34	1399	1188	105	444	838	2.84	.974	159	133
KC	44	16	29	1381	1293	85	405	801	3.24	.981	116	164
CAL	57	18	16	1377	1109	90	620	1000	3.06	.981	114	135
TEX	11	8	34	1374	1258	92	613	868	3.53	.972	166	147
TOTAL	502	193	372	16653					3.06	.979	1535	1770

1972 New York Yankee Pitching Statistics

PLAYER	W	L	ERA	G	GS	CG	SHO	SV	IP	H	R	ER	BB	SO
Mel Stottlemyre	14	18	3.22	36	36	9	7	0	260	250	99	93	85	110
Fritz Peterson	17	15	3.24	35	35	12	3	0	250	270	98	90	44	100
Steve Kline	16	9	2.40	32	32	11	4	0	236	210	79	63	44	58
Mike Kekich	10	13	3.70	29	28	2	0	0	175	172	77	72	76	78
Sparky Lyle	9	5	1.92	59	0	0	0	35	107	84	25	23	29	75
Rob Gardner	8	5	3.06	20	14	1	0	0	97	91	43	33	28	58
Lindy McDaniel	3	1	2.25	37	0	0	0	0	68	54	23	17	25	47

PLAYER	W	L	ERA	G	GS	CG	SHO	SV	IP	H	R	ER	BB	SO
Fred Beene	1	3	2.34	29	1	0	0	3	57	55	21	15	24	37
Ron Klimkowski	0	3	4.02	16	2	0	0	1	31	32	15	14	15	11
Jim Roland	0	1	5.04	16	0	0	0	0	25	27	14	14	16	13
Wade Blasingame	0	1	4.24	12	1	0	0	0	17	14	8	8	11	7
Rich Hinton	1	0	4.86	7	3	0	0	0	16	20	11	9	8	13
Casey Cox	0	1	4.63	5	1	0	0	0	11	13	6	6	3	4
Larry Gowell	0	1	1.29	2	1	0	0	0	7	3	1	1	2	7
Jack Aker	0	0	3.00	4	0	0	0	0	6	5	2	2	3	1
Steve Blateric	0	0	0.00	1	0	0	0	0	4	2	0	0	0	4
Alan Closter	0	0	11.57	2	0	0	0	0	2	2	3	3	4	2
George Medich	0	0	0.00	1	1	0	0	0	0	2	2	2	2	0

1972 New York Yankee Hitting Statistics

PLAYER	AB	R	H	2B	3B	HR	RBI	BB	SO	SB	OBP	SLG	AVG
Bobby Murcer	585	102	171	30	7	33	96	63	67	11	.361	.537	.292
Roy White	556	76	150	29	0	10	54	99	59	23	.384	.376	.270
Horace Clarke	547	65	132	20	2	3	37	56	44	18	.315	.302	.241
Thurman Munson	511	54	143	16	3	7	46	47	58	6	.343	.364	.280
Gene Michael	391	29	91	7	4	1	32	32	45	4	.290	.279	.233
Felipe Alou	324	33	90	18	1	6	37	22	27	1	.326	.395	.278
Ron Blomberg	299	36	80	22	1	14	49	38	26	0	.355	.488	.268
Johnny Callison	275	28	71	10	0	9	34	18	34	3	.299	.393	.258
Celerino Sanchez	250	18	62	8	3	0	22	12	30	0	.292	.304	.248
Bernie Allen	220	26	50	9	0	9	21	23	42	0	.296	.391	.227
Rusty Torres	199	15	42	7	0	3	13	18	44	0	.280	.291	.211
John Ellis	136	13	40	5	1	5	25	8	22	0	.333	.456	.294
Rich McKinney	121	10	26	2	0	1	7	7	13	1	.258	.256	.215
Jerry Kenney	119	16	25	2	0	0	7	16	13	3	.304	.227	.210
Ron Swoboda	113	9	28	8	0	1	12	17	29	0	.341	.345	.248
Hal Lanier	103	5	22	3	0	0	6	2	13	1	.234	.243	.214
Fritz Peterson	82	6	19	1	0	0	9	3	14	0	.259	.244	.232
Mel Stottlemyre	80	3	16	1	1	0	7	3	18	0	.247	.238	.200
Steve Kline	76	5	7	0	0	0	1	4	22	0	.148	.092	.092
Mike Kekich	59	3	8	0	1	0	4	0	14	0	.136	.169	.136
Charlie Spikes	34	2	5	1	0	0	3	1	13	0	.171	.176	.147
Rob Gardner	28	0	3	0	0	0	1	0	16	0	.107	.107	.107
Sparky Lyle	21	2	4	1	0	0	1	1	10	0	.227	.238	.190
Fred Beene	9	0	0	0	0	0	0	0	4	0	.000	.000	.000
Frank Tepedino	8	0	0	0	0	0	0	0	1	0	.000	.000	.000
Lindy McDaniel	7	1	2	0	0	1	2	0	3	0	.286	.714	.286
Ron Klimkowski	6	0	0	0	0	0	0	0	3	0	.000	.000	.000
Rich Hinton	3	0	0	0	0	0	0	0	2	0	.000	.000	.000
Wade Blasingame	2	0	0	0	0	0	0	1	2	0	.333	.000	.000
Steve Blateric	1	0	0	0	0	0	0	0	0	0	.000	.000	.000
Alan Closter	1	0	0	0	0	0	0	0	1	0	.000	.000	.000
Larry Gowell	1	0	1	1	0	0	0	0	0	0	1.000	2.000	1.000
Jim Roland	1	0	0	0	0	0	0	0	0	0	.000	.000	.000

ELEVEN

1973: A Season Filled with Disappointment

While the Yankees' five-game losing streak at the end of the 1972 season had lowered their record to 79–76 and dropped them into fourth place in the final standings, 6½ games out of first, the fact was they had remained in the divisional race for virtually the entire year. With the Baltimore Orioles no longer a dominant team, parity had been reached in the American League East, and New York, Boston, Detroit, and Baltimore were now all very closely bunched. The Orioles had the biggest names in players such as Brooks Robinson, Boog Powell, Paul Blair, Jim Palmer, Mike Cuellar, and Dave McNally, but, with the exception of Palmer, they all appeared to be past their primes. The Tigers were also an aging team, with veterans such as Al Kaline, Norm Cash, Willie Horton, and Bill Freehan forming the nucleus of their squad. It appeared that the Yankees and Red Sox had the brightest futures ahead of them, and that a major acquisition, or two, by either team could put them over the top.

The Yankees took the first step towards improving their roster by making a minor deal on October 27. The trade sent outfielder Danny Walton, who had spent the 1972 season in the minor leagues, to the Twins for reserve catcher Rick Dempsey. The 23–year-old Dempsey had spent parts of the previous four seasons with Minnesota, never coming to the plate more than 40 times in any of them. He was known to have a very strong throwing arm, though, and was an excellent defensive receiver.

Then, on November 24, New York acknowledged their earlier blunder by dealing Rich McKinney and Rob Gardner to the A's for veteran outfielder/first baseman Matty Alou. The younger brother of Felipe, the 34–year-old Matty was the smallest and fastest of the three Alous. He had originally come up with the Giants in 1960, joining Felipe in the San Francisco outfield, and even played briefly with his younger brother, Jesus, in 1963.

After being traded to the Pirates prior to the start of the 1966 season, Matty became a full-time player for the first time in his career and learned how to take better advantage of his running speed by hitting down on the ball. The result was four consecutive years with a batting average of .330, or better, including a National League batting title in 1966, with an average of .342. After his batting average dropped to .297 in 1970, he was traded to the Cardinals, for whom he batted over .300 in each of the next two seasons. However, he was dealt to Oakland late in the 1972 season as part of the A's playoff push. He batted .381 in the League Championship Series and helped Oakland to their first World Championship. With great depth in their outfield, though, the A's viewed him as being expendable and were willing to deal him to New York for the left-handed arm of Gardner and the much younger McKinney. The Yankees hoped that the left-handed line-drive hitter would add another consistent bat to their offense, and planned to play him both at first base and in right field, setting up a three-man rotation with brother Felipe and Johnny Callison.

Just three days later, on November 27, New York pulled off the block-buster deal that they had been hoping to make for more than two years. Knowing that they had not received consistent play at third base since trading away Clete Boyer at the end of the 1966 season, the Yankees had been eyeing Cleveland's Graig Nettles for quite some time. Finally, they were able to persuade the Indians to part with the left-handed slugger, along with back-up catcher Gerry Moses, for four players. Going to Cleveland in the trade were John Ellis, Jerry Kenney, and young outfield prospects Rusty Torres and Charlie Spikes. From Cleveland's perspective, Spikes was really the key to the deal since he was a big right-handed hitter with great power potential who had been a top prospect in the Yankee minor league system for the last few years.

In Nettles, however, the Yankees got a player they truly needed—a left-handed power hitter with a perfect Yankee Stadium stroke, who could also play a solid third base. He had hit more than 25 home runs in two of the last three seasons and had driven in as many as 86 runs in 1971. Moses would be a reliable back-up to Thurman Munson. Although he had been a reserve in Cleveland the prior year, Moses had made the All-Star team as a member of the Boston Red Sox in 1970.

With the Yankees' off-season wheeling and dealing completed, their roster appeared to be pretty much set. The Alou brothers, along with Johnny Callison, would split time at first base and in right field. Horace Clarke, coming off a sub-par season, would return at second base, and he would be joined at shortstop by Gene Michael. Nettles would take over the third base job. Infield reserves would include Bernie Allen, Hal Lanier, and Celerino Sanchez. Thurman Munson would return behind the plate, and he would be backed up by Gerry Moses.

Roy White, coming off his least productive season since he had become a regular in 1968, would patrol left-field once more, while Bobby Murcer, coming off the two most productive seasons of his career, would be in center. Ron Swoboda would be an outfield reserve.

One player whose bat the Yankees clearly needed to get into the lineup more often was Ron Blomberg. When the powerfully-built Blomberg connected, the ball seemed to jump off his bat, and, in the limited amount of action he had seen since coming to the majors, he had proven to be one of the team's most productive hitters. It seemed that he would have more of an opportunity to hit this year since, for the first time in history, the American League had decided to begin using a designated hitter in its games in 1973. The role seemed to suit Blomberg well since he had never proven to be particularly adept in the field, either at first base, or in the outfield.

The starting rotation would be headed by Mel Stottlemyre, Fritz Peterson, and Steve Kline. Although Stottlemyre had lost 18 games the prior year, he had pitched better than his record indicated, and he was still considered by most to be the ace of the staff. Peterson had gotten off to a slow start in 1972, but had rebounded to lead the team with 17 wins. In his first full year as a starter, Kline had been the staff's most consistent pitcher, finishing with a record of 16–9 and an ERA of 2.40.

It was expected that the rotation would be completed by Mike Kekich and George Medich. Kekich had finished with just a 10–13 record in 1972, but had pitched to a respectable 3.70 ERA. While he had yet to live up to his potential, the Yankees hoped that he was finally ready to mature into a top-flight starter. Medich was a young right-hander who had appeared briefly at the end of the 1972 season. He had done very well in the minors while simultaneously preparing to start medical school at Pittsburgh. As a result, his teammates had nicknamed him "Doc."

The bullpen would be led by Sparky Lyle, who had pitched so well in 1972, leading the league with 35 saves, while winning 9 games and compiling a 1.92 ERA. Lindy McDaniel, who had done well in his set-up role the prior year, going 3–1 with a 2.25 ERA, would also be returning. They would be joined by Fred Beene and Casey Cox, the veteran right-hander who had been obtained from Texas during the previous campaign.

However, prior to the start of the regular season, two things happened that would prove to have a major impact on the team. First, on January 3, it was announced that a group of investors, headed by shipbuilder George Steinbrenner, had purchased the Yankees from CBS for $10 million.

The son of a Great Lakes shipping family, the 42–year-old Steinbrenner had become wealthy serving as chairman of the American Shipbuilding Company, a Cleveland-based firm. In his youth, he had been an assistant football coach at Northwestern and Purdue universities, and, later, he had assembled national champions in the National Industrial and American Basketball leagues. Upon purchasing the Yankees, he promised, "I won't be active in the day-to-day operations of the club at all." However, his football-type mentality fostered in him a "win-at-all-cost" attitude and did not permit him to sit idly by and let others control his team's destiny. He would eventually buy out his partners and help to change the face of baseball forever with his aggressive approach to free agency and willingness to spend top-dollar for players he felt could improve his team.

Then, on March 5, the serenity of spring training was broken when pitchers Fritz Peterson and Mike Kekich arrived and announced to others that they had swapped their wives and families. As Roy White points out, "Some of the other players may have had an inkling of what was going on, but it caught others, like myself, completely off guard."[46] More than just a distraction to the team, however, the affair would prove to greatly affect the performance of both pitchers and hasten their departures from New York.

Finally, the regular season opened in Boston, on April 6, with a 15–5 defeat at the hands of the Red Sox. That was followed by three more losses, prior to the Yankees finally earning their first victory of the year in their second game at Yankee Stadium, with Mel Stottlemyre throwing a shutout against Gaylord Perry in New York's 4–0 win over the Indians. The team continued to struggle throughout most of April, collecting just 6 wins in their first 16 games, as of April 25.

Right around this time, the Yankees picked up Jim Ray Hart from the San Francisco Giants. The stocky Hart had once been a top slugger for the Giants as their regular third baseman from 1964 to 1968. During that five-year period, Hart had hit more than 20 homers every year, twice topping 30, had driven in more than 90 runs three times, and had batted at least .285 four times. However, after suffering an injury during the 1968 campaign, he had seen both his productivity and his playing time diminish over the last four seasons, while his weight had increased. Yet, he was still considered to be a dangerous hitter, and the Yankees, still not willing to give Ron Blomberg a chance to hit against left-handed pitching, thought Hart would provide a solid right-handed complement to him at the DH spot.

The team's play began to improve and, after winning their fourth straight game on May 1, they reached the .500–mark for the first time, at 10–10. New York continued to play .500 ball throughout the month of May, compiling a record of 24–24 after play on June 1.

Much of the reason for the team's mediocre performance over the first two months centered around the inability of the starting pitchers to perform as well as they had in past seasons. Mel Stottlemyre and George Medich were solid, with both pitchers winning more than half their starts at this juncture. However, none of the other starters fared as well. Steve Kline, who had won 16 games in 1972, had just 3 wins to his credit, while both Fritz Peterson and Mike Kekich appeared to be having a difficult time focusing following their pre-season disclosure. Peterson had only 4 wins, while Kekich, after being removed from the starting rotation for the season's first month, had only 1.

The Yankees attempted to remedy the situation by making two deals on June 7. First, they traded four minor leaguers—first baseman/outfielder Frank Tepedino, who they had traded once before and later re-acquired, outfielder Wayne Nordhagen, and pitchers Alan Closter and Dave Cheadle—to the Atlanta Braves for Pat Dobson. Then, they purchased Sam McDowell from the San Francisco Giants for $100,000.

The 31–year-old Dobson had originally come up with the Detroit Tigers in 1967. After pitching mostly in relief in his three seasons in Detroit, the right-hander was traded to the San Diego Padres, for whom he went 14–15 in 34 starts, in 1970. After being traded to the Orioles prior to the start of the 1971 season, he became one of a quartet of 20–game winners on Baltimore's staff that year, using a big curveball to compile a record of 20–8 and an ERA of 2.90. After finishing 16–18 with a 2.65 ERA in 1972, he was traded to Atlanta. Prior to being dealt to New York, Dobson had won only three of his ten decisions with the Braves, while pitching to a 4.99 ERA.

The 30–year-old McDowell had once been one of the most dominant pitchers in the American League, striking out more than 300 batters in a season twice for the Cleveland Indians. After first coming up with Cleveland as a 19–year-old in 1962, McDowell became a regular member of the Indians' rotation in 1964. Over the next seven seasons, the big 6'5" left-hander struck out more than 200 batters six times, leading the league in that category five times, won 17 or more games three times, once winning 20, and compiled an ERA of less than 3 runs a game six times, finishing with a mark of 1.81 in 1968. Possessing a blazing fastball, a good change-up, and questionable control, McDowell was the most intimidating pitcher in the American League. However, as he would later admit, he also had a serious drinking problem that began to affect his pitching performance in 1971. That year, he finished the season with a record of 13–17 and an ERA of 3.40. He was subsequently traded to the Giants for Gaylord Perry. His alcoholism continued to affect his performance with San Francisco, as he finished just 10–8, with a 4.33 ERA for the Giants in 1972. When the Yankees acquired him, his record with the Giants was just 1–2, and his ERA was 4.50.

Both Dobson and McDowell were inserted into the rotation shortly thereafter, replacing Kekich and Kline. Kekich would be traded away before the end of the season after making just 4 starts and finishing with a 1–1 record and a 9.20 ERA. Kline had developed a sore arm and would finish the season with a record of just 4–7 and an ERA of 4.01.

The Yankees' play improved and, after play on June 20, their record stood at 35–30 and they had moved into first place in the A.L. East, a position they would hold for the next 20 days. After falling out of first on July 10, the Yankees regained the lead the next day and held onto it as the season's first half came to a close. On July 22, at the All-Star break, the Yankees stood alone in first place, with a record of 57–44.

Three Yankees were selected to the All-Star team. Bobby Murcer, having another superb year, was picked as a starting outfielder for the third straight time. Thurman Munson, also having an excellent season, was selected as a reserve for the second time, while Sparky Lyle was chosen for the first time in his career.

Several other players also contributed prominently to the Yankees' first-half success, though. After being acquired from the Giants, Jim Ray Hart had done a fine job in his role as right-handed DH, providing good power and driving in runs regularly. In fact, he was so successful in his first two months with the team that he was frequently started against right-handed pitching as well, with Ron Blomberg moving to first base.

Although he was still being platooned mostly against right-handed pitching, Ron Blomberg had an exceptional first half, hitting close to .400 for quite some time and providing the team with a third power threat from the left side of the plate, in addition to those posed by Bobby Murcer and Graig Nettles.

Lindy McDaniel and Fred Beene pitched extremely well out of the bullpen, enabling Manager Houk to hold Sparky Lyle back until the game was on the line in the late innings.

After the break, however, New York went into a bit of a tailspin, losing 10 of their next 14 games and falling into third place, two games out of first, with a record of 61–54. In the midst of this slide, an incident occurred in a game against the Red Sox at Fenway Park. With the score tied 2–2 in the top of the ninth inning, Thurman Munson attempted to score from third base on a missed bunt attempt by Gene Michael. In so doing, he crashed into Boston catcher Carlton Fisk, and the two men came up swinging. Boston went on to win the game, 3–2, in the bottom of the inning, knocking the Yankees out of first place for the first time in three weeks.

Without an experienced first baseman on the roster, the Yankees acquired slick-fielding Mike Hegan from Oakland. Hegan had originally come up through the Yankee farm system, even making an appearance for them in the 1964 World Series. After being claimed by the Seattle Pilots in the 1969 expansion draft, he led the team in batting with a mark of .292 in their first year in the league. From there, he had gone to Oakland in 1971, where he was used mostly by the A's in late-inning situations for his defense. He would be used much in the same way by the Yankees during the season's second half, frequently replacing Ron Blomberg or one of the Alous in the latter stages of games. However, he also contributed to the offense, hitting 6 home runs, knocking in 14 runs, and batting .275 in 131 at-bats.

The Yankees seemed to be coming out of their slump when they won 7 of their next 11 games, to improve their record to 68–58. However, an eight game losing streak dropped them into fourth place, 10½ games out of first on August 29, essentially eliminating them from the division race.

On September 6, with the Yankees 10 games out of first place, they sold Felipe Alou to the Montreal Expos and brother Matty to the St. Louis Cardinals. Felipe, in 280 at-bats, had hit 4 home runs, driven in 27 runs, and batted just .236. Matty had hit .296 in his 497 at-bats, but it was a "soft" .296. Hitting mostly in the number two and three spots in the batting order, he had hit just 2 home runs, driven in only 28 runs, and walked just 30 times.

The team made several other roster moves during the season's final month. They acquired veteran catcher/pinch-hitter Duke Sims from the Detroit Tigers. The left-handed hitting Sims was a 10–year veteran who had originally come up with Cleveland, but also had played for the Dodgers before going to Detroit. He had his best year for the Indians in 1970, when, in 345 at-bats, he hit 23 home runs, drove in 56 runs, and batted .264.

They also obtained right-handed pitcher Wayne Granger from the Cardinals. As a rookie reliever with the Cardinals in 1968, Granger had recorded a 4–2 record and a 2.25 ERA. After being traded to the Cincinnati Reds, along with outfielder Bobby Tolan at the end of that season for Vada Pinson, he had been the Reds' closer in both 1969 and 1970, saving 27 games in the first of those years and establishing a record that would later be broken by saving 35 games the following season. However, he had since fallen on hard times and had saved just 5 games for the Cardinals in 1973.

The Yankees also called up from the minors catcher Rick Dempsey, left-handed reliever Jim Magnuson, right-handed pitchers Tom Buskey and Dave Pagan, outfielder Otto Velez, and infielder Fred Stanley. Velez and Stanley were the only ones who saw much action, with Velez hitting 2 home runs, driving in 7 runs, and batting .195 in 77 at-bats, and Stanley hitting 1 home run, knocking in 5 runs, and batting .212 in 66 at-bats. However, Stanley's only home run was a grand slam that turned out to be the last one hit at the "old" Yankee Stadium, before it was remodeled.

The Yankees won just 8 of their final 20 games to finish the season with a record of 80–82, in fourth place, 17 games behind the division-winning Baltimore Orioles. In head-to-head competition with their Eastern Division rivals, the Yankees split the season series with Baltimore, winning 9 of their 18 contests, and won 11 of 18 against Detroit. However, they won only 4 of 18 contests with the second-place Red Sox, failing to win a single game at Fenway Park. They also struggled against the eventual world champion Oakland A's, winning just 4 of their 12 meetings. Of course, the A's featured league MVP Reggie Jackson, who led the league with 32 home runs, 117 runs batted in, and 99 runs scored.

The Yankees' second-half collapse and failure to live up to the expectations that many had for them going into the season can be attributed to a number of factors. For one thing, the offense was not nearly productive enough. While the team's 131 home runs were the sixth highest total in the league and their .261 batting average tied them for fourth best, their 641 runs scored were the tenth highest total in the league. This is a clear indication that there was a lack of timely hitting all season.

Then, there was the lack of overall team speed. Other than Roy White, Horace Clarke, and Bobby Murcer, no one on the team was a particularly good base-runner. As a result, the team's 47 stolen bases were the second lowest total in the league.

Finally, there were the sub-par seasons that several players had. Johnny Callison added virtually nothing to the offense, hitting just 1 home run, knocking in only 10 runs, and batting just .176 in 136 at-bats.

After his fast start, Jim Ray Hart slumped badly during the season's second half. Although his numbers at season's end were not particularly bad—13 home runs, 52 runs batted in, and a .254 batting average in 339 at-bats—most of his home runs and RBIs were accumulated prior to the All-Star break.

While Graig Nettles hit 22 home runs and knocked in 81 runs, he batted only .234 and committed 26 errors at third base.

Roy White finished fourth on the team in home runs, with 18, and led in runs scored, with 88, and stolen bases, with 16, but his .246 batting average was his lowest mark since becoming a regular in 1968.

Then, there were pitchers Fritz Peterson and Mike Kekich, both of whom were clearly affected by what was going on in their personal lives. While Kekich was traded away before the end of the year, Peterson finished with a record of 8–15 and an unusually high ERA of 3.95.

However, as a whole, the pitching staff was effective. The team ERA of 3.34 was the third lowest in the league, and the starters combined for 16 shutouts, tying them for the second highest total in the league.

Mel Stottlemyre finished with a record of 16–16, but his ERA was a solid 3.07 and, with a little more run support, he probably could have won between 18 and 20 games. He led the staff with 273 innings pitched, 19 complete games, and 4 shutouts.

George Medich was, perhaps, the team's most consistent starter, finishing the season with a 14–9 record and a 2.95 ERA, good enough for fifth best in the American League.

Fred Beene excelled in his role as middle reliever/spot-starter, going 6–0 with a 1.68 ERA in 91 innings of work.

Lindy McDaniel was superb as Sparky Lyle's set-up man, finishing the season with a record of 12–6 and a 2.86 ERA, saving 10 games, and even getting 3 starts.

While not quite as dominant as he had been in 1972, Sparky Lyle, once again, ranked among the top relievers in baseball. Although his won-lost record was only 5–9, he finished the season with a 2.51 ERA, and his 27 saves were the second highest total in the league.

The offense had its outstanding performers as well. Although he wasn't able to maintain his torrid pace from the season's first half, Ron Blomberg finished with 12 home runs, 57 runs batted in, and a .329 batting average in just 301 at-bats. Projected over an entire season of approximately 500 at-bats, that comes out to about 20 home runs and 95 runs batted in. In addition, he led the team in both on-base percentage (.395) and slugging percentage (.498).

Thurman Munson had his finest all-around year as a hitter. For the first time in his young career, he showed that he had the ability to turn on the ball and hit for power while still maintaining a high batting average. He finished third on the team in home runs (20), runs batted in (74), and runs scored (80), and second in batting average (.301) and hits (156). Among the regulars, he led in slugging percentage, and his mark of .487 was the fifth highest in the American League. At season's end, he was selected to *The Sporting News* All-Star team, was awarded his first Gold Glove, and finished twelfth in the league MVP voting.

Once again, though, the star of the team was Bobby Murcer, who tied Graig Nettles for the team lead with 22 home runs, and led in runs batted in (95), batting average (.304), and hits (187), while finishing second to Roy White with 83 runs scored. He finished fourth in the American League in batting, third in hits, and seventh in runs batted in. At season's end, he was selected to *The Sporting News* All-Star team for the third consecutive year and finished ninth in the league MVP voting.

Nevertheless, the season had been a disappointing one for the Yankees. After playing so well prior to the All-Star break, the team had fallen apart during the season's second half. Changes needed to be made if New York was going to seriously contend for the divisional title in 1974. Unfortunately for Lindy McDaniel, one of those changes involved him, as he would be dealt to Kansas City during the off-season.

For a good portion of his 21–year major league career, Lindy McDaniel was among the top two or three relief pitchers in the game. When he retired at the end of the 1975 season, he had more relief appearances (987) than anyone in history, with the exception of Hall of Famer Hoyt Wilhelm, and he was fourth on the all-time saves list, with 172.

McDaniel bypassed the minor leagues completely after signing with the Cardinals in 1955 as a 19–year-old. As a starter with St. Louis in 1957, he compiled a record of 15–9 and a 3.49 ERA. However, after struggling through the following season with a record of just 5–7 and an ERA of 5.80, McDaniel was moved to the bullpen in 1959. There, he appeared in 62 games, finished with a record of 14–12, and led the National League with 15 saves. The following year was his finest, though, as McDaniel compiled a record of 12–4, saved a league-leading 26 games, pitched to a brilliant 2.09 ERA, was selected to the All-Star team for the only time in his career, and finished third in the Cy Young voting and fifth in the league MVP voting.

After two more years in St. Louis, McDaniel was traded to the Chicago Cubs prior to the start of the 1963 season. That year, he led the National League in saves for the third and final time in his career, with 22, while also winning 13 games in relief. Following two mediocre seasons with the Cubs in 1964 and 1965, McDaniel was dealt to the Giants, for whom he won 10 games in 1966, while pitching to an ERA of 2.66.

After a sub-par year with the Giants in 1967, McDaniel was traded to the Yankees during the 1968 campaign for pitcher Bill Monbouquette. In New York, McDaniel experienced a resurgence, dominating American League hitters with his patented forkball and superb control. League hitters, unfamiliar with McDaniel's delivery and assortment of pitches, had an extremely difficult time making solid contact with the tall right-hander's best pitch, which broke down and away from left-handed batters. Over the season's second half, he compiled a record of 4–1, picked up 10 saves, pitched to a 1.75 ERA, and struck out 43 batters in 51 innings of work. After a mediocre year in 1969, McDaniel was, once again, in top form in 1970. That year, he finished with a 9–5 record, compiled a 2.01 ERA, and saved a career-high 29 games— second most in the American League.

Following McDaniel's sub-par 1971 season, the Yankees obtained Sparky Lyle from Boston to be their closer. As a result, McDaniel's role was a lesser one in his last two years in New York. However, he fared extremely well in each, going 3–1, with a 2.25 ERA in 1972, and finishing 12–6, with 10 saves and a 2.86 ERA in his final season in pinstripes.

After being traded to Kansas City following the 1973 season, McDaniel pitched two more years before finally retiring. Prior to that, though, he had helped to stabilize the bullpens of four different teams, and, although largely overlooked, had been one of the top relief pitchers of his era.

Season Highlights, Outstanding Performances, and Memorable Moments

April 6   On Opening Day at Fenway Park, the Yankees lose to the Red Sox, 15–5. However, Ron Blomberg makes history by becoming the first official DH in the major leagues, walking with the bases loaded in his first at-bat against Luis Tiant.

April 11   After losing their first four games, the Yankees earn their first victory of the season, defeating the Indians, 4–0, at Yankee Stadium. Mel Stottlemyre throws a two-hit shutout, beating last year's Cy Young winner, Gaylord Perry, who surrenders three hits to Bobby Murcer.

April 12   Steve Kline throws a two-hitter, as the Yankees shut out the Indians again, this time by a score of 5–0.

April 18   At Baltimore's Memorial Stadium, the Yankees score five times in the ninth inning to overcome a 4–2 deficit and defeat the Orioles, 7–4. The big blows are two-run homers by Thurman Munson and Felipe Alou.

One of the top relief pitchers of his era, Lindy McDaniel helped to stabilize the Yankees bullpen for six seasons.

April 28   At Yankee Stadium, the Yankees homer four times and collect 14 hits in defeating the Twins, 11–3. Bobby Murcer homers twice and drives in five runs, and he is joined by Matty Alou and Graig Nettles, who also hit round-trippers. Alou goes 4–for-5, while Thurman Munson and Murcer each collect three hits.

April 29   The Yankees complete a three-game sweep of the Twins by taking both ends of a doubleheader played at Yankee Stadium, by scores of 6–3 and 11–1. In the first game, Mel Stottlemyre goes the distance, Horace Clarke collects three hits, and Graig Nettles homers. In the nightcap, Ron Blomberg goes 4–for–4 and drives in three runs, while Thurman Munson knocks in three more with two hits.

May 1   At Yankee Stadium, the Yankees defeat the Royals, 6–1, to reach the .500–mark for the first time this season, at 10–10. Steve Kline gets the victory, and Bobby Murcer provides the big blow with a three-run home run in the seventh inning.

May 8   At Metropolitan Stadium, the Yankees pound out 14 hits and score 14 times to defeat the Twins, 14–4. Ron Blomberg drives in four runs on two hits, including his first home run of the season, and Thurman Munson chips in with three hits of his own.

May 13   At Yankee Stadium, the Yankees split a doubleheader with the Orioles, winning the first game, 4–0, and losing the nightcap, 9–6. Mel Stottlemyre pitches a shutout in the opener and New York ties a major-league record by hitting four home runs in a shutout game in which no other runs are scored. Bobby Murcer, Roy White, Ron Blomberg, and Graig Nettles all connect for New York.

May 16   The Yankees defeat the Brewers at Yankee Stadium by a score of 11–4. The hitting star is Thurman Munson, who goes 3–for–4, with a home run and four runs batted in.

May 17   The Yankees come from behind to defeat the Brewers in 11 innings, by a score of 4–2. Trailing 2–0 in the bottom of the ninth, New York scores twice to send the game into extra innings. Bobby Murcer's dramatic two-out homer ties the game, and Graig Nettles' two-run homer in the eleventh provides the margin of victory.

May 20   At Municipal Stadium in Cleveland, the Yankees sweep a doubleheader from the Indians, winning the first game by a score of 4–2, and taking the nightcap, 7–3. In the opener, Ron Blomberg goes 3–for–3 and Graig Nettles homers, while Roy White's grand slam provides the winning margin in the second game.

May 22   At Tiger Stadium in Detroit, the Yankees defeat the Tigers, 7–2, as Jim Ray Hart goes 4–for-5, with a home run and three runs batted in, to support the five-hit pitching of Mel Stottlemyre.

May 26   At Yankee Stadium, the Yankees defeat the Rangers, 10–5, as Ron Blomberg drives in three runs with three hits, Bobby Murcer homers and knocks in four runs, and Gene Michael homers for the second day in a row.

June 6   At Arlington Stadium in Texas, the Yankees defeat the Rangers, 5–2, for their fourth straight victory. The win puts the Yankees four games over .500 for the first time all year, at 28–24.

June 8   The Yankees hit four home runs at Royals Stadium to defeat Kansas City, 8–1. Jim Ray Hart homers twice, and Roy White and Bobby Murcer also homer.

June 9   At Royals Stadium, New York rallies for five runs in the ninth inning to defeat Kansas City, 6–4. Newcomer Pat Dobson pitches five innings in relief, allowing just one hit, to earn his first victory in pinstripes. The win improves the Yankees' record to 30–25 and puts them into first place.

June 20   At Yankee Stadium, Mel Stottlemyre allows just two singles by Bobby Grich in New York's 2–1 victory over the Orioles. The Yankees score their only two runs on a seventh inning double by Jim Ray Hart.

June 24   At Yankee Stadium, the Yankees sweep a doubleheader from the Tigers, winning the first game, 3–2, and taking the night-cap, 2–1. Fred Beene pitches four scoreless innings of one-hit relief to earn the victory in the opener, with Sparky Lyle throwing a perfect ninth to pick up his 19th save. In the second game, Graig Nettles homers off Mickey Lolich in the bottom of the ninth to break a 1–1 tie and give reliever Lindy McDaniel his sixth victory of the year. The victories improve New York's record to 40–30, extend their winning streak to a season-best eight games, and strengthen their hold on first place.

June 29   The Yankees hit three home runs off of Gaylord Perry at Yankee Stadium as they defeat the Indians, 7–2. Roy White homers twice, Bobby Murcer adds another, and George Medich goes the distance as New York puts an end to their two-game losing streak.

July 1   At Yankee Stadium, the Yankees take two from the Indians, winning the opener, 5–2, behind Pat Dobson, and taking the second game, 11–3, behind rookie Dave Pagan. Both Horace Clarke and Gerry Moses collect three hits in the first game, while Bobby Murcer, Ron Blomberg, and Roy White all homer in the nightcap. The victories put the Yankees 12 games over .500, at 45–33, and keep them comfortably in first place.

July 13   At Yankee Stadium, Bobby Murcer hits three home runs and knocks in all five runs in New York's 5–0 win over Kansas City. Mel Stottlemyre throws the shutout — the 39th of his career.

July 20   The Yankees go 13 games over .500 for the first time all year, sweeping the White Sox in a doubleheader at Yankee Stadium, 12–2 and 7–0. George Medich and Sam McDowell are the winning pitchers, with McDowell throwing a two-hit shutout in the second game. Meanwhile, knuckleballer Wilbur Wood starts and loses both games for Chicago. Celerino Sanchez goes 4–for-5 in the opener, while Roy White's grand slam is the big blow in the nightcap. New York's record now stands at 56–43.

July 26   The Yankees defeat the Brewers, 1–0, in 12 innings at Yankee Stadium. Pat Dobson pitches 11 shutout innings, scattering just five hits. Sparky Lyle works a perfect 12th to earn the victory, while losing pitcher Jim Colborn goes all the way for Milwaukee. Thurman Munson goes 4–for-5 and drives in the game's only run with a single in the bottom of the 12th.

July 27   The Yankees' record improves to a season-best 15 games over .500 with a 7–6 victory over the Brewers at Yankee Stadium. Thurman Munson collects three more hits, and Graig Nettles adds two, including his 14th home run of the year. New York's record is now 59–44.

August 4   The Yankees defeat the Tigers, 3–2, in 14 innings at Tiger Stadium. After New York starter Fritz Peterson leaves the game in the second inning with a muscle pull, reliever Lindy McDaniel comes in and works the next 13 innings, allowing just one run and six hits, to earn the victory. Horace Clarke's home run is the game winner.

August 13   At Yankee Stadium, Roy White homers from both sides of the plate as the Yankees defeat the Angels, 6–0. George Medich throws the shutout.

Sept. 3   The Yankees win for only the second time in 12 games, defeating the Tigers in Detroit by a score of 4–3. Thurman Munson homers twice off of losing pitcher Joe Coleman, with his two-run homer in the 8th inning being the winning blow.

Sept. 8   The Yankees crush the Brewers at Yankee Stadium by a score of 15–1. Graig Nettles homers and drives in six runs, while shortstop Fred Stanley hits a grand slam.

Sept. 15   At Memorial Stadium, Mel Stottlemyre throws the 40th shutout of his career, blanking the Orioles, 3–0. The shutout ties Stottlemyre with Red Ruffing for second place on the all-time Yankee list, behind only Whitey Ford (45). It will also turn out to be the final one of his career.

Sept. 23   In Cleveland, the Yankees sweep a doubleheader from the Indians, winning the first game, 9–1, behind Mel Stottlemyre, and taking the nightcap, 2–1, behind George Medich. In the opener, both Ron Blomberg and Otto Velez homer twice against Cleveland starter Dick Tidrow.

1973 American League Final Team Standings and Offensive Statistics

TEAM	G	W	L	PCT	GB	R	H	2B	3B	HR	BB	SO	SB	AVG	OBP	SLG
EAST																
BAL	162	97	65	.599	—	754	1474	229	48	119	648	752	146	.266	.348	.389
BOSTON	162	89	73	.549	8	738	1472	235	30	147	581	799	114	.267	.340	.401
DET	162	85	77	.525	12	642	1400	213	32	157	509	722	28	.254	.322	.390
NY	162	80	82	.494	17	641	1435	212	17	131	489	680	47	.261	.324	.378
MIL	162	74	88	.457	23	708	1399	229	40	145	563	977	110	.253	.327	.388
CLE	162	71	91	.438	26	680	1429	205	29	158	471	793	60	.256	.317	.387
WEST																
OAK	162	94	68	.580	—	758	1431	216	28	147	595	919	128	.260	.336	.389
KC	162	88	74	.543	6	755	1440	239	40	114	644	696	105	.261	.342	.381
MINN	162	81	81	.500	13	738	1521	240	44	120	598	954	87	.270	.344	.393
CAL	162	79	83	.488	15	629	1395	183	29	93	509	816	59	.253	.320	.348
CHI	162	77	85	.475	17	652	1400	228	38	111	537	952	83	.256	.326	.372
TEX	162	57	105	.352	37	619	1397	195	29	110	503	791	91	.255	.320	.361
TOTAL						8314	17193	2624	404	1552	6647	9851	1058	.259	.331	.381

Team Pitching and Fielding Statistics

TEAM	CG	SH	SV	IP	H	HR	BB	SO	ERA	FA	E	DP
EAST												
BAL	67	14	26	1461	1297	124	475	715	3.07	.981	119	184
BOSTON	67	10	33	1440	1417	158	499	808	3.65	.979	127	162
DET	39	11	46	1447	1468	154	493	911	3.90	.982	112	144
NY	47	16	39	1427	1379	109	457	708	3.34	.976	156	172
MIL	50	11	28	1454	1476	119	623	671	3.98	.977	145	167
CLE	55	9	21	1464	1532	172	602	883	4.58	.978	139	174
WEST												
OAK	46	16	41	1457	1311	143	494	797	3.29	.978	137	170
KC	40	7	41	1449	1521	114	617	790	4.19	.974	167	192
MINN	48	18	34	1451	1443	115	519	879	3.77	.978	139	147
CAL	72	13	19	1456	1351	104	614	1010	3.53	.975	156	153
CHI	48	15	35	1456	1484	110	574	848	3.86	.977	144	165
TEX	35	10	27	1430	1514	130	680	831	4.64	.974	161	164
TOTAL	614	150	390	17396					3.82	.977	1702	1994

1973 New York Yankee Pitching Statistics

PLAYER	W	L	ERA	G	GS	CG	SHO	SV	IP	H	R	ER	BB	SO
Mel Stottlemyre	16	16	3.07	38	38	19	4	0	273	259	112	93	79	95
George Medich	14	9	2.95	34	32	11	3	0	235	217	84	77	74	145

PLAYER	W	L	ERA	G	GS	CG	SHO	SV	IP	H	R	ER	BB	SO
Fritz Peterson	8	15	3.95	31	31	6	0	0	184	207	93	81	49	59
Lindy McDaniel	12	6	2.86	47	3	1	0	10	160	148	54	51	49	93
Pat Dobson	9	8	4.17	22	21	6	1	0	142	150	72	66	34	70
Sam McDowell	5	8	3.95	16	15	2	1	0	95	73	47	42	64	75
Fred Beene	6	0	1.68	19	4	0	0	1	91	67	21	17	27	49
Sparky Lyle	5	9	2.51	51	0	0	0	27	82	66	30	23	18	63
Steve Kline	4	7	4.01	14	13	2	1	0	74	76	39	33	31	19
Jim Magnuson	0	1	4.28	8	0	0	0	0	27	38	17	13	9	9
Tom Buskey	0	1	5.40	8	0	0	0	1	16	18	12	10	4	8
Wayne Granger	0	1	1.76	7	0	0	0	0	15	19	7	3	3	10
Mike Kekich	1	1	9.20	5	4	0	0	0	14	20	15	15	14	4
Dave Pagan	0	0	2.84	4	1	0	0	0	12	16	4	4	1	9
Casey Cox	0	0	6.00	1	0	0	0	0	3	5	3	2	1	0

1973 New York Yankee Hitting Statistics

PLAYER	AB	R	H	2B	3B	HR	RBI	BB	SO	SB	OBP	SLG	AVG
Roy White	639	88	157	22	3	18	60	78	81	16	.329	.374	.246
Bobby Murcer	616	83	187	29	2	22	95	50	67	6	.357	.464	.304
Horace Clarke	590	60	155	21	0	2	35	47	48	11	.317	.308	.263
Graig Nettles	552	65	129	18	0	22	81	78	76	0	.334	.386	.234
Thurman Munson	519	80	156	29	4	20	74	48	64	4	.362	.487	.301
Matty Alou	497	59	147	22	1	2	28	30	43	5	.338	.356	.296
Gene Michael	418	30	94	11	1	3	47	26	51	1	.270	.278	.225
Jim Ray Hart	339	29	86	13	2	13	52	36	45	0	.324	.419	.254
Ron Blomberg	301	45	99	13	1	12	57	34	25	2	.395	.498	.329
Felipe Alou	280	25	66	12	0	4	27	9	25	0	.256	.321	.236
Johnny Callison	136	10	24	4	0	1	10	4	24	1	.197	.228	.176
Mike Hegan	131	12	36	3	2	6	14	7	34	0	.309	.466	.275
Hal Lanier	86	9	18	3	0	0	5	3	10	0	.244	.244	.209
Otto Velez	77	9	15	4	0	2	7	15	24	0	.326	.325	.195
Fred Stanley	66	6	14	0	1	1	5	7	16	0	.288	.288	.212
Celerino Sanchez	64	12	14	3	0	1	9	2	12	1	.239	.313	.219
Gerry Moses	59	5	15	2	0	0	3	2	6	0	.270	.288	.254
Bernie Allen	57	5	13	3	0	0	4	5	5	0	.290	.281	.228
Ron Swoboda	43	6	5	0	0	1	2	4	18	0	.191	.186	.116
Rick Dempsey	11	0	2	0	0	0	0	1	3	0	.250	.182	.182
Duke Sims	9	3	3	0	0	1	1	3	1	0	.500	.667	.333
Lindy McDaniel	2	0	0	0	0	0	0	0	2	0	.000	.000	.000

TWELVE

1974: The Great Pennant Race

The Yankees' second-half collapse in 1973 was a clear indication that the team was still a few players away from being a true contender in the American League East. While New York fans had overestimated the talent of their own club, they had underestimated the Orioles, who, after a one-year hiatus, had recaptured the divisional title. With an infusion of energy from young and talented players such as Bobby Grich, Rich Coggins, and A.L. Rookie of the Year Al Bumbry, plus solid seasons from veterans Brooks Robinson, Paul Blair, Mike Cuellar, Dave McNally, and Cy Young Award winner Jim Palmer, Baltimore had silenced their critics by winning the divisional crown by a comfortable eight-game margin.

Meanwhile, the Yankees had gaping holes to fill at several vital positions. With the sale of the Alou brothers during the season's last month and the subsequent release of outfielder Johnny Callison, New York was in dire need of both a first baseman and a right-fielder. The team was also in need of at least one more starting pitcher to complement Mel Stottlemyre, George Medich, and Pat Dobson with. Fritz Peterson, distracted by the rather unusual circumstances surrounding his personal life, was coming off a miserable 8–15 season, Steve Kline had not returned to his earlier form, and Sam McDowell was no longer the dominant pitcher he had been earlier in his career with Cleveland. In addition, the front office was always looking to improve the team in the middle infield, since it had never been fully satisfied with either Horace Clarke at second or Gene Michael at short.

General Manager Gabe Paul addressed the right-field situation with his first deal of the off-season on December 7, acquiring outfielder Lou Piniella and relief pitcher Ken Wright from the Kansas City Royals for Lindy McDaniel.

Piniella was a 30–year old, solid right-handed hitter who had originally come up through the Oriole farm system. After being dealt to Cleveland, he had been left unprotected in the expansion draft and had been picked up by the Royals prior to the start of the 1969 season. In Kansas City's first year of existence, Piniella batted .282, hit 11 home runs, and knocked in 68 runs to win Rookie of the Year honors. He topped the .300–mark in both 1970 and 1972, but, after hitting just .250 in 1973, the Royals decided that he was expendable.

Wright was a 27–year-old right-hander who had spent four seasons with Kansas City. Pitching primarily in relief, Wright had compiled a 6–5 record and a 4.91 ERA in 1973.

Then, on March 19, New York was involved in a three-team deal with Cleveland and Detroit. The deal saw veteran right-hander Jim Perry go from the Tigers to the Indians, where he would join his brother, Gaylord. Meanwhile, the Yankees sent back-up catcher Gerry Moses to Detroit and received outfielder Walt "No-Neck" Williams from the Indians, and pitchers Ed Farmer and Rick Sawyer from the Tigers.

From the Yankees' perspective, Williams was the key to the deal. The 5'6", 185–lb Williams was a professional right-handed hitter who had been a part-time player for most of his career. After starting out in the Astros organization, he had gone to the White Sox prior to the start of the 1967 season. He spent the next six years with Chicago, collecting more than 400 at-bats only once, in 1969. However, that year, Williams batted .304, topping .300 for the only time in his career. He was traded to the Indians after 1972 for infielder Eddie Leon. With Cleveland in 1973, Williams batted .289 in 350 at-bats. He had little power and, despite his small stature, he rarely walked. Yet, the Yankees planned to use him primarily as a pinch-hitter and late-inning defensive replacement, since he was a solid defensive outfielder.

Just four days later, on March 23, the Yankees purchased outfielder Elliott Maddox from the Texas Rangers for $60,000. The right-handed hitting Maddox had originally come up with the Tigers in 1970. After being used mostly as a utility player in his only year in Detroit, both in the outfield and at third base, Maddox was traded to the Senators, along with Denny McLain. He remained with the Senators after they moved to Texas and changed their name to the Rangers. However, Maddox was unable to break into the starting lineup and failed to collect as many as 300 at-bats in any season with Texas. He had a reputation for being a very good outfielder, but a below-average hitter. The Yankees thought he would be a good player to have on their bench since he could play any of the outfield positions, or even third base.

Prior to the start of the regular season, Paul also made what appeared to be two other minor moves, acquiring shortstop Jim Mason and utility man Bill Sudakis from the Texas Rangers in separate deals.

The left-handed hitting Mason had been a part-time player with the Rangers in each of the last two seasons. Having batted just .197 in 147 at-bats in 1972 and just .206 in 238 at-bats the following year, he had yet to prove that he was capable of hitting major-league pitching. However, he was, at 23, 12 years younger than Gene Michael and appeared to pose the most serious threat to him as the team's starting shortstop since Michael first claimed the job in 1969.

The powerfully-built Sudakis had originally come up with the Dodgers in 1968. After hitting 14 home runs and driving in 53 runs as the Dodgers' starting third baseman in 1969, the versatile switch-hitter was converted to catcher the following year. After hitting 14 homers and knocking in 44 runs in just 269 at-bats as the team's starting catcher in 1970, Sudakis broke a finger and, subsequently, became a utility player in his next several seasons. Appearing at third base, first base, and catcher, he played for the Dodgers in 1971, the Mets in 1972, and the Rangers in 1973. He saw the most action for Texas, hitting 15 home runs, knocking in 43 runs, and batting .255 in 235 at-bats. It was thought that he would compete with Mike Hegan for the first base job, since the Yankees had not been able to find anyone else to play the position.

These moves were not nearly as significant, though, as a number of events that occurred around the team during the off-season. First, as soon as the 1973 regular season ended, Ralph Houk resigned as Yankee manager. After more than a quarter-of-a-century in the Yankee organization in one capacity or another, Houk had decided that it was time to leave since he could not manage under George Steinbrenner.

Following his years as a back-up catcher with the team, Houk had become a coach under Casey Stengel. However, after Stengel was fired following the Yankee defeat in the 1960 World Series, Houk had been named manager and had led the team to one of its greatest seasons in 1961. Following two more years as Yankee manager, Houk moved into the front office prior to the start of the 1964 season, naming Yogi Berra as the new manager. When New York was defeated in seven games by the Cardinals in the World Series that year, however, the Yankees fired Berra and replaced him with Cardinal manager Johnny Keane. A little over one year later, Houk replaced Keane with himself and took over the managerial reins for the next eight years. As both GM and manager, Houk had grown accustomed to having a great deal of control over the team, and he clearly was not comfortable managing under Steinbrenner, who insisted on meddling in the team's affairs and on being consulted before any move could be made. Therefore, Houk left the only major league organization he had ever known and signed a three-year contract to manage the Detroit Tigers just 11 days later.

On December 18, the Yankees announced the signing of Dick Williams as manager. Williams had led the Oakland A's to the last two world championships. However, he had grown weary of having to deal with meddlesome owner Charlie Finley and had left the team despite having one year remaining on his contract. Finley contested the move, however, demanding compensation from New York in the form of players. Two days later, American League president Joe Cronin ruled that, since Williams was still technically under contract to the A's, he could not be signed by New York. As a result, the Yankees turned to Bill Virdon, the former centerfielder, who had earlier coached and managed for the Pittsburgh Pirates.

Another huge development was the fact that, for the first time in more than 50 years, the Yankees would be playing their home games in somewhere other than Yankee Stadium. With the Stadium being remodeled, the Yankees would be spending the next two seasons playing in Shea Stadium, as tenants of the Mets. With its different dimensions and swirling winds, Shea would have a major impact on the team, and on some of its players in particular. In addition, the Yankees' home attendance would suffer somewhat, since Queens had long been a stronghold for Mets fans.

Finally, just two days prior to the start of the regular season, owner George Steinbrenner was indicted for making illegal campaign contributions on behalf of Richard Nixon.

By the time Opening Day finally arrived, the Yankee team had a very different look about it. First base would be shared by Mike Hegan and Bill Sudakis. Horace Clarke would, once again, be the starting second baseman. However, Gene Michael had been relegated to back-up status by Jim Mason, who had won the starting shortstop job during spring training. Graig Nettles would start at third, with reserves in the infield including Michael and Fred Stanley.

The Yankees were looking for a big year from Thurman Munson behind the plate. After hitting a career-high 20 home runs in 1973, it was thought that a move out of Yankee Stadium, with its distant fences in left and left-center field, would add perhaps another 10 homers to his total and increase his run production as well. He would be backed up by Rick Dempsey.

Roy White would start in left-field, Bobby Murcer would patrol center, and Lou Piniella would start in right. Back-up outfielders would include Elliott Maddox and Walt Williams. Ron Blomberg and Jim Ray Hart would platoon at the DH spot.

The starting rotation would be comprised of Mel Stottlemyre, Doc Medich, Pat Dobson, Fritz Peterson, and Steve Kline. The bullpen would be headed by Sparky Lyle. He would be joined by Fred Beene, Tom Buskey, and Ken Wright. Sam McDowell would be available for long relief and spot-starting assignments.

The Yankees opened the regular season with a 6–1 victory over the Indians before only 20,744 fans at Shea Stadium. Graig Nettles hit a two-run homer for the Yankees' first runs of the year, and Mel Stottlemyre went all the way for the win, defeating Gaylord Perry in the process. New York won their next three games as well to start the season off 4–0. However, they won only four of their next eleven contests, leaving their record at 8–7.

As the Yankees continued to play .500 ball through the season's first month, Manager Bill Virdon ruffled some feathers by restructuring the outfield. Not completely satisfied with Bobby Murcer in centerfield, he decided to shift the team's best player to right and install Elliott Maddox in center. Though not happy with the switch, Murcer accepted the move without complaining. Virdon simultaneously moved Lou Piniella from right-field to left and began using Roy White more as a designated hitter against left-handed pitching, platooning him with Ron Blomberg. Jim Ray Hart, batting only .053 with just one hit in his first 19 at-bats, was released.

In making these moves, Virdon was stating, in no uncertain terms, that this was *his* team, and that he was going to do whatever it took to help it win. While this upset certain players initially, in the end it helped to establish his authority and improve team chemistry. The shifting of Murcer to right turned out to be a very wise move because, while Murcer was a good center-fielder, he was an excellent right-fielder. More importantly, though, it gave Elliott Maddox the chance to play everyday for the first time in his career and to show what an outstanding centerfielder he was. Maddox had more range than Murcer and was better suited to play the position.

However, Virdon showed less wisdom in his handling of White, who was the team's best defensive left-fielder. From the beginning of the season, it seemed that the new Yankee manager was not particularly impressed with White's abilities. He used him only occasionally in the outfield, preferring to play Lou Piniella in left instead. In fact, on those rare occasions when White did start the game in left-field, he was frequently removed for defensive reasons in the late innings in favor of Walt Williams. White performed admirably, though, when his name was on the lineup card, and, to his credit, later in the year, Virdon admitted he had made a mistake in his original assessment of White's abilities.

On April 27, with the Yankees' record at 11–9, Gabe Paul made the team's biggest trade of the year. Not satisfied with the play the team was getting out of Mike Hegan and Bill Sudakis at first base, he dealt four pitchers—Fritz Peterson, Steve Kline, Fred Beene, and Tom Buskey—to the Cleveland Indians for first baseman Chris Chambliss and pitchers Dick Tidrow and Cecil Upshaw. While Tidrow and Upshaw were both considered to be valuable pick-ups, Chambliss was the player the Yankee front office really wanted.

With the Indians in 1971, Chambliss had been named the American League's Rookie of the Year for hitting .275 with 9 homers and 48 runs batted in. He led Cleveland in batting in each of the next two seasons, hitting .292 in 1972 and .273 the following year. Although he was more of a line-drive hitter who had not yet shown the ability to hit a lot of home runs, it was thought that, when the team eventually moved back into Yankee Stadium, the left-handed hitting Chambliss would be able to take advantage of the ballpark's short right-field porch and become a legitimate home run threat and RBI-man. He was batting .328 with Cleveland at the time of his trade to New York.

Tidrow broke in with the Indians in 1972, winning 14 games with a poor Cleveland club. As the number two man behind Gaylord Perry in the Indians' starting rotation that year, he finished with an ERA of 2.77 and was named *The Sporting News*' Rookie Pitcher of the Year. He finished 14–16, with a 4.42 ERA for Cleveland in 1973 and was 1–3, with a 7.11 ERA at the time of the trade.

The 6'6" Upshaw had once been a top closer for the Atlanta Braves. Employing a tough side-arm delivery, he had helped the Braves to the division title in 1969 with 27 saves. However, the following spring he nearly severed a finger on his pitching hand while showing teammates how to dunk a basketball. As a result, he missed the entire 1970 campaign before returning the following year to post a record of 11–6, 17 saves, and an ERA of 3.51. He was not the same pitcher, though, that he had been prior to the injury and, over the last two seasons with Atlanta and Houston, he had a combined 5–9 record and only 14 saves. With Cleveland prior to the trade, he was 0–1, with a 3.38 ERA.

The deal seemed to upset many of the veterans on the team who felt that they were already good enough to compete for the division title without having to trade away almost half of their pitching staff. In fact, the newcomers were greeted with a certain amount of indifference, causing the sensitive Chambliss to struggle in his first year in pinstripes.

Nevertheless, the team finished the month of April with a record of 13–10, in second place, two games out of first. Particularly effective during this period were Mel Stottlemyre, George Medich and Graig Nettles. Stottlemyre had posted 5 wins against only 1 loss, while Medich's record stood at 4–1. Nettles carried the offense in the early-going, finishing the month with a major-league record-tying 11 home runs.

In early May, the Yankees acquired two more pitchers. The first was right-hander Dick Woodson, who had spent his entire four-year career with the Minnesota Twins. After pitching out of the Twins' bullpen in each of his first two seasons, Woodson became a regular member of the starting rotation in 1972, going 14–14, with a 2.72 ERA. After experiencing some arm problems the following season, he finished 10–8, with a 3.95 ERA. He fell out of favor with Minnesota management prior to the start of the 1974 season, though, by becoming the first major league player to invoke the new arbitration procedure established to settle contract disputes between clubs and their players. His record with the Twins prior to the trade was 1–1, with a 4.33 ERA.

The other pitcher New York picked up was left-handed reliever Mike Wallace, who they acquired from the Phillies. He had only been in the majors since 1973, and the Yankees viewed him as a middle-inning reliever.

New York struggled during the month of May, and into early June, finishing play on June 7 with a record of just 26–30, in fifth place, 4½ games out of first. The bat of Graig Nettles had cooled off, Bobby Murcer's power numbers were down, Jim Mason wasn't hitting, and Mel Stottlemyre had slumped, losing six of his last seven decisions, to lower his record to 6–7.

More importantly, however, was the fact that Stottlemyre was experiencing a great deal of pain in his right shoulder. It was discovered that he had a torn rotator cuff that would prevent him from pitching for the better part of the year. In fact, his career even seemed to be in jeopardy.

Prior to finding out about Stottlemyre, however, the Yankee front office had made another deal, sending Duke Sims to the Rangers for pitcher Larry Gura.

The 26–year-old Gura had first come up with the Cubs in 1970. Shuffling back and forth between the majors and minors over the next four seasons, the left-hander had been used mostly in relief by Chicago. Although he was not a particularly hard thrower, Gura's ability to change speeds made his fastball look faster than it actually was, and he also had a fine assortment of breaking pitches. Nevertheless, in parts of four seasons with the Cubs, he had been able to compile a record of just 3–7 and had yet to show that he had the ability to pitch in the majors on a regular basis. Yet, he was still young, and Gabe Paul believed he was capable of eventually becoming a fourth or fifth starter.

The Yankees also acquired utility infielder Fernando Gonzalez from Kansas City. Gonzalez first came up with the Pirates at the end of the 1972 season and appeared in 37 games the following year, batting .224 in his 49 plate appearances. He had the ability to play either third base or second and had been used sparingly by the Royals, appearing in only nine games and collecting just 21 at-bats.

With Mel Stottlemyre perhaps lost for the season, the team continued to look for another starter to join Pat Dobson, Doc Medich, and Dick Tidrow in the rotation. On June 15, with New York hovering around the .500–mark, they purchased left-hander Rudy May from the California Angels.

May had always been a bit of an enigma since he appeared to have all the tools to be a superb pitcher yet had never been able to put it all together. The 29–year-old had spent his entire major league career with the Angels and had compiled an overall record of just 51–76. His best season with California had come in 1972, when he finished 12–11 with a 2.94 ERA. Yet, with his outstanding fastball and excellent curve, he had all the skills to become a top winner.

The Yankees inserted May into the rotation and he won his first start in pinstripes. However, the team went on a seven-game losing streak and, after play on July 3, their record stood at 35–42, and they were in sixth place, eight games out of first.

Things began to change, though, and, after winning their sixth straight game on July 13, New York improved their record to 44–43, and they were only 3½ games out of first place. Key to the effort were Lou Piniella, Elliott Maddox, and the improved play of Jim Mason. Piniella and Maddox were the team's most consistent offensive performers all year, and Maddox was also providing excellent defense in centerfield. Mason had started to hit and, in a game against Texas on July 8, he tied a major league record with four doubles.

That same day, the Yankees purchased infielder Sandy Alomar from the Angels. The versatile Alomar had played every position but pitcher and catcher in the major leagues. He had originally come up with the Braves in 1964, but had also played for the Mets and White Sox before becoming the Angels' regular second baseman in 1969. Although he led A.L. second basemen in errors in 1968 and 1969, most observers felt that his error totals were the result of the exceptional range that he possessed. He was California's everyday second baseman for five years, playing in 648 consecutive games from 1969 to 1973, and stealing more than 20 bases in each of those seasons. His best year was 1971 when he batted .260 and stole 39 bases. However, his average had fallen to .239 and .238 the next two years and the Angels felt that he didn't add enough to their offense. Meanwhile, the Yankees loved his range and felt that he would be an improvement over Horace Clarke and Gene Michael, who had been splitting time at second base. They inserted Alomar into the everyday lineup and dealt Clarke to the San Diego Padres. Alomar seemed to add a spark, playing solid defense while batting .269 and driving in 27 runs in his 279 at-bats with the Yankees.

New York played .500 ball in the remaining games leading into the All-Star break, and, at the break, their record stood at 48–47, and they were in fourth place. However, they were just two games out of first.

The Yankees were represented on the All-Star team by Bobby Murcer and Thurman Munson. Murcer was having a difficult time coping with the deeper right-field fence and swirling winds at Shea, and had yet to hit a home run in his home ballpark. Balls he hit that typically would have landed four or five rows back in the right-field seats at Yankee Stadium were merely long fly balls to the warning track in Shea. As the season progressed, Murcer seemed to grow more and more frustrated with his inability to hit one out. Yet, he was still hitting for average and was doing a fine job defensively in right-field. Munson seemed more intent than he usually was on pulling the ball, and, as a result, his batting average had taken a bit of a dip. He still was arguably the best catcher in the league, though, so his selection to the team was a valid one.

After the break, the Yankees continued to play mediocre ball, and, after play on August 13, their record stood at 56–59, and they were in fourth place, 7½ games out of first. The team got hot, though, and went on to win 15 of their next 18 games to improve their record to 71–62 and move them into second place, just one game out of first.

Critical to the success of the team during this stretch was the improvement in the starting pitching. After being acquired from the Angels, Rudy May won six of his first seven decisions with the Yankees. Pat Dobson, whose record had once been 8–13, won four straight starts during this period to improve his record to 14–14. Larry Gura was inserted into the rotation and went on to win his first five decisions.

Also prime contributors were Roy White and Ron Blomberg. White responded to the increased playing time he was seeing, and Blomberg was extremely productive whenever he was in the lineup.

The Yankees took over first place for the first time since early May with a 3–0 victory over the Brewers on September 4. They won three of their next five games before purchasing former American League batting champion Alex Johnson from the Texas Rangers on September 9.

Johnson was an extremely talented, but equally troubled player who had developed a reputation over the years for being surly, taciturn, and lazy. After coming up with the Phillies in 1964, he had been peddled first to the Cardinals, then to the Reds, then to the Angels, then to Cleveland, and, finally, to Texas. He was extremely fast, but he rarely hustled. In fact, Johnson was thought to be, quite possibly, the fastest right-handed hitter going from home to first base. In spite of the fact that he had never hit more than 17 home runs in a season, Johnson also had great power. In 1970, as a member of the Angels, he had become only the third player in history to hit a ball into the centerfield bleachers in Chicago's Comiskey Park. The first two men to accomplish the feat were Jimmie Foxx and Hank Greenberg.

After hitting .300 three times in the National League, Johnson switched leagues in 1970, joining the California Angels. That year, he led the A.L. in batting with a mark of .329. However, the Angels were forced to trade him away at the end of the following season, in spite of his exceptional natural ability, due to a number of bizarre events.

First, in June of 1971, Johnson accused teammate Chico Ruiz of pulling a gun on him in the Angels' clubhouse. However, there were no witnesses, and Ruiz denied any knowledge of the incident. Just two weeks later, Johnson was suspended by the team for his failure to hustle, following five benchings and 29 fines. Finally, in September of that year, Johnson was awarded nearly $30,000 in back salary from the Angels when an arbitrator ruled that he was "emotionally incapacitated" during the events that led to his June suspension. As a result, the arbitrator reasoned that Johnson should have been treated as if he were a physically disabled player.

In spite of his erratic behavior, the one constant that Johnson offered was his ability to hit a baseball. After batting .287 with Texas in 1973, he had compiled a .291 average in 453 at-bats with the team in 1974. Johnson paid immediate dividends for New York following their September 9 purchase of him. Arriving in Boston during the Red Sox-Yankee game the next day, he came up in the 12th inning with the score tied 1–1 and promptly hit a home run to win the game for the Yankees, 2–1.

The victory helped New York hold onto first place, something they did for several more days. However, the Orioles were also playing excellent ball and were hot on the Yankees' trail. Finally, after sweeping New York in a three-game series at Shea in mid-September, Baltimore overtook the Yankees.

The two teams continued to play inspired ball over the final two weeks of the season. After their fourth consecutive victory on September 22, the Yankees' record stood at 84–70, and they were in first place, a half game ahead of the Orioles, with just eight games left on the schedule. However, on September 24, New York dropped a doubleheader to Boston, and Baltimore reclaimed the lead.

Even though the Yankees won their next four games, they were unable to make up any ground on the Orioles, who also refused to lose. So, the Yankees traveled to Milwaukee to complete their schedule with a two-game series against the Brewers, while Baltimore had three games remaining with the Tigers. With just a half game separating the two teams, the Yankees knew they had to win their remaining two games, and they had to hope that the Tigers would beat the Orioles at least once.

The pressure that the team was under surfaced shortly after the Yankees arrived in Milwaukee. After checking into the hotel, a scuffle broke out between Bill Sudakis and Rick Dempsey. Apparently, Sudakis, who was known for being a good needler, had been teasing Dempsey because of his lack of playing time. With the division title at stake, Thurman Munson was catching virtually every game down the stretch, and Dempsey hadn't been seeing very much action. So, Sudakis decided to try to get under the back-up catcher's skin. He succeeded in doing so, and Dempsey ended up taking a swing at him, causing a fight to break out. In an attempt to break up the battle, Bobby Murcer injured a finger, and it was not known if he would be able to play in the team's final two games.

Murcer ended up not playing, but it really didn't matter. While the Yankees lost their first game to Milwaukee, 3–2, in 10 innings, the Orioles defeated the Tigers, 7–6, to clinch the American League East title. Baltimore also won their final game of the season, so, even if the Yankees had won both of their contests, they still would have finished a game behind the Orioles. The Yankees did win their last game and finished the year with a record of 89–73, in second place, just two games out of first.

While the Yankees feasted against the Western Division in 1974, compiling a winning record against every team in the division, they did not fare nearly as well against their Eastern Division rivals. New York finished with a 7–11 record against Baltimore, and with the same mark against both Boston and Detroit.

In almost a complete reversal of what had happened the previous year, the Yankees improved their play dramatically during the season's second half, winning 33 of their final 47 contests. Even though the team came up just a bit short, their effort during the final two months of the season appeared to be something they could build on for next year. There were several key contributors to the success that the team experienced during the second half of the season, and to the improvement they showed over the prior year.

On the pitching staff, after coming over from Cleveland in the big seven-player trade, Dick Tidrow finished 11–9, with a 3.87 ERA. George Medich finished the season 19–15, and led the staff with 4 shutouts and 17 complete games, while finishing second in strikeouts (154) and innings pitched (279). Pat Dobson came on strong in the season's second half, winning 11 of his last 13 decisions to finish 19–15, and leading the team with 157 strikeouts and 281 innings pitched, while compiling a 3.07 ERA. Rudy May finished 8–4 and led all New York starters with an outstanding 2.28 ERA. Larry Gura won five of his six decisions and compiled an ERA of 2.41. Mike Wallace excelled in his role as middle-inning reliever, going 6–0 with a 2.41 ERA. While Sparky Lyle saved just 15 games, he finished 9–3 with a superb 1.66 ERA in 66 appearances.

As for the offense, after a rocky start, Jim Mason performed much better during the season's second half, finishing the year with a .250 batting average. In just 264 at-bats, Ron Blomberg was, once again, extremely productive, hitting 10 home runs, knocking in 48 runs, and batting .311. His .481 slugging percentage led the team, and his .375 on-base percentage was second best.

The two most consistent players, though, were Lou Piniella and Elliott Maddox. Piniella finished fourth in the American League with a .305 batting average and finished third on the team in runs batted in (70) and runs scored (71), and second in hits (158). Maddox finished fifth in the league in batting (.303) and fourth in on-base percentage (.397). He also led the team in runs scored (75) and provided excellent defense in centerfield, rivaling Baltimore's Paul Blair as the best defensive centerfielder in the league. At season's end, he finished eighth in the league MVP voting.

The team may have done even better, though, if it had gotten greater production from a few other players.

Bobby Murcer led the team with 88 runs batted in and 166 hits, and finished second to Roy White (15) in stolen bases, with 14. However, he hit only 10 home runs, batted just .274, and scored only 69 runs. Yet, he did an excellent job in right-field, collecting 21 assists and handling the move to his new position with dignity and class. Little did he know, however, that he had played his last game with the Yankees for more than four years.

While Graig Nettles led the team with 22 home runs and finished second in runs batted in, with 75, and runs scored, with 74, he batted only .246 and hit only 11 home runs after the month of April. Unhappy with the infield at Shea Stadium, he also committed 21 errors.

It was thought that Thurman Munson would thrive at Shea, and that his power numbers would increase dramatically. However, he hit only 13 home runs, drove in just 60 runs, and batted only .261. He also committed 22 errors in the field, most of which came on errant throws to second base on attempted steals by opposing base-runners. In the latter stages of the season, he was frequently replaced in the late innings of close games by Rick Dempsey for defensive reasons. Yet, at season's end, Munson was awarded his second consecutive Gold Glove. He was also selected to *The Sporting News* All-Star team.

Chris Chambliss did not adapt well to his new environment. In 400 at-bats, he hit only 6 home runs, drove in just 43 runs, and batted only .243. Some people were starting to question whether or not Gabe Paul had made a mistake by acquiring him in the first place.

The Yankees were hurt most, though, by the absence of Mel Stottlemyre, who had been the ace of the pitching staff for almost a decade. Although he made one relief appearance shortly before the end of the season to test his injured pitching shoulder, he was essentially lost to the team for two-thirds of the year. More importantly, though, he would discover during the off-season that his pitching career was over. He would join Horace Clarke, Gene Michael, Fritz Peterson, and Bobby Murcer as longtime Yankees who had begun the 1974 season as members of the team, but who would no longer be in pinstripes by the time 1975 rolled around.

Perhaps more than that of any other player, Horace Clarke's name has become synonymous with this particular period in Yankee history. In fact, there are those who even refer to the period of 1965 to 1975 as *The Horace Clarke Years.* This is truly a misnomer since, while Clarke was never an all-star, he was a pretty decent player, and was actually one of the better ones on some of those Yankee teams.

The switch-hitting Clarke, a native of St. Croix in the Virgin Islands, first came up to New York in 1965 and filled in at second, short, and third. The following year, with Bobby Richardson in his final season as Yankee second baseman and starting shortstop Ruben Amaro out for most of the year with an injury, Clarke saw extensive duty at shortstop. Even though he was forced to play out of position, he handled himself well, committing only 8 errors in 63 games there and hitting .266 in 312 at-bats.

With Richardson retiring at the end of the 1966 season, Clarke took over the second base job the following year and led the team in batting average (.272), stolen bases (21), runs scored (74), and hits (160). After a sub-par 1968 season, Clarke had his finest year in 1969, establishing career highs in batting (.285), runs scored (82), hits (183), stolen bases (33), doubles (26), and triples (7). In fact, his 183 hits were the second highest total in the American League that year. While Clarke never again hit any higher than .263, he remained a solid base-runner and decent leadoff hitter in his final four seasons with the Yankees. In his seven years as a regular in New York, he led the team in stolen bases four times, and in triples, runs scored, and base hits twice each. Although he had little power, Clarke was an extremely pesky hitter. In 1970 alone, he broke up three no-hitters in the ninth inning, thwarting bids by Joe Niekro, Sonny Siebert, and Jim Rooker.

However, the knock on Clarke was not so much with his offense, but rather his defense. It was often said that he did not have a lot of range and that he was not very good at turning the double play. While the accuracy of these statements is somewhat debatable, the numbers are not. Clarke set an A.L. record by leading league second basemen in assists six consecutive years, from 1967 to 1972. He also led in putouts from 1968 through 1971. While there were those who questioned his range, Clarke was one of the more surehanded second basemen in the league. In 1967, he committed only 8 errors in 140 games, leading all league second basemen with a .990 fielding average.

While Clarke's greatest strength was not in turning the double play, he worked very hard on that aspect of his game and improved himself quite a bit. In fact, with Clarke at second base and Gene Michael at shortstop, the Yankees led the league with 179 double plays in 1972. Yet, his critics continued to speak out against him until he was finally dealt to the Padres during the 1974 campaign. Clarke finished out his career that year, then retired unceremoniously to the Virgin Islands.

While he never let it show, the quiet, humble, and sensitive Clarke had to be hurt by many of the things that were said about him during his time in New York. Roy White came up with him through the minor leagues and was one of Clarke's closer friends on the team. He said of his former teammate: "I always thought Horace was a solid player. He hit .260 — .270 every year and stole between 20 and 30 bases. One year, he and Gene Michael led the league in double plays. I think he took the brunt of a lot of abuse for the bad times. I think it was mostly because he wasn't the most graceful player … he didn't look as great in a uniform as Bobby Richardson, or some of the other guys who preceded him did. I think they kinda' used Horace as a scapegoat because he had the funny stance, you know, real bow-legged guy, but he was a pretty good player."[47]

Although it always seemed that the Yankees were trying to find someone to replace Gene Michael as the team's starting shortstop, he held onto

Horace Clarke was New York's starting second baseman and leadoff hitter from 1967 to 1973. Frustrated Yankees fans of that generation would later refer to this period in the team's history as *The Horace Clarke Years.*

the position for five seasons, mostly because of his smooth fielding and alert play.

The 6'2" Michael, nicknamed "Stick" for his tall and slender physique, was a college basketball star at Kent State University. Even though he was coveted by several NBA teams, Michael chose to play baseball instead. He was originally signed by the Pittsburgh Pirates but had a difficult time making it to the major leagues because of his light hitting. After several years in the Pittsburgh minor league system, he was traded, along with former bonus baby Bob Bailey, to the Dodgers for Maury Wills at the end of the 1966 season. However, with Los Angeles in 1967, Michael batted only .202 in 223 at-bats. He was subsequently sold to the Yankees at the end of the season.

Given an opportunity in New York to win the starting shortstop job in 1968, the 29–year-old Michael failed to impress, batting just .198 in 116 at-bats. He was removed from the everyday lineup early in the season, in favor of Tom Tresh, who remained the starter for the rest of the year. When Tresh struggled early during the 1969 campaign, though, Michael was given another chance, and he made the most of it. Inserted into the starting lineup approximately one month into the season, Michael ended up hitting a career-high .272 and doing a fine job in the field.

However, after his batting average fell off to a more typical .214 the following year, the team began its search for his replacement. Over the next four seasons, Michael had to ward off challenges from Frank Baker, Hal Lanier, Jerry Kenney, and Fred Stanley, which he was able to do successfully, mostly because of his good glove work and heads-up-play. In particular, he became noted for pulling off the hidden-ball-trick, something he did on more than one occasion. While he was neither extremely fast on the bases nor spectacular in the field, Michael did everything with a certain graceful elegance. Whether he was running the bases or fielding his position, everything appeared to be effortless. While he never won a Gold Glove for his work at shortstop, he was among the American League's better fielders at the position throughout much of his Yankee career.

Finally, Michael lost his starting job to Jim Mason in 1974 and ended up going to Detroit the following year, finishing up his playing career as a back-up for the Tigers under former Yankee manager Ralph Houk.

Michael later returned to the Yankee organization, though, first as a minor league manager, then as a coach, then as General Manager, and finally as manager. However, he eventually got caught up in the revolving door of Yankee managers under owner George Steinbrenner. First, after Dick Howser had led the team to 103 victories in 1980, Michael replaced him as skipper at the end of the season. He was then replaced by Bob Lemon on September 6, 1981, only to be rehired as manager just 14 games into the following season. After being fired again by Steinbrenner in August of 1982, Michael left the organization he had been with for most of the past 15 seasons and joined the Chicago Cubs, for whom he also managed for more than one year before being fired by Cub GM Dallas Green.

Michael later returned to the Yankee organization and became the GM once again during the late 1980s. In that role, he helped to rebuild the team that had become the laughing stock of the American League due to a number of ill-advised moves made by the front office. Over the next several seasons, he made many sagacious moves, including trading for Paul O'Neill and David Cone, and signing Wade Boggs to a free agent contract. More importantly, however, he, more than anyone else, helped to con-

GENE MICHAEL
Coach

Clarke's double play partner for five seasons was smooth-fielding, light-hitting, shortstop Gene Michael.

vince Steinbrenner that it would be wise not to deal away so readily the organization's top minor league talent for aging veterans, and to rebuild the team from within. As a result, the Yankees held on to prospects such as Bernie Williams, Andy Pettite, Derek Jeter, and Mariano Rivera and, once again, became a dominant team. Michael, as much as anyone, is responsible for that. Although Steinbrenner replaced him as GM with Bob Watson at the end of the 1995 season, Michael's influence on the team can still be seen, both in the work he did as GM and the fine job he is doing today as top scout and talent evaluator.

While, over the years, Fritz Peterson's name has become associated more than anything else with his rather bizarre swapping of wives with teammate Mike Kekich, this is actually an injustice to him since he was a very solid pitcher throughout most of his career in pinstripes.

As a rookie with the last-place Yankees in 1966, Peterson tied Mel Stottlemyre for the team lead with 12 victories, and led New York starters in ERA for the first of three times. After suffering through a poor sopho-more season in 1967, Peterson pitched very well in each of the next five seasons, winning 20 games once, 17 twice, and 15 once. The fact that he finished only one or two games over .500 in most of those years was due almost entirely to the fact that he received very little in the way of run support. Three times during that period he compiled an ERA of less than 3 runs a game, and twice he finished among the top five pitchers in the league in that category.

Peterson's best year was 1970, when he won 20 games for the only time in his career. That year, he finished with a record of 20–11 and an ERA of 2.90, and was selected to the league

One of the Yankees' best pitchers for much of this period was left-hander Fritz Peterson, who had his finest season in 1970, when he won 20 games, helping to lead New York to a second-place finish.

All-Star team for the only time. The left-hander showed his flaky side during the season's final game — a 4–3 victory over the Red Sox at Fenway Park. With the Yankees up by a run late in the game, Peterson was removed for a relief pitcher. With his 20th victory hanging in the balance, he couldn't stand the pressure and decided to listen to the remainder of the game on the radio in manager Ralph Houk's office, sitting underneath Houk's desk.

Peterson was not a very hard thrower, and his curveball was merely average. However, what made him so effective was his outstanding control. He usually walked only about 40 batters a year, reaching a low in 1968, when he walked just 29 men in 212 innings. He led American League pitchers three years in a row, from 1968 to 1970, in fewest bases on balls allowed per nine innings, and, over the course of his major league career, walked just 426 batters in 2,218 innings (or, just 1.73 batters per 9 innings).

During the early 1970s, the Yankees' best player, and one of the best in the American League, was outfielder Bobby Murcer.

Also, after his first few seasons, Peterson developed a screwball, which made him even more effective.

After winning 15 games in 1971 and another 17 the following year, Peterson became distracted with his marital situation, and his record slipped to just 8–15 in 1973. After being dealt to Cleveland early in the 1974 campaign as part of that big seven-player trade, he pitched only three more years, compiling only one more winning season. With the Indians in 1975, Peterson finished with a record of 14–8 and an ERA of 3.94. However, after starting off the next season 0–3, he was traded to Texas, with whom he finished out the remainder of the year before retiring at season's end.

It is unfortunate that many people remember Fritz Peterson mostly because of the unusual circumstances surrounding his marriage because he was a very solid pitcher, and one of the better players on many of the Yankee teams he played for.

Bobby Murcer had several things in common with Mickey Mantle. Like Mickey, Murcer was from Oklahoma, was signed by scout Tom Greenwade, originally came up as a shortstop, first appeared in a Yankee uniform at the tender age of 19, and was heralded as the team's next great player. While he never attained the level of greatness that his predecessor did, Murcer was a fine player for several seasons, and, at the peak of his career, was among the very best players in the game.

Murcer was first brought up by New York near the end of the 1965 season, just as the Yankee dynasty was beginning to crumble. He also made a brief appearance at the end of the following season, playing all his games at shortstop. He failed to distinguish himself in either of those years, batting just .243 and .174, respectively, and struggling, in particular, against left-handed pitching. He also performed erratically in the field and seemed to be, just as Mantle had been when he first arrived in the big city, somewhat intimidated by his new surroundings.

Murcer spent both 1967 and 1968 in the army and came out a new man. Not only had he matured mentally, but he was no longer the skinny 20–year-old who had been with the team two years earlier. He had developed into a man physically as well and appeared ready to fulfill what many perceived to be his inevitable destiny as the team's next great player. He was even given Mantle's old locker, since Mickey had retired at the end of the previous season.

With the similarities in their backgrounds, the comparisons between Mantle and Murcer were inevitable. However, in truth, they were extremely unfair since few players, if any, were blessed with the natural talents that Mantle possessed in his youth. Not that Murcer was not a gifted athlete. He had fine speed and good power. But, at 5'11" and barely 180 pounds, he lacked Mickey's awesome power, and also did not have the blinding speed that Mantle had when he first came up to the big leagues.

The comparisons placed undue pressure on the youngster, yet he seemed to take them in stride and actually handled himself rather well in his first two seasons. After starting out 1969 as a third baseman, Murcer was shifted to centerfield, where he felt far more comfortable. As he learned his new position, Murcer put up some fairly impressive offensive numbers. While he struck out more than 100 times in both 1969 and 1970, Murcer combined for 49 homers, 160 runs batted in, and 177 runs scored those two years. Yet, his batting averages of .259 and .251 were not what either Yankee management or the fans were expecting from him and, as was the case with Mantle early in his career, he occasionally heard boos emanating from the stands at his home ballpark.

All of that changed, though, in 1971, when Murcer became the darling of the fans. In his first two seasons, the left-handed hitting Murcer constantly tried to take advantage of the short right-field porch at Yankee Stadium by pulling the ball. Opposing pitchers, subsequently, tried to pitch him outside to make his task more difficult. As a result, Murcer frequently either struck out or hit weak ground balls to the right side of the infield.

However, in 1971, he began hitting the ball more to left-field, and, as a result, became a complete hitter and one of the best players in baseball. His batting average jumped 80 points, to .331, and he finished a close second to Tony Oliva in the American League batting race. He also hit 25 home runs, drove in 94 runs, scored 94 others, and cut his strikeout total down to just 60. Murcer led the American League with a .427 on-base percentage, finished second with a .543 slugging percentage, second in runs scored, third in total bases, and fourth in runs batted in. He was selected to both the American League and *The Sporting News* All-Star teams for the first time in his career, and, at season's end, finished seventh in the league MVP voting. That year, he was arguably the best centerfielder and one of the five best all-around players in the game.

Murcer had another outstanding season in 1972, establishing career highs in home runs (33), runs batted in (96), runs scored (102), triples (7), and doubles (30), and batting .292. He led the American League in runs scored and total bases, finished second to MVP Dick Allen in home runs, third in runs batted in, doubles, and slugging percentage (.537), and fourth in triples. He was selected to the American League and *The Sporting News* All-Star teams for the second consecutive year, won the only Gold Glove of his career for his outstanding defense in centerfield, finished fifth in the league MVP voting, and was, once again, arguably the best centerfielder and one of the five best players in baseball.

After another fine season in 1973 in which he hit 22 homers, knocked in 95 runs, batted .304, finished ninth in the league MVP voting, and earned his third straight A.L. and *Sporting News* All-Star selections, Murcer's performance slipped somewhat in 1974. With the team moving to Shea Stadium for the next two seasons, Murcer had a difficult time adjusting to the elements and more distant right-field fence in Queens. Many balls he pulled to right-field that would have been home runs in Yankee Stadium were caught on the warning track in Shea and, as a result, he hit only 10 home runs all year. He also scored just 69 runs and batted only .274. Yet, he still managed to lead the team with 88 runs batted in, do an excellent job in right-field after surrendering his prestigious spot in centerfield to Elliott Maddox, and get selected to his fourth straight A.L. All-Star team.

Following the 1974 season, however, in a move that stunned Murcer and most Yankee fans alike, the team traded the popular outfielder to the San Francisco Giants for star outfielder Bobby Bonds. Distraught after hearing of the trade, Murcer swore he would never forgive the Yankees, who he had always held close to his heart.

As despondent as he was about leaving New York, Bobby had a solid season for the Giants in 1975. Playing in cold and windy Candlestick Park, he hit only 11 home runs but knocked in 91 runs, batted .298, struck out only 45 times in 526 at-bats while walking 91 times, and was selected to the National League All-Star team. After another productive season with the Giants in which he hit 23 homers and drove in 90 runs, Murcer was traded to the Cubs, ostensibly, for third baseman Bill Madlock, who had won the N.L. batting title in each of the past two seasons.

After posting good numbers in Chicago in both 1977 and 1978, the 32-year-old Murcer began to see his playing time diminish in 1979, as he collected only 190 at-bats during the first half of the season. Finally, on June 26, he returned to the team and to the city that he loved so much, as the Yankees reacquired him for a minor league pitcher and cash. His return was truly a stroke of fate, since it reunited him with former teammate and close friend Thurman Munson a little more than one month before the Yankee captain would die tragically in a plane crash. It is hard to believe that this was purely coincidental, since the end result would be a string of emotional events that no true Yankee fan will ever forget.

On the field, however, Murcer briefly took over the starting centerfield job for the recently-departed Mickey Rivers, who had just been traded to Texas for Oscar Gamble. He then moved to left-field to make room for young outfield prospect Bobby Brown. Playing regularly the remainder of the season, Murcer hit 8 home runs, knocked in 33 runs, and batted .273 in 264 at-bats with the Yankees. He remained with the team for the next four seasons, serving mostly as a part-time designated hitter and pinch-hitter. He retired early during the 1983 campaign to make room on the roster for a young prospect named Don Mattingly. Murcer was immediately given a job in the broadcast booth as an announcer, a position he has held for the last 20 years.

While Bobby Murcer never quite developed into the great player that some predicted he would, he was a very fine one for a good portion of his career. He was selected to five league All-Star teams and three *Sporting News* All-Star teams. He finished his career with 252 home runs, 1,043 runs batted in, 972 runs scored, and a .277 batting average.

However, former teammate Roy White feels that, if Murcer had remained in New York throughout his entire career, his numbers would have been even better. He suggests, "If Bobby would have had a chance to play his whole career with the Yankees, he would have had some great numbers. He probably could have added close to another 150 home runs onto his home run total because he had a great swing for Yankee Stadium — a very compact, short stroke. Him getting traded and going to the other teams, I think it hurt his overall numbers. I think he could have been that much greater a player if he could have been with us. Plus, he was really upset about leaving New York. In his heart, he was all Yankee."[48]

Another thing about Murcer was that he always seemed to have a flair for the dramatic. Several times during his career, there were moments when he did something truly special and, when, for that particular moment, he was indeed a great player. Twice as a Yankee, he hit three home runs in one game. In fact, on the first of those occasions, in a doubleheader against the Indians in June of 1970, he hit four home runs on the day. In August of 1972, he became the first Yankee to hit for the cycle since Mickey Mantle accomplished the feat 15 years earlier.

However, perhaps his most memorable achievement came on August 6, 1979, just four days after his close friend Thurman Munson had been killed in a plane crash. Earlier that very same day, Bobby and Lou Piniella had both delivered eulogies at their team captain's funeral. The team had actually considered canceling that evening's game against the Orioles, but decided not to after Murcer went to George Steinbrenner and told him of Diane Munson's request. Bobby had spent the previous evening at the Munson home and Thurman's widow had told him that she wanted the team to play the next day because Thurman was always a gamer and he would have wanted it that way. Piniella was too distraught to play, but, even though he had broken into tears while delivering his eulogy, Murcer told manager Billy Martin that he didn't feel tired and felt the need to play.

With the Yankees trailing Baltimore 4–0 in the bottom of the seventh inning, Murcer hit a three-run homer to right-field to close the gap to 4–3. Then, coming up in the bottom of the ninth with runners on second and third and no one out, Bobby lined a single to left field to score both runners and win the game. So, on an evening when many men would not even have been able to play, Murcer knocked in all five runs and, essentially, won the game all by himself. The scene of Bobby and Lou Piniella embracing, while practically in tears, as the Yankee players left the field at the end of the game, is one that will remain in the hearts and minds of Yankee fans forever.

In their rich history, the Yankees have had many fine pitchers, several of whom are in the Hall of Fame. However, through the years, none has been more overlooked or underrated than Mel Stottlemyre. For, had he pitched for the team in almost any other era, he, undoubtedly, would have received far more credit and been ranked among their all-time best.

Stottlemyre was first called up to New York from Richmond of the International League in early August of 1964. The right-hander had dominated at the triple A level, posting a record of 13–3 and an ERA of 1.42

with Richmond. With the Yankees in the midst of a pennant race and in dire need of another reliable starter to complement Whitey Ford, Jim Bouton, and Al Downing with, the 22–year-old rookie was immediately inserted into the starting rotation. Handling himself like an experienced veteran, Stottlemyre proceeded to compile a 9–3 record and a 2.06 ERA, while helping the team to win their fifth consecutive American League pennant.

The two things that stood out most about Stottlemyre from the very beginning were his great sinkerball and his tremendous poise. While he also had a fastball that had good movement on it and an excellent slider, Stottlemyre threw a sinker that looked like it fell right off a table, breaking almost straight down as it approached home plate. As a result, when he was most effective, most of his outs would come on ground balls. Stottlemyre's ball broke the most when his arm was a little tired, so he usually seemed to get stronger as the game progressed. Therefore, if he was able to make it out of the first couple of innings unscathed, the opposing team was usually in for a long game.

Mel's other primary attribute was his poise. He never seemed to be affected by what was happening on the field, and he always maintained his composure. That poise was first demonstrated in his rookie season when he pitched so admirably under the extreme pressure of a pennant race. It surfaced once more in the World Series that year, when he started three games against the Cardinals. He defeated Bob Gibson in Game Two, going all the way in the Yankees' 8–3 victory. He left Game Five for a pinch-hitter in the bottom of the seventh inning, trailing Gibson, 2–0. Although New York eventually lost the game in extra innings, Stottlemyre was not charged with the loss because Tom Tresh tied the game in the bottom of the ninth inning with a two-run homer. He also started the seventh game, on just two days' rest, because Whitey Ford was unable to pitch due to arm problems he was experiencing. He surrendered three runs in the fourth inning and went on to lose the game to Gibson and the Cardinals. Little did he know, however, that he would never again appear in the post-season.

When Stottlemyre first joined the Yankees, he certainly must have felt that he would have many opportunities to pitch in the World Series. After all, the team was on the verge of winning their fifth consecutive American League pennant and still featured stars such as Mickey Mantle, Roger Maris, Elston Howard, and Whitey Ford. Unfortunately for Mel, though, the dynasty was about to end and he would spend the remainder of his career pitching for mediocre or weak teams. Yet, no matter what the team around him played like, Stottlemyre always stood out as a class performer and remained a link to the team's greatness of the past.

In 1965, with New York finishing in sixth place, Stottlemyre posted a record of 20–9 and an ERA of 2.63. He finished second in the league in wins and shutouts (4), and led in innings pitched (291) and complete games (18). At that time, only one Cy Young Award was still being presented for both leagues combined, and that year's winner was Sandy Koufax. However, if the American League had its own award, in all probability, Stottlemyre would have won it. He was also a 20–game winner in 1968 and 1969. In the first of those seasons, Mel finished 21–12, with a 2.45 ERA, 19 complete games, 279 innings pitched, and 6 shutouts. The following season, he was 20–14, with a 2.82 ERA, 303 innings pitched, and a league-leading 24 complete games. In each of those years, he was among the four or five best pitchers in the American League.

Stottlemyre also pitched extremely well in 1967, 1971, and 1973, but his won-lost record in each of those years does not reflect just how effective he truly was. Unfortunately, throughout most of Mel's career, the Yankees were either at, or near, the bottom of the American League in runs scored. Receiving very little in the way of run-support, his career won-lost record of 164–139 was not nearly as impressive as it could have been had he pitched for better teams.

Nevertheless, Stottlemyre was still able to amass some pretty good numbers. In addition to winning more than 20 games three times, he won at least 15 four other times. He ended his career with an outstanding 2.97 ERA. In each of his nine full seasons, he pitched at least 250 innings. He completed at least 18 games five times, threw at least 6 shutouts three times, and finished with an ERA of less than 3 runs a game six times. Stottlemyre was selected to the American League All-Star team five times, and was selected to *The Sporting News* All-Star team once (1965). He finished tenth in the league MVP voting in 1968 and made it into the top 20 two other times. Stottlemyre finished second in the American League in wins once, and third on two other occasions. He led the league in innings pitched once, and finished in the top five two other times. Mel led the league in complete games twice, and finished among the league leaders four other times. He also finished among the league leaders in shutouts six times.

Mel was also an excellent fielder and, in his early years, a good-hitting pitcher. Had it not been for the presence of Jim Kaat, who had a lock on the Gold Glove Award for pitchers every year, Stottlemyre, undoubtedly, would have won his fair share. He was an excellent athlete who was always in perfect fielding position when he completed his delivery. As a hitter, Mel once accomplished the rare feat of hitting an inside-the-park grand slam. However, his finest overall performance probably came on September 26, 1964. That day, pitching against the Senators in Washing-

Mel Stottlemyre won 20 games three times pitching for mediocre Yankees teams. Had he played in almost any other era, he would have gone down as one of the very best pitchers in team history.

ton, Mel threw a two-hit shutout, winning 7–0, and went 5-for-5 at the plate.

On the all-time list of Yankee pitchers, Mel is tied for second with Hall of Famer Red Ruffing, behind only Whitey Ford, in shutouts, with 40. He is also third in innings pitched, fifth in strikeouts, sixth in wins, eighth in complete games, and eighth in ERA (for pitchers with over 800 innings). Yet, when the names of some of the finest pitchers to ever wear a Yankee uniform are mentioned, Stottlemyre's name rarely comes up.

This is truly an injustice because, had he not pitched for the team during this period of mediocrity, his name would be much more prevalent in the minds of most people.

In his book *Few and Chosen*, Whitey Ford says, "If he had been with the teams I played on, he would have been a 20–game winner several more times and might have been regarded as the greatest right-handed pitcher in Yankees history."

Roy White says of his former teammate, "I think Mel's been very underrated. He was really a dominant pitcher for the Yankees until he got hurt. He broke more bats than anybody. He had that great sinkerball, a good slider, and good control. He was a big-game pitcher. He was a lot like Catfish Hunter, personality-wise, in that he was always the same. After a game, you couldn't tell whether he won or lost. He was one of those guys who wouldn't go into a shell after he lost a game, get mad, and not talk to the press, or anything like that. He was the same guy all the time. But, when you talk about great Yankee pitchers, he's usually never mentioned. People have kind of forgotten about him, but this guy was really tough."[49]

Unfortunately, pitching all those innings for nine seasons took their toll on Mel's right arm and, during the 1974 campaign, he tore the rotator cuff in his shoulder, ending his pitching career. Perhaps the greatest injustice was that, just two years later, the team would win the American League pennant, and, just three years later, they would win their first world championship in 15 years. Along with Roy White, Mel deserved to be there for both of those events more than any other player. While Roy was fortunate enough to have been on the team from 1976 to 1978, it is sad that Stottlemyre's career ended before that.

It is fitting, though, that, after winning a world championship ring as the pitching coach for the Mets in 1986, Mel was brought back to the Yankees by Joe Torre in 1996. In his second tour of duty with the Yankees, this time as pitching coach, he has been an important part of four world championship teams and has collected four more championship rings with the team he spent his entire playing career with.

Season Highlights, Outstanding Performances, and Memorable Moments

April 6   The Yankees open their two-year stay at Shea Stadium with a 6–1 Opening Day victory against the Indians. The Yankees score their first two runs of the season in the fourth inning on a Graig Nettles home run. They subsequently score four more times in defeating Cleveland starter Gaylord Perry, who will go on to win his next 15 decisions. New York starter Mel Stottlemyre gets the victory.

April 14   At Cleveland's Municipal Stadium, the Yankees split a doubleheader with the Indians, winning the first game, 9–5, and losing the nightcap, 9–6. New York third baseman Graig Nettles homers four times on the day, and will go on to tie the major-league record with eleven home runs in the month of April.

May 26   The Yankees sweep a doubleheader from the Orioles at Shea Stadium, winning the first game, 6–5, and taking the second, 7–5. Thurman Munson and Bill Sudakis hit home runs in the opener, while Elliott Maddox and Ron Blomberg each collect three hits in the nightcap.

June 2   At Metropolitan Stadium, the Yankees defeat the Twins, 11–1, banging out 18 hits in the process. Ron Blomberg, Lou Piniella, and Graig Nettles all collect three hits, and Blomberg, Piniella, and catcher Rick Dempsey each homer. The winning pitcher is New York starter Mel Stottlemyre, who evens his record at 6–6. The victory will end up being the last of his career.

June 11   At Shea Stadium, the Yankees lose to the Angels, 5–4. Yankee starter Mel Stottlemyre leaves the game after the third inning due to pain in his right (pitching) shoulder. The start will be the final one of Stottlemyre's career, which will end prematurely due to a torn rotator cuff. He will end his last season in pinstripes with a record of 6–7.

June 17   The Yankees top the .500–mark for the first time in more than a month with a 5–1 victory over the Angels at Anaheim Stadium. Gene Michael, starting at second base, collects three hits, and Lou Piniella homers. Mike Wallace picks up the win, while Frank Tanana is tagged with the loss. New York's record now stands at 33–32.

July 5   At Arlington Stadium in Texas, the Yankees explode for 14 runs and 20 hits in drubbing the Rangers, 14–2. The New York offense is led by Elliott Maddox and Thurman Munson, each of whom collects four hits, and Graig Nettles, who chips in with three. Munson and Nettles also homer.

July 8   The Yankees crush the Rangers once again in Texas, this time by a score of 12–5. New York shortstop Jim Mason ties a major-league single-game record with four doubles, and Roy White and Ron Blomberg each collect four hits.

July 10 In Kansas City, the Yankees defeat the Royals, 9–4. Bobby Murcer homers twice, Thurman Munson adds one, and Chris Chambliss collects three hits. The nine runs give New York a total of 64 in their last six games.

July 13 At Shea Stadium, the Yankees score six times against Vida Blue and go on to defeat the A's, 12–6. Roy White collects four hits and Graig Nettles adds three, while Bobby Murcer gets two hits, scores twice, and knocks in three runs.

August 16 The Yankees split a doubleheader with the White Sox at Shea Stadium, winning the first game, 9–8, and losing the second, 4–2. In the opener, with New York trailing 8–7 in the bottom of the 13th inning, Thurman Munson hits a two-out, two-run homer to win the game.

August 23 The Yankees defeat the Angels, 10–4, at Shea Stadium. Roy White goes 4–for–5, knocks in four runs, scores twice, and just misses hitting for the cycle, as he homers, triples, and collects two singles.

August 25 At Shea Stadium, the Yankees defeat the Angels, 2–1. New York starter Larry Gura out-duels Nolan Ryan to pick up his first win as a Yankee.

August 31 At Comiskey Park, the Yankees batter the White Sox, 18–6. Roy White goes 5–for–7, Gene Michael collects four hits, and Thurman Munson goes 4–for–5, with a homer and 5 runs batted in. George Medich is the recipient of New York's offensive outburst. The victory puts the Yankees, at 69–62, seven games over .500 for the first time all season.

Sept. 2 At Shea Stadium, the Yankees defeat the Brewers, 3–1, in the first game of a doubleheader to extend their winning streak to six games. The victory also is New York's eleventh in their last twelve games, moving them to within just one game of first place. Rudy May picks up his sixth win in a Yankee uniform, against just two losses. However, New York's winning streak comes to an end in the second game as Milwaukee comes away with a 3–2 victory.

Sept. 4 The Yankees move into first place in the A.L. East for the first time since May 11 with a 3–0 win against the Brewers at Shea. George Medich throws the shutout for his 17th victory of the year.

Sept. 10 The Yankees complete a two-game sweep of the Red Sox at Fenway Park with a thrilling 2–1, 12–inning victory. One day after being purchased from the Texas Rangers, Alex Johnson joins New York during the game and wins it with a home run.

Sept. 15   At Tiger Stadium, New York defeats Detroit, 10–2, as Larry
            Gura earns his fourth victory of the year against no losses. Lou
            Piniella goes 4–for-4, with 3 runs batted in.

Sept. 20   After falling out of first place for one day, New York regains
            the A.L East lead by sweeping a doubleheader against the Indi-
            ans at Shea Stadium. The Yankees win the first game, 5–4, with
            Bobby Murcer going 3–for-5 with 3 runs batted in and Sparky
            Lyle picking up the win in relief. In the nightcap, Larry Gura
            wins his fifth game, against no losses, by out-pitching former
            Yankee Fritz Peterson, 3–0.

Sept. 21   The Yankees pick up their third consecutive victory against the
            Indians, defeating the Tribe, 14–7, at Shea Stadium. Roy White
            goes 3–for-5, with a home run, 5 runs batted in, and 4 runs
            scored, while Bobby Murcer collects 3 hits, 3 runs batted in,
            and hits his first home run all year at Shea.

Oct. 1   The Yankees are officially eliminated from the A.L. East race
            when they drop a 3–2 decision to the Brewers in Milwaukee.
            The loss leaves New York two games behind the first-place Ori-
            oles, with only one game remaining.

1974 American League Final Team Standings and Offensive Statistics

TEAM	G	W	L	PCT	GB	R	H	2B	3B	HR	BB	SO	SB	AVG	OBP	SLG
EAST																
BAL	162	91	71	.562	—	659	1418	226	27	116	509	770	145	.256	.325	.370
NY	162	89	73	.549	2	671	1451	220	30	101	515	690	53	.263	.328	.368
BOSTON	162	84	78	.519	7	696	1449	236	31	109	569	811	104	.264	.336	.377
CLE	162	77	85	.475	14	662	1395	201	19	131	432	756	79	.255	.312	.370
MIL	162	76	86	.469	15	647	1335	228	49	120	500	909	106	.244	.310	.369
DET	162	72	90	.444	19	620	1375	200	35	131	436	784	67	.247	.304	.366
WEST																
OAK	162	90	72	.556	—	689	1315	205	37	132	568	876	164	.247	.324	.373
TEX	160	84	76	.525	5	690	1482	198	39	99	508	710	113	.272	.338	.377
MINN	162	82	80	.506	8	673	1530	190	37	111	520	791	74	.272	.338	.378
CHI	160	80	80	.500	9	684	1492	225	23	135	519	858	64	.268	.333	.389
KC	162	77	85	.475	13	667	1448	232	42	89	550	768	146	.259	.329	.364
CAL	162	68	94	.420	22	618	1372	203	31	95	509	801	119	.254	.323	356
TOTAL						7976	17062	2564	400	1369	6135	9524	1234	.258	.325	.371

Team Pitching and Fielding Statistics

TEAM	CG	SH	SV	IP	H	HR	BB	SO	ERA	FA	E	DP
EAST												
BAL	57	16	25	1474	1393	101	480	701	3.27	.980	128	174
NY	53	13	24	1455	1402	104	528	829	3.31	.977	142	158
BOSTON	71	12	18	1455	1462	126	463	751	3.72	.977	145	156
CLE	45	9	27	1445	1419	138	479	650	3.80	.977	146	157
MIL	43	11	24	1457	1476	126	493	621	3.76	.980	127	168
DET	54	7	15	1455	1443	148	621	869	4.16	.975	158	155
WEST												
OAK	49	12	28	1439	1322	90	430	755	2.95	.977	141	154
TEX	62	16	12	1433	1423	126	449	871	3.82	.974	163	164
MINN	43	11	29	1455	1436	115	513	934	3.64	.976	151	164
CHI	55	11	29	1465	1470	103	548	826	3.94	.977	147	188
KC	54	13	17	1471	1477	91	482	731	3.51	.976	152	166
CAL	64	13	12	1439	1339	101	649	986	3.52	.976	147	150
TOTAL	650	144	260	17448					3.62	.977	1747	1954

1974 New York Yankee Pitching Statistics

PLAYER	W	L	ERA	G	GS	CG	SHO	SV	IP	H	R	ER	BB	SO
Pat Dobson	19	15	3.07	39	39	12	2	0	281	282	111	96	75	157
George Medich	19	15	3.60	38	38	17	4	0	279	275	122	112	91	154
Dick Tidrow	11	9	3.87	33	25	5	0	1	190	205	99	82	53	100
Rudy May	8	4	2.28	17	15	8	2	0	114	75	36	29	48	90
Sparky Lyle	9	3	1.66	66	0	0	0	15	114	93	30	21	43	89
Mel Stottlemyre	6	7	3.58	16	15	6	0	0	113	119	54	45	37	40
Cecil Upshaw	1	5	3.02	36	0	0	0	6	59	53	25	20	24	27
Larry Gura	5	1	2.41	8	8	4	2	0	56	54	17	15	12	17
Mike Wallace	6	0	2.41	23	1	0	0	0	52	42	18	14	35	34
Dave Pagan	1	3	5.11	16	6	1	0	0	49	49	29	28	28	39
Sam McDowell	1	6	4.69	13	7	0	0	0	48	42	27	25	41	33
Dick Woodson	1	2	5.79	8	3	0	0	0	28	34	19	18	12	12
Steve Kline	2	2	3.46	4	4	0	0	0	26	26	12	10	5	6
Tippy Martinez	0	0	4.26	10	0	0	0	0	12	14	7	6	9	10
Fred Beene	0	0	2.70	6	0	0	0	1	10	9	4	3	2	10
Fritz Peterson	0	0	4.70	3	1	0	0	0	7	13	4	4	2	5
Tom Buskey	0	1	6.35	4	0	0	0	1	5	10	4	4	3	3
Ken Wright	0	0	3.18	3	0	0	0	0	5	5	2	2	7	2
Rick Sawyer	0	0	16.20	1	0	0	0	0	1	2	3	3	1	1

1974 New York Yankee Hitting Statistics

PLAYER	AB	R	H	2B	3B	HR	RBI	BB	SO	SB	OBP	SLG	AVG
Bobby Murcer	606	69	166	25	4	10	88	57	59	14	.332	.378	.274
Graig Nettles	566	74	139	21	1	22	75	59	75	1	.316	.403	.246
Lou Piniella	518	71	158	26	0	9	70	32	58	1	.341	.407	.305
Thurman Munson	517	64	135	19	2	13	60	44	66	2	.316	.381	.261
Roy White	473	68	130	19	8	7	43	67	44	15	.367	.393	.275

PLAYER	AB	R	H	2B	3B	HR	RBI	BB	SO	SB	OBP	SLG	AVG
Elliott Maddox	466	75	141	26	2	3	45	69	48	6	.395	.386	.303
Jim Mason	440	41	110	18	6	5	37	35	87	1	.302	.352	.250
Chris Chambliss	400	38	97	16	3	6	43	23	43	0	.282	.343	.243
Sandy Alomar	279	35	75	8	0	1	27	14	25	6	.302	.308	.269
Ron Blomberg	264	39	82	11	2	10	48	29	33	2	.375	.481	.311
Bill Sudakis	259	26	60	8	0	7	39	25	48	0	.296	.344	.232
Gene Michael	177	19	46	9	0	0	13	14	24	0	.313	.311	.260
Fernando Gonzalez	121	11	26	5	1	1	7	7	7	0	.258	.298	.215
Rick Dempsey	109	12	26	3	0	2	12	8	7	1	.288	.321	.239
Otto Velez	67	9	14	1	1	2	10	15	24	0	.345	.343	.209
Mike Hegan	53	3	12	2	0	2	9	5	9	1	.317	.377	.226
Walt Williams	53	5	6	0	0	0	3	1	10	1	.127	.113	.113
Horace Clarke	47	3	11	1	0	0	1	4	5	1	.294	.255	.234
Fred Stanley	38	2	7	0	0	0	3	3	2	1	.244	.184	.184
Alex Johnson	28	3	6	1	0	1	2	0	3	0	.214	.357	.214
Jim Ray Hart	19	1	1	0	0	0	0	3	7	0	.182	.053	.053
Duke Sims	15	1	2	1	0	0	2	1	5	0	.188	.200	.133
Terry Whitfield	5	0	1	0	0	0	0	0	1	0	.200	.200	.200
Jim Deidel	2	0	0	0	0	0	0	0	0	0	.000	.000	.000

THIRTEEN

1975: One Last Year of Mediocrity

With their outstanding play during the second half of the 1974 season, it appeared that the Yankees had finally turned the corner and were ready to seriously contend for the American League East title. The team had won 33 of their final 47 games and been eliminated from the pennant race on the next-to-last day of the season. In addition, for the first time in many years, there did not seem to be any major holes that needed to be filled on the roster.

While some within the organization expressed concern over Chris Chambliss' poor performance after he came over from Cleveland in late April of the previous year, Gabe Paul still felt that the young first baseman had a bright future ahead of him. After all, he was only 26 years old, had only been in the majors for four years, and, because of the circumstances surrounding the trade that had brought him to New York, had been made to feel unwelcome by some of his new teammates. There had been some talk during the off-season of moving Roy White to first base, but Chambliss clearly needed to be given more of any opportunity to succeed in New York.

The front office seemed satisfied with the team's new double play combination of Sandy Alomar at second and Jim Mason at short. Alomar had more range than Horace Clarke, and had added a spark to the team after he was acquired at mid-season. Mason had struggled during the first half of 1974, but seemed to find himself during the season's second half. He was now thought to be the team's shortstop of the future.

After his fast start in April, Graig Nettles had faltered badly during the last five months of the season. Yet, he had hit 22 home runs in each of his first two years in New York, was a left-handed power threat the team desperately needed, and was one of the better third basemen in the league.

While Thurman Munson's first year at Shea Stadium had been a some-what disappointing one, he had still managed to win a Gold Glove and get elected to *The Sporting News* All-Star team at season's end. He was gener-ally acknowledged to be, along with Boston's Carlton Fisk, the best catcher in the American League.

The team also had four solid outfielders in Roy White, Lou Piniella, Elliott Maddox, and Bobby Murcer. Piniella and Maddox had been New York's most consistent performers in 1974, and the latter had shown that he was among the elite defensive centerfielders in the game. Although White had seen less playing time than he was accustomed to, he had done a fine job whenever he was in the lineup. Murcer's power numbers and run production had dropped off dramatically as a result of the move to Shea, but he had still been selected to the American League All-Star team for the fourth consecutive time, and he was considered to be the Yankees' best all-around player.

There was also depth on the roster at every position. Fred Stanley could play any of the infield positions, Walt Williams was an adequate reserve outfielder, and Rick Dempsey was a fine defensive receiver and solid back-up to Munson behind the plate.

New York also had two rather potent bats to use at the DH spot. From the left side of the plate, there was Ron Blomberg, while, from the right side, the Yankees could insert former A.L. batting champ Alex Johnson into the lineup.

The pitching staff did not appear to be as deep, but, despite losing their ace, Mel Stottlemyre, early in the season, they had done a good job in 1974, finishing third in the league with a team ERA of 3.31. Pat Dobson and Doc Medich were solid starters, both having won 19 games the pre-vious year. After being acquired during the season's first half, Rudy May had been the team's most effective starter for the remainder of the season, finishing 8–4, with a 2.28 ERA. Dick Tidrow had done a good job after coming over from Cleveland, and Larry Gura had gone 5–1 after being inserted into the rotation in late August.

In the bullpen, Sparky Lyle had finished 9–3, with 15 saves and a 1.66 ERA, and Mike Wallace had gone 6–0, with a 2.41 ERA. After them, though, there were only youngsters Dave Pagan and Tippy Martinez, both of whom were talented, but also extremely inexperienced.

Pagan was a hard-throwing right-hander who had been brought up by the team during the 1974 season. In 16 appearances, six of them starts, he had compiled just a 1–3 record and a 5.11 ERA. He also seemed to have a propensity for developing blisters on his pitching hand that would keep him out of action for weeks at a time. Yet, the Yankees loved the velocity he had on his fastball and hoped that he would eventually be able to claim a spot in the starting rotation.

Martinez had also been brought up by the team for the first time the previous year. In just 12 innings of work, all in relief, the left-hander had finished with a record of 0–0 and an ERA of 4.26. He had been a relief specialist throughout much of his minor league career, and the Yankees envisioned him as eventually being a set-up man for closer Sparky Lyle.

It seemed that the Yankees' primary need was for another arm in the bullpen, or for an ace starter to replace Mel Stottlemyre, who, unfortunately, was unable to make it back from his torn rotator cuff. New York had cut the veteran right-hander from their roster prior to the start of spring training, and, although he had been given a tryout by his former manager Ralph Houk in Detroit, it was clear that his playing career was over. While Dobson and Medich were both good pitchers, neither was a true staff "ace," the kind around which a starting rotation could be built. That was something Stottlemyre had been since 1965, and something the team was now lacking.

The Yankees addressed their greatest need on December 31, when they signed Jim "Catfish" Hunter to an historic five-year, $3.75 million contract. Hunter, the ace of the three-time world champion Oakland A's pitching staff, was coming off his finest season. In 1974, he had led the American League in wins (25) and ERA (2.49), and been awarded the Cy Young. However, on December 13, he had been declared a free agent by arbitrator Peter Seitz after submitting a breach-of-contract claim against Oakland owner Charlie Finley, who had failed to pay $50,000, half of Hunter's salary, to a life insurance fund. The $750,000 annual salary the Yankees gave Hunter was three times more than any other major league player was making at the time. However, New York, obviously, felt he was worth it.

Hunter had first come up with the A's when they were still in Kansas City, back in 1965. Pitching for poor teams his first five seasons, he failed to post a winning record in any of those years. However, with young and talented players such as Reggie Jackson, Joe Rudi, and Sal Bando all coming up to the A's during the late '60s, the team, and Hunter's record, improved dramatically. After winning 18 games in 1970, the right-hander won 21 games in each of the next three seasons before winning 25 in 1974. By the time he signed with the Yankees, Hunter had already been named to the All-Star team six times, finished in the top five in the Cy Young voting three times, and finished in the top ten in the league MVP voting twice.

Catfish had a reputation for giving up the long ball, but, more than anything else, that was because hitters were not afraid to dig in against him at home plate because they knew he had such outstanding control.

He had a good fastball, and a good assortment of off-speed pitches, but it was his ability to throw strikes, and the movement he had on his pitches, that made him so effective.

Hunter also had a reputation for being a big-game pitcher. In seven World Series appearances with the A's from 1972 to 1974, he compiled a record of 4–0, with one save. He was also extremely popular with his teammates because they knew they could take him at face value. With Hunter, there was no pretense — what you saw was what you got. While he was soft-spoken and humble, he also had a sort of country boy charm that appealed to almost everyone.

The signing of Hunter had a ripple effect on the rest of the pitching staff. With him as the number one starter, Dobson and Medich could now be slotted into the number two and three spots, which they were better suited for. Rudy May and Larry Gura would complete the starting rotation, and Dick Tidrow could be moved to the bullpen, where another arm was desperately needed for middle and long relief.

However, Hunter's signing was just the second of two major moves the Yankees made during the off-season. Two months earlier, on October 22, the team had traded Bobby Murcer to the San Francisco Giants for Bobby Bonds in an exchange of star outfielders. The deal was a rather controversial one since Murcer, in addition to being the team's best player, had been such a fan favorite throughout his career in New York. Yet, Bonds was an extremely talented player who was viewed by some as being a right-handed version of Reggie Jackson.

Bonds had spent his entire seven-year major league career with San Francisco, first coming up in 1968 and playing alongside his hero Willie Mays in the Giants' outfield. In his first full season, 1969, he hit 32 home runs and stole 45 bases, reaching the 30–30 plateau for the first time in his career. After putting up good numbers in each of the following three seasons, Bonds had his greatest year in 1973, when he came within one home run of becoming the first player in major league history to hit 40 homers and steal 40 bases in the same season. That year, he hit 39 home runs, stole 43 bases, batted .283, and led the National League with 131 runs scored. However, he ended the season in a bit of a slump that carried over to 1974, when he was benched and fined by manager Charlie Fox. While Bonds eventually regained his batting eye and was able to finish the year with respectable numbers (21 homers, 71 RBIs, .256 batting average, 97 runs scored), he had apparently worn out his welcome in San Francisco. As a result, the Giants decided to trade away the man who had been selected to three All-Star teams and been awarded three Gold Gloves. He was also considered by many to be the fastest player in baseball.

Yet, in spite of his immense talent, Bonds did come with a certain amount of baggage. Even though he had very good power, having hit more than 30 homers three times with the Giants, he had batted leadoff throughout most of his career. As the Yankees would later discover, that had a great deal to do with his propensity for striking out — especially with men on base. Three times, he had led the National League in strikeouts, and in two consecutive seasons—1969 and 1970 — he had established a new major league record for most strikeouts in a season, with 187 and 189, respectively. In addition, it would later surface that he had a drinking problem that figured prominently in his inability to ever fully live up to his great potential. Nevertheless, the Yankees decided that his tremendous natural talent was something they just could not pass up.

New York's final move of the off-season was a less significant one, as they acquired reserve catcher Ed Herrmann from the Chicago White Sox. The left-handed hitting Herrmann had spent most of his six seasons in Chicago as a platoon player, never appearing in more than 119 games with the White Sox. He typically batted somewhere between .240 and .260, but he had some power, hitting a career-high 19 home runs in just 297 at-bats in 1970. However, just as Bobby Bonds was considered by many to be the fastest player in the game, Herrmann may well have been the slowest. Over six major league seasons, the 6'1", 210 lb. Herrmann had stolen a total of just five bases. The Yankees planned to use him occasionally behind the plate and at the DH spot, and to have him come off the bench as a lefty pinch-hitter.

With these three moves, the New York roster was pretty much set. The only other off-season event of any note occurred on November 27 when baseball commissioner Bowie Kuhn suspended George Steinbrenner from the game for two years as a result of his conviction for making illegal campaign contributions to Richard Nixon, among others. Steinbrenner was not to have any involvement in the day-to-day operations of the Yankees during the entire length of his suspension, and was not even allowed to attend games in person. However, few believed that "The Boss" would not remain in close contact with the team's front office executives and manager.

The regular season opened on April 8 with a 5–3 loss to the Indians in Cleveland. However, that game holds a great deal of historical significance since Frank Robinson made his managerial debut in it, thereby becoming the first black manager in major league history.

After losing their next two games at Shea Stadium, the Yankees had to wait until the season's fourth game to gain their first victory of the year, defeating the Tigers, 6–0, behind George Medich. However, the team then lost its next three games at home to start the season off with a record of just 1–6. New York continued to struggle throughout much of April, with Catfish Hunter failing to earn a victory in any of his first four starts. Finally, with his record 0–3, Hunter won his first game as a Yankee on April 27, defeating the Brewers in the second game of a doubleheader to improve the team's record to 7–9.

New York reached the .500–mark for the first time on May 1, defeating the Orioles and Jim Palmer, 5–0, on a Hunter shutout. That left their record at 10–10. However, they then proceeded to lose 10 of their next 12 games, dropping them to 12–20, and into fifth place in the division, 7½ games out of first.

While Hunter had evened his record at 4–4 by this point, several other players were not performing as well as they were expected to. Pat Dobson's record was just 2–5, and George Medich was just 3–6. Meanwhile, Jim Mason and Lou Piniella were struggling at the plate, and Bobby Bonds was in the midst of a terrible slump. Inserted into the third spot in the batting order, he was striking out frequently, leaving a lot of men on base. The change in leagues appeared to be bothering him since American League pitchers did not generally challenge hitters with fastballs as much as their counterparts in the National League did. Bonds, looking for fastballs on certain counts, was instead being thrown breaking balls. He seemed ill-prepared to deal with them, and usually found himself waving at them meekly.

The team, and Bonds, began to play better, though, especially after manager Virdon rearranged his lineup. He took Bonds out of the number three slot and moved him into the leadoff position. Elliott Maddox remained the number two hitter, but, depending on who was pitching, Virdon went to a rotation of Roy White, Thurman Munson, Ron Blomberg, and Lou Piniella in the three through five spots. The team won 16 of their next 20 games, improving their record to 28–24, and moving them into second place, just two games out of first. Dobson had won his last four decisions, Hunter was now 8–5, Rudy May was 6–2, Munson was driving in runs out of the cleanup spot, and Bonds, more comfortable in his familiar role as leadoff hitter, was igniting the offense.

However, early in June at Chicago's Comiskey Park, in the midst of an eight-game winning streak, Bonds injured his leg chasing down a fly ball on the warning track in right field. Although he missed only a few games, the injury seemed to set Bonds back since, prior to that, he had been the team's hottest hitter. Even though he stayed in the lineup the remainder of the season, Bonds was not at full speed the rest of the year and was unable to get back into the groove he had been in prior to sustaining the injury.

The team suffered an even greater blow one week later when, in a game at Shea Stadium against the White Sox on June 13, Elliott Maddox sustained a season-ending injury when he tore cartilage in his knee falling on the wet outfield turf. At the time of the injury, Maddox was batting .307, and was leading the team with 36 runs scored and a .382 on-base percentage. More importantly, though, it forced New York to restructure their outfield and use the already injured Bobby Bonds in centerfield, where he was not as effective as Maddox, and use a combination of Lou Piniella and Walt Williams in right. Ordinarily, this would not have been such a hardship, but Piniella was suffering through the worst season of his major league career. Due to equilibrium problems he was experiencing as a result of an inner ear infection, Piniella ended up hitting only .196 in just 199 at-bats on the year.

To compensate for the loss of their regular centerfielder and for the slump that Piniella was in, New York experimented with a number of other players the remainder of the year in an attempt to find the right outfield mix. First, they acquired speedster Rich Coggins from the Montreal Expos.

As a 23–year-old with the Baltimore Orioles in 1973, Coggins had finished runner-up to teammate Al Bumbry in the A.L. Rookie of the Year voting. That year, the lefty-hitting Coggins hit .319 in 389 at-bats and stole 17 bases. However, when he batted only .243 the following season, he was dealt to the Expos, along with Dave McNally, for Ken Singleton and Mike Torrez prior to the start of the 1975 campaign. He was batting .270 with the Expos prior to being picked up by the Yankees. In 107 at-bats with New York, he hit only .224, hit just 1 home run, and drove in only 6 runs.

New York also brought up from the minors a 28–year-old career minor leaguer named Rick Bladt, whose only prior major league experience had come with the Cubs six years earlier when he hit .154 in 13 at-bats. With the Yankees, he came to the plate 117 times, hit 1 home run, knocked in 11 runs, and batted .222.

In spite of the loss of Maddox and the ineffectiveness of Piniella, the Yankees continued to play outstanding ball throughout most of June. In fact, at the end of play on June 25, after winning their fifth consecutive game, the Yankees' record stood at 40–29, and they were in first place in the A.L. East.

The team was being carried by the pitching of Catfish Hunter, Pat Dobson, and Rudy May, and by the hitting of Thurman Munson. After slow starts, Hunter had improved his record to 11–6, while Dobson had raised his mark to 8–5. May picked up right where he had left off in 1974, compiling a record of 7–3. Munson was among the hottest hitters in the league and was now considered to be the team's best player, hitting for a high average and driving in runs with regularity.

However, the team soon slumped, losing as many as seven consecutive games at one point, and slipped out of first place. At the All-Star break on July 12, the Yankees' record stood at 46–41, and they were in third place, four games out of first.

New York was well represented on the All-Star team, fielding four players. Munson, Bonds, and Nettles were selected as starters, and Hunter was chosen as one of the pitchers. Munson and Nettles were having their finest seasons and were clearly deserving of their selections. Hunter's record was 12–8, so he was also deserving. However, Bonds' selection to the starting team was somewhat questionable since, aside from a brief hot streak from the end of May into early June, he was not having one of his better seasons, and since Reggie Jackson in Oakland, and rookies Fred Lynn and Jim Rice in Boston were all having exceptional years.

The Yankees continued to struggle after the break, losing 10 of their next 14 games to drop below .500 for the first time in almost two months on July 28, with a record of 50–51. The team had also fallen to 11 games out of first place and appeared to be in desperate trouble. Finally, on August 1, with the team in the middle of a five-game winning streak, manager Bill Virdon was fired and replaced with Billy Martin.

Martin, who had spent the better part of his playing career with the Yankees, had always been a Yankee at heart and relished the opportunity to return to the team he had started his career with. After his playing days were over, he had become first a minor league manager in the Minnesota Twins organization, then a third base coach for the Twins, then, finally, the team's manager. After managing the team to two A.L. West titles in 1969 and 1970, he was fired by owner Calvin Griffith for personal differences between the two men. He was also let go by Tiger management after leading the team to the A.L. East title in 1972, and by the Texas front office after taking the team from a last-place finish in 1973 to second place the following season. Martin's greatest problem seemed to be that he had a self-destruct mechanism inside of him that did not permit him to enjoy success, and a huge ego (insecurity) that always caused him to strive to make himself the central figure on any team he was associated with. He also enjoyed challenging authority. It seemed that, considering the personality of Yankee owner George Steinbrenner, the match would prove to be a highly combustible one. Yet, more than anything, Steinbrenner wanted to win, and Martin had a track record that was not approached by many. Also, more than anything, Martin wanted to manage the Yankees.

The change in managers didn't seem to help, though, and, after losing their fifth straight game on August 21, the Yankees' record stood at 62–62, and they had been all but eliminated from the pennant race. They were 12½ games behind the first-place Boston Red Sox who were being led by the brilliant rookie tandem of Fred Lynn and Jim Rice. Lynn was having a fabulous season in centerfield, and would go on to become the first player in major league history to win the Rookie of the Year and Most Valuable Player Awards in the same season.

Meanwhile, Billy Martin set about configuring his team for 1976 and finding the kind of players who fit into his system. The first thing he did was replace Jim Mason at shortstop with Fred Stanley. Mason, who was having a horrendous year, ended up hitting just .152 in 223 at-bats. Stanley batted only .222 in 252 trips to the plate, but had to remind Martin a little of himself since he was an overachiever who played the game with a great deal of spirit.

Martin also acquired one of his former Detroit players, shortstop Ed Brinkman, from Texas. Brinkman had first come up with the Washington Senators in 1961. A good fielder, but a notoriously weak hitter throughout most of his career, Brinkman saw his batting average jump 80 points, to .266, when new manager Ted Williams changed his batting style in 1969. After a .262 season with the Senators in 1970, Brinkman was traded to Detroit, along with third baseman Aurelio Rodriguez and pitchers Joe Coleman and Jim Hannan, for Denny McLain, Elliott Maddox, third baseman Don Wert, and pitcher Norm McRae. Brinkman failed to hit any higher than .237 in his four years with the Tigers, but, playing under Billy Martin in 1972, he won a Gold Glove while setting four single-season records for shortstops: consecutive errorless games (72), consecutive errorless chances (331), fewest errors (7), and best fielding percentage (.990). Brinkman had begun 1975 as a member of the Cardinals, and had played one game with the Rangers prior to being picked up by New York. In 63 at-bats with the Yankees, he batted .175, with no home runs and 2 runs batted in.

New York also called up four players from the minor leagues— outfielders Terry Whitfield, Dave Bergman, and Kerry Dineen, and pitcher Ron Guidry. Whitfield, who had made a brief appearance with the club at the end of the previous season, was considered to be one of the organization's top prospects. He had good speed and was a solid hitter. In 81 at-bats, he hit .272 and knocked in 7 runs. Bergman had little power, but was a batting champ and league MVP in each of his first two minor league seasons. He came to the plate 17 times, but failed to get a hit. The speedy Dineen also had little power, but was considered to be a good outfielder and base-runner. He had 8 hits in 22 at-bats, for a .364 batting average.

The 24–year-old Guidry had been kept out of the majors by New York's policy of acquiring pitchers either through trades or free agent signings. Some within the organization also felt that, at 5'11" and 160 lbs., he was too small to pitch effectively at the major league level. Yet, his supporters felt that he had the kind of arm that could one day make him a top starter. He appeared in 10 games, lost his only start, finished with an ERA of 3.45, and struck out 15 batters in 15 innings of work.

New York hovered around the .500–mark the remainder of the season, finishing with a record of 83–77, in third place, 12 full games behind the first-place Red Sox and 7½ games behind the second-place Orioles. In head-to-head competition with their Eastern division rivals, they finished 10–8 against Baltimore, but won only 5 of 16 contests against Boston.

There were several reasons why the Yankees failed to perform as well in 1975 as they had during the second half of the prior season. As was mentioned earlier, shortstop Jim Mason and outfielder Lou Piniella both had terrible seasons. Sparky Lyle had a sub-par year, finishing with a record of 5–7, an ERA of 3.12, and, more importantly, with just 6 saves. Pat Dobson finished just 11–14, and his 4.07 ERA was a run a game higher than it had been in 1974. Due to a series of injuries that kept him out of the lineup for much of the year, Ron Blomberg came to the plate just 106 times, hit just 4 home runs, knocked in only 17 runs, and batted just .255. Unfortunately, he would suffer an even more serious injury in spring training the following year that would put him out for most of the season and, essentially, end his baseball career.

Bobby Bonds put up good numbers. He led the team in home runs (32), runs scored (93), and stolen bases (30), and finished fourth in the league in both home runs and runs scored. He also finished third on the team with 85 runs batted in. However, those who watched him play every day had to be somewhat disappointed in his overall performance. His 137 strikeouts established a new Yankee record, and many of those came in important situations with men on base. In addition, he had a very strong throwing arm, but it was inaccurate at times, and he often failed to hit the cut-off man. He had so much natural ability that, at season's end, his offensive numbers were always good, but he truly was not as effective as his numbers indicated. Perhaps that is why he ended up spending his last eight major league seasons with eight different teams, in spite of putting up solid numbers in five of those years.

More than anything, though, the Yankees were hurt by the absence of Elliott Maddox for two-thirds of the season. Batting .307, leading the team in both on-base percentage and runs scored, and playing a marvelous centerfield at the time of his injury, Maddox was fast-becoming one of the team's most complete and important players. His ability to get on base, and his great defense in centerfield were critical to the team's success. When he went down for the season in mid-June with a knee injury, New York's chances were greatly diminished.

The year was not without its bright spots, however. The pitching staff, once again, finished with the third lowest team ERA in the American League. Tippy Martinez and Dick Tidrow pitched well out of the bullpen. Martinez appeared in 23 games, compiled an ERA of 2.68, and led the team with 8 saves. Tidrow made 37 appearances, all in relief, and finished 6–3, with 5 saves and a 3.12 ERA. Rudy May made 31 starts, threw 13 complete games, and compiled a record of 14–12 with an ERA of 3.06. It appeared that he was finally maturing as a pitcher.

However, the team's best pitcher was Catfish Hunter. After losing his first three decisions, Hunter ended up leading the team in virtually every pitching category. He finished the season with a record of 23–14, an ERA of 2.58, 30 complete games, 7 shutouts, 177 strikeouts, and 328 innings pitched. He led the league in complete games and innings pitched, and tied Jim Palmer for the league lead in wins. He also finished second in earned run average and shutouts. At seasons's end, he finished runner-up to Palmer in the Cy Young voting and twelfth in the league MVP voting.

The offense also had its share of outstanding performers. No longer forced to bat cleanup, as he had done earlier in his career with the Yankees, Roy White did a fine job taking over the number two spot in the order from Elliott Maddox. He hit 12 home runs, knocked in 59 runs, batted .290, finished third on the team with 16 stolen bases and 81 runs scored, and finished second in doubles (32) and on-base percentage (.372).

Chris Chambliss, feeling much more comfortable in New York, had a much better year at first base. He knocked in 72 runs, led the team with 38 doubles, finished second in batting (.304) and hits (171), and vindicated Gabe Paul for making the trade that brought him to the Yankees.

Graig Nettles had his finest season to-date in New York. He finished second on the team with 21 home runs and 91 runs batted in, raised his batting average to .267, and provided steady defense at third base. At season's end, he was selected to *The Sporting News* All-Star team for the first time in his career.

The team's best player, though, was Thurman Munson, who established himself as the team's leader and best clutch hitter. Although he hit only 12 home runs, he knocked in a team-leading 102 runs, led the team with a .318 batting average and 190 hits, and finished second with 83 runs scored. Munson finished third in the league in batting and base hits, and fifth in runs batted in. At season's end, he was awarded his third consecutive Gold Glove, was selected to his third straight *Sporting News* All-Star team, and finished seventh in the league MVP voting.

When the season ended, Ron Blomberg's Yankee career was essentially over. However, players such as Chris Chambliss, Lou Piniella, Graig Nettles, Sparky Lyle, Thurman Munson, and Roy White, who had been with the team through some of these "lean years," unknowingly, were about to take part in the next great period of Yankee excellence.

Ron Blomberg had a chance to be something really special — a Jewish baseball star with the New York Yankees. While Joe Gordon had excelled for the team during the late 1930's and early '40's, he had always kept his heritage a secret since anti-Semitism was so prevalent during the era in which he played. So, Blomberg had an opportunity to be the first known star of Jewish origin to ever play for the most famous team in sports, in a city with a huge Jewish population.

While the Yankees made Blomberg the first overall pick in the 1967 amateur draft, baseball was actually not the Atlanta, Georgia native's first love. In fact, he had always planned on playing basketball or football — or both — in college. When New York selected him first in 1967, Blomberg had literally hundreds of scholarship offers to play either one, or both, of the other two major sports. He actually signed an offer from John Wooden, the coach of the UCLA Bruins, but later chose to play baseball instead when he was drafted number one in the country by the Yankees.

Although he appeared briefly in a New York uniform at the end of the 1969 season, it wasn't until 1971 that Blomberg arrived in the big leagues to stay. With his hustling style of play, enthusiasm for the game, and obvious natural gifts, Blomberg became an instant fan favorite. At 6'1" and 205 lbs, he was powerfully built, and he had a quick and powerful left-handed swing that seemed perfect for Yankee Stadium. There were two areas, though, that Blomberg was lacking in.

The first was his defensive play. In his first season in New York, Blomberg was used exclusively in the outfield. While he was extremely fast and had a strong throwing arm, Blomberg possessed neither the quickness nor the instincts to play the outfield. In his second season, the Yankees tried him at first base, but he showed that he lacked the hands to play that position, committing 13 errors in just 95 games there. Finally, in 1973, when the American League decided to begin using the designated hitter in its games, Blomberg had a spot that he was well suited for. In fact, he will prob-

Although Ron Blomberg swung a menacing left-handed bat, injuries and an inability to hit southpaws prevented him from ever becoming an everyday player.

ably always be remembered as having been the first designated hitter in history. It was a spot that was created for players like him because hitting was one area he definitely was not lacking in.

Blomberg's other shortcoming was his inability to hit left-handed pitching. While he hit right-handers very well, Blomberg had a difficult time against lefties. As a result, he was a platoon player throughout his entire career and was never able to accumulate more than about 300 at-bats in any season. Needless to say, this greatly limited his offensive productivity and kept him from ever putting up the kinds of numbers the Yankees were hoping to get from him. Yet, against right-handed pitching, he wielded perhaps the most potent bat in New York's lineup.

While Blomberg was very strong, he truly was not a big home run hitter. Rather than always trying to pull the ball, he preferred to use the entire field and hit the ball where it was pitched. As a result, he was more of a gap hitter who hit hard line drives to all fields. Yet, with his quick swing, and the power he generated from it, he was not an infrequent visitor to the right field seats at Yankee Stadium. In his first season in New York, he hit 7 home runs, knocked in 31 runs, and batted .322 in just 199 at-bats. His batting average dropped to .268 the following year, but, in just 299 at-bats, he managed to hit 14 home runs and drive in 49 runs.

Blomberg's third season, 1973, was his best, though. After pulling a hamstring just three days before breaking training camp prior to the start of the regular season, he was forced to shorten his stride at home plate and hit the ball more to the opposite field, and up the middle. As a result, Bloomberg maintained a batting average close to .400 for much of the first half of the season. Although he wasn't able to keep up that pace for the entire year, he ended up batting .329, while collecting 12 homers and 57 RBIs in just 301 at-bats. He also established career-highs in on-base (.395) and slugging (.498) percentage.

Blomberg batted .311 the following year, but slumped to just .255 in 1975, when he came to the plate just 106 times due to an assortment of muscle injuries. He was hopeful of seeing more action the following year, but, unfortunately, his plans, and his career, were short-circuited by an injury that occurred in spring training. Chasing after a fly ball, he ran into an outfield wall, injuring himself seriously. After not playing in either 1976 or 1977, Blomberg attempted a comeback with the Chicago White Sox in 1978. However, in 156 at-bats, he hit just 5 home runs, drove in only 22 runs, and batted just .231. Blomberg called it quits at the end of the year.

Roy White recalls how disappointing it was that his former team-mate's promising career had to be cut short the way it was: "Ronnie could really swing the bat. He was really a good hitter. It's unfortunate that he had to run into that wall. I was playing center that day in Winter Haven when he ran into that cement wall out in left-center field trying to run down a fly ball. That really cut short his career."[50]

White also remembers something else about Blomberg: "Great eating exploits…. He once ate 50 hamburgers, or something ridiculous like that…. There was also a restaurant in Fort Lauderdale during spring training that served something like a 36 or 70–ounce sirloin steak — something huge like that. Anyway, if you could eat it, you didn't have to pay. He did it two times and then was banned from the restaurant."[51]

Although his initial season in New York was an extremely difficult one, Chris Chambliss ended up being a very productive player and a pillar of strength and stability on the turbulent Yankee teams that won three consecutive American League pennants from 1976 to 1978.

Chambliss was drafted twice by the Cincinnati Reds, first in 1967, then again in 1969. However, he decided to stay in school and attend UCLA for a year before signing with the Cleveland Indians when he was drafted a third time in 1970. When Chambliss led the American Association in hitting with a mark of .342 at Wichita in 1970, he became the first player to lead that league in batting in his first pro season. The following year, he was named the American League's Rookie of the Year when he batted .275, while hitting 9 home runs and driving in 48 runs in 415 at-bats with the Indians.

After leading Cleveland in batting in each of the next two seasons with averages of .292 and .273, he was traded to the Yankees early in the 1974 season as part of a seven-player deal. Yankee GM Gabe Paul, who had been serving in that very same capacity in Cleveland just a few years earlier when Chambliss first signed with the Indians, was extremely happy to have him since he felt that the young first baseman had a bright future ahead of him. However, many of New York's players were not as thrilled about his arrival since Paul had traded away almost half of the team's pitching staff to acquire him. To show their displeasure, some of the veterans on the team treated Chambliss with a certain aloofness when he joined the squad, thereby making his adjustment to the big city even more difficult than it would have been otherwise. In his first season in New York, Chambliss hit just 6 home runs, drove in only 43 runs, and batted just .242 in 400 at-bats.

While rumors circulated during the off-season about possibly trying to find a replacement for him, Chambliss came to camp in 1975 determined to prove his critics wrong. He succeeded in doing so, finishing the year with 72 runs batted in, batting .304, leading the team with 38 doubles, and establishing himself as New York's first baseman of the future.

The following year, Chambliss began a string of three consecutive seasons in which he was, quite possibly, the team's most consistent and reliable performer. During that period, he hit 17 homers twice, averaged 92 runs batted in a year, never driving in fewer than 90, and posted batting averages of .293, .287, and .274, respectively. He also missed just 11 games over that three-year stretch, was selected to the league All-Star team in 1976, finished fifth in the league MVP voting that same season, and won a Gold Glove in 1978 by leading all league first basemen with a .997 fielding average.

Of course, Chambliss is best-remembered for having hit one of the most important home runs in team history, and one of the most dramatic in baseball history. On October 14, 1976, leading off the bottom of the ninth inning of Game Five of the ALCS, with the scored tied 6–6 against the Kansas City Royals, Chambliss homered against Mark Littell to end New York's 12–year pennant drought and send Yankee Stadium into a frenzy. The home run was Chambliss' second of the series and culminated a brilliant performance in which he batted .524 and either tied or broke

The acquisition of first baseman Chris Chambliss during the 1974 season was one of the moves that helped to return the Yankees to prominence during the late 1970s.

five LCS records for hits (11) and RBIs (8). Although the Yankees were subsequently swept by the Reds in the World Series, Chambliss, once again, performed admirably, batting .312 and collecting 5 hits in the four games.

Chambliss was also extremely productive in each of the next two seasons, when the Yankees won back-to-back World Series titles. However, his contributions to the team could not be measured by statistics alone. On a team fraught with turmoil and friction, Chambliss remained as steady as a rock, always providing a calming influence. While George Steinbrenner battled with Billy Martin, Martin fought with Reggie Jackson, and Jackson argued with Thurman Munson, among others, even-tempered men such as Chambliss, Catfish Hunter, Roy White, and Willie Randolph helped to hold the team together.

Nevertheless, after hitting 18 homers and batting .280 in 1979, Chambliss was traded to Toronto at the end of the year. From there, he was sent quickly to Atlanta, where he hit a career-high 20 homers in both 1982 and 1983. After ending his playing career with the Braves in 1986, he returned to New York as the Yankees' hitting coach in 1988, a position he held for more than a decade before being relieved of his duties at the end of the 2000 season.

When the Yankees traded for Lou Piniella at the end of the 1973 season, they not only acquired one of the best pure hitters in the American League, but an extremely intelligent player whose knowledge and passion for the game made him an invaluable member of the team for the next 11 years.

Piniella was originally signed by the Cleveland Indians in 1962. However, he was drafted by the Washington Senators the following year before being picked up by the Orioles in 1964. He remained in the Oriole system the next few seasons, until the Indians reacquired him in 1968. Piniella was then left unprotected prior to the expansion draft of 1969, and, after being claimed by the Seattle Pilots, was dealt to the expansion Kansas City Royals. So, by the time Piniella arrived in the big leagues to stay, he had already been with five different organizations and was 25 years old.

Piniella quickly showed that he belonged, though, winning American League Rookie of the Year honors in 1969, with a .282 batting average, 11 homers, and 68 runs batted in. He followed that up with 11 home runs, 88 runs batted in, and a .301 average in 1970. After a less-productive year in 1971, Piniella had another solid season in 1972, finishing second to Rod Carew in the A.L. batting race with an average of .312, leading the league with 33 doubles, and making the All-Star team for the only time in his career. However, after his average slipped to .250 the following year, he was traded to New York for reliever Lindy McDaniel.

Piniella's first season in pinstripes was a good one as he became a regular member of the Yankee outfield, batted .305, and amassed more than 500 at-bats for the only time in his Yankee career. He remained in New York for 11 seasons, platooning in most of those years with some very fine players. In his years with the team, he split time in both the outfield and at the DH position with the likes of Roy White, Oscar Gamble, and Bobby Murcer. He led the team in batting three times, with his highest marks coming in the championship seasons of 1977 (.330) and 1978 (.314).

On the Yankee teams of the mid-to-late 1970's, it was Piniella, along with Thurman Munson, who provided protection for the many left-handed hitters in the lineup. While opposing managers usually preferred to throw left-handers at the Yankees in an attempt to neutralize the left-handed bats of Reggie Jackson, Graig Nettles, Chris Chambliss, and Mickey Rivers, they always had to be wary of Piniella's right-handed bat. Though not known as a slugger, Piniella was a very solid line-drive hitter, and was, perhaps, the best pure hitter on those Yankee teams. When the game was on the line in the late innings, there was no one on the team, with the possible exception of Thurman Munson, who Yankee fans would rather have seen up at the plate.

While Piniella's ability as a hitter was common knowledge, he was actually quite underrated as an outfielder. Though not particularly graceful, nor very fast, he was extremely reliable and caught virtually everything that was within his reach. He also seemed to have a knack for making big plays. In fact, it was Piniella's defense in right-field that helped preserve the Yankees' 5–4 victory against the Red Sox in 1978's one-game playoff.

First, he robbed Fred Lynn of an extra-base hit and two runs batted in with a fine running catch in the sixth inning. Then, in the bottom of the ninth, with the tying run on first base in the person of Rick Burleson, Piniella prevented the Boston shortstop from advancing to third base on a single by Jerry Remy. With the Yankees leading by a run, Burleson was on first base with one man out. Remy hit a line drive in Piniella's direction that the right-fielder lost in the sun. However, he had the presence of mind to go to the spot where he thought the ball might land. From there, he lunged at the ball, fielded it on the first hop, turned quickly, and made a strong throw in the direction of third base. Piniella's alert play prevented Burleson from going to third. As a result, when the next batter, Jim Rice, hit a long fly ball to Piniella in right, Burleson, instead of being able to score the tying run, was only able to advance to third base. Carl Yastrzemski subsequently popped up to end the game, and the rest is history. So, while Bucky Dent has always received much of the credit for New York's victory in that game (which he deserves), Piniella was really the unsung hero.

That game was, to a large extent, a microcosm of Piniella's career. He did not do the kinds of things that grabbed everyone's attention. He didn't hit a lot of home runs; he didn't steal a lot of bases; he didn't make a lot of spectacular catches in the outfield. But he played the game as hard as he could and to the best of his ability every day. He was an intelligent player who did the little things to help his team win. He also played the game with a great deal of passion. Although not particularly fast, he was one of the team's most aggressive base-runners. It was this passion and aggressiveness, as well as his clutch-hitting, that made Piniella so popular with the fans of New York.

When he finally retired from the game in 1984, Piniella remained in the Yankee organization for several more years. After serving as both a scout and batting instructor, he took over as manager in 1986 and led the team to consecutive winning seasons. Under Piniella in 1986, New York finished 90–72 and in second place. The following year, they won 89 games, but finished fourth in the division.

Lou Piniella gave the Yankees a solid right-handed bat in the middle of their lineup for 11 seasons. His clutch play and passion for the game made him a real fan favorite.

Piniella was subsequently replaced as manager by Billy Martin and "promoted" to General Manager. He was later asked to manage the team once again by George Steinbrenner, and, out of loyalty to the organization, he agreed to do so. However, Piniella eventually grew tired of the instability and unpredictability associated with managing in New York and moved elsewhere, first managing the Cincinnati Reds to a world championship in 1990, and then taking over the managerial reigns in Seattle. After several successful years with the Mariners, Piniella moved on to the Tampa Bay Devil Rays, for whom he is currently managing.

In late November of 1972, the Yankees traded young outfield prospects Charlie Spikes and Rusty Torres, along with back-up infielder Jerry Kenney and reserve catcher John Ellis to Cleveland for Graig Nettles and back-up catcher Gerry Moses. The deal has to rank as one of the greatest New York ever made since, while none of the other players involved ever truly distinguished themselves in the major leagues, Nettles went on to become the greatest third baseman in franchise history.

Originally from San Diego, Nettles saw his first major league action with the Minnesota Twins in 1967, when he was called up briefly at the end of the season. He appeared in 22 games for the team the following season, mostly as an outfielder, before being called up for good in 1969. After playing for Billy Martin in Denver in the minors, the new Twins' manager brought him up that year and used him mostly in the outfield and as a pinch-hitter, since Minnesota's regular third baseman was Harmon Killebrew.

Prior to the start of the 1970 season, though, Nettles was traded to Cleveland as part of a six-player deal that sent, among others, Luis Tiant to Minnesota and former Cy Young Award winner Dean Chance to the Indians. Nettles had three productive years in Cleveland, with his best year coming in 1971 when he hit 28 homers, knocked in 86 runs, and batted .261. The Yankees had been eyeing him for quite some time, though, thinking that his left-handed power bat would be a welcome addition to their lineup. Although he later admitted to being strictly a guess-hitter, Nettles was also an excellent fastball hitter who had a perfect Yankee Stadium stroke. When New York finally acquired him at the end of the 1972 season, they felt like they had their third baseman for the next 10 years.

While Nettles put up decent numbers his first two seasons in New York, many fans were somewhat disappointed in his overall performance. Although he hit 22 homers both years, while driving in 81 and 75 runs, respectively, he posted batting averages of just .234 and .246, and committed 26 errors the first year and 21 the next. In 1975, however, Nettles developed into the player Yankee fans were hoping their team had acquired three seasons earlier. That year, the third baseman hit 21 homers, knocked in 91 runs, raised his batting average more than 30 points to .267, brought his error total down to a respectable 19, and made the All-Star team for the first time in his career. He was also selected to *The Sporting News* All-Star team for the first time. After struggling during the first half of 1976, Nettles caught fire in the second half and ended up leading the American League with 32 homers, while knocking in 93 runs and playing solid defense at third.

It was in 1977 and 1978, though, that Nettles truly distinguished himself. In the first of those years, he established career highs in home runs (37), runs batted in (107), and runs scored (99), while reducing his error total to just 12. He was selected to both the A.L. and *The Sporting News* All-Star teams for the second time, finished fifth in the league MVP voting, and won his first Gold Glove Award. The following season, Nettles

GRAIG NETTLES
Third Baseman

Graig Nettles gave the Yankees another left-handed power bat they so desperately needed. The greatest third baseman in team history almost singlehandedly turned around the 1978 World Series with his great glove work in Game Three.

hit 27 homers, drove in 93 runs, batted a career-high .276, committed just 11 errors, was selected, once again, to both the A.L. and *The Sporting News* All-Star teams, finished sixth in the league MVP voting, and won his second consecutive Gold Glove. Yet, it was his performance in the World Series that year that he is probably best remembered for.

With the Yankees trailing the Dodgers two games to none, the Series shifted back to New York for the next three games. In Game Three, the Yankees sent 25–game winner Ron Guidry to the mound in the hope that he might change the momentum of the Series. However, it was Nettles' defensive heroics that turned the tide. While Guidry pitched well, he found himself in at least three difficult situations in which Los Angeles had put men in scoring position. Each time, though, the man at the plate made the mistake of hitting the ball in the direction of Nettles, who saved at least four runs with his great glove work. Whether he was lunging to his glove side or diving to his back-hand, Nettles put on a clinic at third, spearing several hot smashes by Dodger batters and turning them into outs. His performance preserved the Yankees' 5–1 victory, completely changed the momentum of the Series, and gave New York the impetus to go on and win the next three games as well and come away with their second consecutive world championship.

This kind of performance is a perfect example of why Nettles was so valuable to the Yankees for so many years. For, while he was a dangerous hitter, his defense was what set him apart from other third basemen. It was an aspect of his game that he worked extremely hard at, since he had not always played third base, and since it did not come as naturally to him as it did to someone like Brooks Robinson. In fact, the Yankees' two years at Shea Stadium were not pleasant ones for Nettles since the infield was never in very good condition. Both New York teams were playing there, and the infield was usually rock hard because it wasn't getting enough water.

Nevertheless, Nettles turned himself into a superb fielder and one of the most vital members of the Yankees. In fact, with the possible exception of Thurman Munson, he might well have been the most indispensable player on the team. Chris Chambliss, Willie Randolph, Roy White, Mickey Rivers, and Reggie Jackson were certainly key members of the team as well. But the Yankee bench was always stocked with decent talent at each of the positions those men played. However, if Nettles was lost for a substantial period of time, the team was in trouble. Perhaps that is why, from 1973 to 1978, he never appeared in fewer than 155 games or collected fewer than 552 at-bats. He was a true iron-man and one of the primary reasons why New York was able to win two straight world championships.

However, after being diagnosed with hepatitis in 1980 and missing 67 games, Nettles was not quite himself when he returned to the team just prior to New York's three-game playoff loss to the Royals. He also was injured during the following year's World Series, when the Yankees lost in six games to the Dodgers. Although he remained a home run threat in his final two years in New York, Nettles failed to come to the plate as many as 500 times or hit more than 20 homers. He was traded to San Diego in 1984 and was a prime contributor to the Padres' first pennant, hitting 20 homers and knocking in 65 runs, in just 395 at-bats. After two more years in San Diego, Nettles was dealt to Atlanta, where he spent one season before ending his career with the Expos in 1988.

When all was said and done, Nettles had hit 390 home runs and driven in 1,314 runs. His 319 homers as an American League third baseman are a record, and he played on six pennant-winners and two world champions. He was selected to six All-Star teams and won two Gold Gloves.

As for his fielding, Lou Piniella, who played with Nettles for 10 seasons in New York, says of his former teammate, "... Great glove. He knew how to play the position. In the years that I played, he probably played the position second only to Brooks Robinson — and not a distant second."[52]

Not bad for someone who was a disappointment to most Yankee fans his first two years in New York.

Although he was preceded by other outstanding relief pitchers such as Joe Page, Hoyt Wilhelm, and Lindy McDaniel, Sparky Lyle, along with Rollie Fingers, was baseball's first true "closer." For, while the other pitchers mentioned all started games early in their careers, Lyle was bred exclusively for relief, never having started a game in the major leagues.

Lyle first came up with the Boston Red Sox in 1967 and had his first outstanding season for the team the following year, when he compiled a record of 6–1, with 11 saves and a 2.74 ERA. After saving 53 games over the next three seasons, he was traded to New York for Danny Cater at the end of the 1971 season.

With the Yankees, Lyle developed into one of the very best relief pitchers in the game. Lyle's first season in New York was a magnificent one as he led the American League with 35 saves, compiled a record of 9–5, pitched to a brilliant 1.92 ERA, and finished third in the league MVP voting. Although he was less effective the following year, Lyle returned to top form in 1974, winning 9 games while losing only 3, compiling a 1.66 ERA, and being selected to the league All-Star team for the second of three times in his career. Lyle's best season, though, was 1977 when he finished with a record of 13–5, with 26 saves and a 2.17 ERA en route to becoming the first relief pitcher ever to win the A.L. Cy Young Award. He also made, perhaps, his most memorable pitching performance in the playoffs that year.

With the Yankees down two games to one to the Royals in the ALCS and on the verge of being eliminated, Lyle came in to relieve starter Ed Figueroa in just the fourth inning. He went the rest of the way, allowing just two hits and no runs in 5⅔ innings, to preserve New York's 6–4 victory. He also pitched 1⅓ innings of scoreless relief the very next day in the Yankees' come-from-behind 5–3 victory that propelled them into the World Series. He finished that post-season with a record of 2–0 and an ERA of 0.96 in just over nine innings of work.

In spite of Lyle's outstanding work during the 1977 season, owner George Steinbrenner decided to pursue free-agent closer Rich Gossage during the off-season. When Gossage signed with the Yankees, Lyle's role became a far less important one, and, even though he finished the season with a record of 9–3, he saved only nine games. At the end of the year, he was dealt to the Texas Rangers as part of a big ten-player trade that brought Dave Righetti to New York. Lyle spent four more years in the big leagues, pitching for the Rangers, Phillies, and White Sox, but never again achieved the success he had in New York.

While Lyle was one of the finest relief pitchers of his time, he was also one of the most charismatic. In 1972, his first season in New York, it became a ritual around Yankee Stadium that, when Lyle entered a game in the latter innings, the organist would begin playing *"Pomp and Circumstance."* The Yankee reliever, upon reaching the infield, would throw his warm-up jacket down and stride to the mound in a menacing manner, with a huge chaw of tobacco protruding from his jaw. The fans loved it, and Lyle's entrance into a game quickly became akin to a theatrical event.

Lyle had the perfect makeup for a top relief pitcher. He had the type of disposition where nothing phased him, the swagger and self-confidence that all closers need, and the guts of a riverboat gambler. He also had a tremendous slider that he used so effectively against right-handed hitters. While Lyle's slider was not thrown with the same velocity as Ron Guidry's, it broke down-and-in to right-handers just as sharply. In fact, it was actually Sparky who helped Guidry develop the pitch that made him as successful as he was.

Former outfielder Tom Grieve said of Lyle: "For a guy that really didn't have an exceptional fastball, he saved a lot of games with guts, determination, and a hard slider that he could throw to right-handed hitters."[53]

Willie Randolph says of his former teammate, "I never faced Sparky, but I know he had to be hellacious. You knew the slider was coming, but you still could hardly hit it." He adds, "He had ice water in his veins; he didn't care; he left it on the field and had a good time doing it."[54]

Another thing Sparky had was an outrageous sense of humor. He soon developed a reputation among his teammates for possessing a rather unusual hobby. For some odd reason, it seemed that Lyle had an affinity for sitting in birthday cakes in the nude. Needless to say, this spoiled many a clubhouse birthday celebration, as well as many a player's appetite.

Lyle's most elaborate prank, however, occurred at the very beginning of spring training one year. After not seeing most of his teammates during the entire off-season, Sparky encased his left (pitching) arm in a cast and entered the Yankees' spring training complex in that fashion. When the manager and other players on the team first saw him approaching, there was a feeling of great concern, since that left arm of Lyle's was so important to the success of the team. However, after a few moments of considering who they were dealing with, they all realized that it was just a joke, and everyone broke into laughter.

While Lyle's Yankee career did not end exactly as he would have liked it to, he made his feelings about what it was like playing for the team well known in a book he wrote with Peter Golenbock in 1979 called *The Bronx Zoo*. In it, he discussed some of his teammates and also touched on what he and many others perceived to be the insanity that went on within the Yankee organization during much of his time there. While his book was not considered to be nearly as controversial as Jim Bouton's *Ball Four*, it certainly presented an interesting insight into some of the characters on those teams, and into some of the relationships between certain members of the organization. So, in a sense, it could be said that Lyle, the prankster, once again had the last laugh.

Sparky Lyle was the team's closer from 1972 to 1977. However, after winning the American League Cy Young award in 1977, Lyle was relegated to the role of set-up man for the newly acquired Goose Gossage. A year later, Lyle was traded away to Texas, prompting Graig Nettles to quip that "Sparky went from Cy Young to Sayonara" (National Baseball Hall of Fame Library, Cooperstown, N.Y.).

Thurman Munson arrived in New York as a brash and cocky 22–year-old, brimming with so much self-confidence that he annoyed not only many opposing players, but even surprised some of his own teammates with his cockiness. However, by the mid-1970's, he was admired and respected by virtually every player he competed against and was, quite possibly, more beloved by his teammates than any other Yankee player.

Munson was born in Akron, Ohio, on June 7, 1947. After starring in baseball, football, and basketball in high school, he attended Kent State University on a baseball scholarship. Upon his graduation, he was drafted and signed by the Yankees, for whom he appeared in fewer than 100 minor league games before being called up to the majors for good in August of 1969. In 86 at-bats with New York that year, Munson batted .256 and hit his first major league home run. He also made enough of an impression on the Yankee brass to have them trade away Frank Fernandez during the off-season and begin envisioning having Munson behind the plate for many years to come.

The trust that the Yankee front office placed in Munson, however, was not as great as the amount of confidence the young man had in his own abilities. Former teammate and close friend, Bobby Murcer, who was in his first full major league season when Munson was called up to New York in 1969, says of Thurman, "He felt like he belonged the first time he stepped on the field here at Yankee Stadium.... The late '60s and early '70s, rookies were supposed to be seen and not heard. Thurman was a different kind of rookie — he was seen *and* heard."[55]

Thurman Munson's arrival in 1970 was a sign that things were about to change. The heart and soul of the team, Munson would help lead the Yankees to three pennants and two world championships.

Fellow Kent State alumnus, Gene Michael, who roomed with Munson his first few years in the league, says, "Thurman got away with more things as a rookie than most players would. For some reason, they accepted Thurman quickly ... his brashness and that. But he really wasn't that way. He was very concerned and compassionate in a lot of ways."[56]

The confidence that Munson had in himself helped him make it through the difficult early days of his 1970 rookie season. Off to a terrible start, he continued to believe in himself, as did manager Ralph Houk, who stuck with him in spite of his early slump. Munson rewarded Houk by finishing the season with a .302 batting average and winning American League Rookie of the Year honors. Although his average dropped to .251 the following season, Munson made the All-Star team for the first of seven times and displayed remarkable quickness and agility behind the plate. While he did not possess an extremely strong throwing arm like Johnny Bench, Munson had probably the quickest release in baseball, and was just as agile coming out from behind the plate on slowly-hit balls.

Mel Stottlemyre, who pitched to Munson in the latter's early years on the team, says, "He was so sure of himself, and so sure of what he could do behind the plate. He was known for his quickness behind the plate. He was as quick as anybody I've ever seen coming out from behind that crouch on bunted balls and on his throws to second base."[57]

When most people think of Munson's defense, they probably have a clearer image in their minds of the way he fielded during his last several seasons, when, due to a sore shoulder and the usual bruises that come with being an everyday catcher, his throwing efficiency was greatly reduced. But, early in his career, Munson was a tremendous defensive player. In fact, in 1971, he committed only one error all year, and that came on a collision at home plate when the ball was knocked out of his glove by Oriole catcher Andy Etchebarren.

In the early days of his career, Munson didn't hit for very much power, and was not nearly as good at driving in runs as he would become in later years. He failed to hit more than 10 home runs or drive in more than 53 runs in any of his first three seasons. At that time, he was more of a line drive hitter who got the majority of his hits to right and right-center field. Of course, playing in the "Old" Yankee Stadium, with its "Death Valley" in left-center and centerfield, had as much to do with that as anything. As a result, he usually batted second in the Yankee lineup. However, Munson began to find his power-stroke in 1973, when he hit 20 home runs, knocked in 74 runs, and batted .301. He had learned how to turn on an inside pitch and had also learned how to relax more when coming to the plate with men on base.

Another thing Munson had become was a true team leader. Extremely competitive, and with a burning desire to win, he challenged his teammates to work as hard as they possibly could, always seeking to bring out the best in them.

Outfielder Elliott Maddox, who had his best major league season in his first year with the team in 1974, spoke of the kind of leader Munson was and of the influence he had on him: "If Thurman was on your case and telling you, 'You have to apply yourself more, you have to do this, or you have to do that because you know you're capable of it', it meant he liked you. So, he *loved* me because he never gave me a moment's peace.... So, you would want to do it, just to get him off your back."[58]

Munson reached his peak during the mid-1970s, batting over .300 and driving in more than 100 runs in three consecutive seasons (1975–1977). He hit a career-high .318 in 1975, then followed that up by winning the American League's Most Valuable Player Award in 1976 by hitting 17 home runs, driving in 105 runs, batting .302, and leading the Yankees to their first pennant in 12 seasons. The following year, Munson hit 18 homers, knocked in 100 runs, and batted .308. However, due to the number of injuries his body had sustained over the years from catching more than 130 games a season for practically his entire career, Munson's productivity started to decline in 1978. Although he batted .297, he hit only 6 home runs and knocked in just 71 runs. Yet, for the second season in a row, he helped lead his team to the world championship with his clutch hitting, superb handling of the pitching staff, and tremendous leadership qualities. In fact, many of his teammates felt that he was the most important and indispensable player on the team — in essence, the glue that held the rest of the team together.

Ron Guidry, who first became a regular member of the starting rotation in 1977, says, "Having him there, everybody kind of revolved around him, because you could take me out of a game and they could still play and win. You could take somebody else out and they could probably still win. But, if you took Thurman out, our chances of winning were half as good."[59]

Guidry also speaks of the confidence that Munson instilled in his pitchers: "Pitching was made easier because I got to throw to a guy like Thurman. He made pitchers that were average ones good. He made them win a lot of games because of his ability to take all the pressure and call the game. We all felt like: 'That's the best pitch to throw. I'm not gonna' second-guess it and say it's not'. I could have thrown a guy 20 sliders and made him look foolish, but, if he called for a fastball, that's what I threw."[60]

Willie Randolph, who joined the Yankees in Munson's MVP season of 1976, talks of his all-around ability: "When you think of Thurman Munson, you think about the total package. This man could even run. Most catchers back then would just go base to base. Thurman would take you first to third in a minute. If you needed an RBI, he could hit that patented line drive to right to drive in runs. If you needed a home run, he could turn on you and take you deep. The total package. I don't think, even when you talk about the great catchers of the game — and he was obviously up there — none of those guys really did *everything* well like Thurman did. He did everything that was necessary to win."[61]

While, in his last two seasons, Thurman's offensive productivity was starting to decline, he had already accomplished enough to allow him to be grouped with the great Yankee catchers who preceded him. In fact, Munson was quite proud of his linkage to Bill Dickey, Yogi Berra, and Elston Howard. Like Berra and Howard, he was named league MVP. He also finished in the top ten in the voting two other times, and, in addition to being selected to the American League All-Star team a total of seven

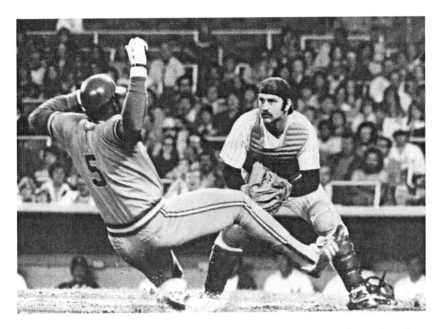

Here, Thurman Munson prepares to block the plate against George Scott, then playing for the Milwaukee Brewers.

times, he was selected to *The Sporting News* All-Star team four times and was awarded three Gold Gloves.

The first Yankee captain since Lou Gehrig, Munson was also one of the finest clutch performers of his time. In 14 ALCS games, he hit 2 home runs, knocked in 10 runs, and batted .339. In 16 World Series contests, he hit 1 homer, drove in 12 runs, and batted .373. Even though the Yankees were swept by Cincinnati in the 1976 World Series, Munson batted .529 and had six hits in his final six at-bats.

Illustrating the kind of admiration and respect that many of Munson's opponents had for him, Reds' catcher Johnny Bench says, "I was always totally amazed at Thurman. I thought he was one of the greatest competitors I've ever known."[62]

One particular moment that has to stand out in the minds of many Yankee fans from that era as an example of Munson's competitive spirit and clutch play is the third game of the 1978 ALCS against the Royals. As the result of a badly damaged shoulder and a bruised and battered body, Munson had failed to hit a home run in more than two months. Yet, with the Series tied at a game apiece and the Yankees down by a run late in the game, Thurman hit a ball about 30 feet over the 430–foot sign in deepest left-center field at Yankee Stadium, off of Doug Bird, to win the game. Perhaps it was that kind of intestinal fortitude that prompted Reggie Jackson to write in his autobiography, "Had he lived, I bet we would have won two more World Series in New York, both in 1980, and in 1981."[63]

Unfortunately, Thurman was not there in either of those years because, on August 2, 1979, while practicing takeoffs and landings in his private plane in Akron, Ohio, Munson perished when the plane hit a tree. Thurman's tragic death left his teammates and Yankee fans alike stunned and deeply saddened. Perhaps Ron Guidry expressed everyone's feelings best when he said: "I had the feeling that it would never be the same. I said to myself: 'I'm gonna' win games, but it will never be the same again, because you can't replace him'. There was no way to replace that man."[64]

While it has now been almost a quarter-of-a-century since Thurman Munson last played for the Yankees, his presence is still felt around Yankee Stadium — especially in the clubhouse. Thurman's locker remains empty — unused by anyone since his death.

Current manager Joe Torre — one of the architects of the latest Yankee dynasty — has this to say: "The way he played the game exemplifies what we have been about.... I just sense that Thurman is in everybody's ear during the course of the season. There's no question his presence in the clubhouse is felt because of his locker."[65]

Roy White is unique in that he was with the Yankees when they reached their nadir during the mid-1960's, yet was able to persevere and make it to the championship years of 1976–1978. Horace Clarke and Mel Stottlemyre were also with the team in 1965, but they were both gone by the end of the 1974 season. White's Yankee career, however, spanned the 15 seasons from 1965 to 1979.

White began his minor league career in 1962, as an 18–year-old switch-hitting second baseman with the Greensboro Yankees in the Class B Carolina League. The following season, as the team's leadoff hitter, he batted .309, led the league with 117 runs scored, and was named to the league's All-Star team. After spending the entire 1964 season and most of the following year in the minors, White was finally called up to New York towards the end of 1965. When he arrived, one of the first things manager Johnny Keane did was convert him to an outfielder.

"Bobby Richardson's presence on the team was the primary reason, but there were other reasons as well," recalls White. "When I came up, Johnny Keane was the manager. When I was first called up in September

"The Quiet Yankee," Roy White, was the only man to play on every team from 1965 to 1975. His perseverance allowed him to take part in the celebrations that followed the championship seasons of 1977 and 1978.

of 1965, Bobby Murcer was also a call-up and Keane said he didn't want to play us both in the infield because there are some teams that are hesitant to have two rookies out there at second and at short. So, he said that he might use me in the outfield. I ended up playing virtually all the games that I played at the end of the season in the outfield. Then, when I came back in 1966, he had a vision of me being like a Curt Flood, who he had in centerfield in St. Louis. He thought that, with my speed, I could convert to the outfield."[66]

White got off to a fast start in 1966, but eventually slumped and ended up the season batting just .225, and on the bench. He also saw limited action the following year, splitting his time between the outfield and third base, a position the team was looking to fill after trading away Clete Boyer at the end of the 1966 season. In 1967, he hit just .224 in 214 at-bats.

However, White finally blossomed in 1968, developing into the Yankees' best all-around player. That year, he led the team in virtually every offensive category and finished second to Mickey Mantle, with 17 home runs. He also did an excellent job in left-field after being given the everyday job by manager Ralph Houk.

As to why it took him four years to develop into the solid player he would end up being throughout the remainder of his career, White says, "I think it was switching positions … from being an infielder, to an outfielder, to an infielder, back to an outfielder. I think that affected my hitting. Actually, in 1966, I was leading the Yankees in hitting and in home runs about six weeks into the season. Then, I got home run happy. I started thinking that it was easy. Then, I got myself into a terrible slump and ended up being on the bench by June. I had seven home runs in May and, at the end of the season, I still had seven. I ended up hitting around .220 in a couple of hundred at-bats. All of the position switching started around then, and I just had trouble finding a spot where I finally got comfortable."[67]

White says that manager Houk changed all that, though, in 1968: "In spring training of 1968, Ralph Houk said, 'You're just going to be an outfielder now. Let's not worry about going back into the infield. Just stay out there and learn how to play it to the best of your ability'. That was kind of a load off of my mind, knowing that I was going to be in the outfield and that I had nothing else to concentrate on."[68]

After seeing some action in both right-field and center early that season, White was made the everyday left fielder by Houk, who saw the speedy White as an ideal candidate to patrol Yankee Stadium's roomy power alley."

That same season, after being moved around the lineup quite a bit in the early-going, White was made the Yankees cleanup hitter. Asked what it was like batting fourth, behind Mickey Mantle, he says, "That was really amazing ... pretty shocking actually. That was after another meeting with Ralph. He called me in and said, 'Roy, I'm gonna' hit you number four. I just don't have anybody else. They're pitching around Mickey. He's not getting very many good pitches to hit, and you're the most reliable guy on the club, so I'm gonna' hit him three and hit you four'."[69]

White continued to bat fourth in the Yankee order for the next half-dozen seasons, having his two best years while batting cleanup. In 1970, he established career highs in home runs (22), runs batted in (94), runs scored (109), base hits (180), and batting (.296), and was selected to the American League All-Star team for the second consecutive year. The following season, he hit 19 homers, drove in 84 runs, scored 86 others, and batted .292.

Nevertheless, White, at 5'10" and 170 lbs, was far from your prototypical cleanup hitter. His most natural position was probably the number two spot in the order, since it allowed him to better use his ability to get on base, score runs, work the count, hit-and-run, steal bases, and do the little things to help the team win. He was an extremely patient hitter, finishing among the top ten players in the league in bases on balls seven times during his career, and even leading the league in that department in 1972, with 99. He also led the league in runs scored once, and finished in the top ten in that category five other times as well. White would also have made an excellent leadoff hitter, a role he often assumed in 1974 when the team contended for the A.L. East title with the Orioles.

However, throughout much of Roy's career, the Yankees just didn't have anybody else who could do a better job batting fourth. He, himself, admits, "I was pretty well miscast in the number four slot. I had to change my mentality, especially batting left-handed in Yankee Stadium, with the shorter porch in right. If it was a tie ballgame, or, if we were down by a run in the latter innings, I had to look for a pitch that maybe I could try to pull and that I had a chance to hit out. That wasn't really the type of player that I was."[70]

In White's last several seasons with the team, though, he had a better supporting cast and was able to move to his more natural number two spot in the order. Batting second for the pennant-winning Yankees in 1976, he batted .286, stole a career-high 31 bases, and led the American League with 104 runs scored.

By that time, he had also greatly improved himself as a right-handed hitter. Ironically, in the early stages of his career, White was a far better hitter from the left-hand side of the plate than he was from his natural (right-handed) side. His first few seasons, he usually batted well over .300 as a left-handed hitter, but struggled to keep his average over .230 from the right side. As he tells it, "That was something I really had to work on. It was kind of a neglected factor. I just wasn't taking enough batting practice right-handed. I kind of figured it out myself because I'd look at the averages and see .230 right-handed and .330 or .340 left-handed. It occurred to me that, sooner or later, I might not be playing against lefties if I didn't get better. So, whereas, I tried to pull the ball early as a right-handed hitter, I started going the other way, choking up on the bat, and trying to get on base from the right-hand side. That was my natural side, so I felt like I was stronger … but I really wasn't. So, when I started doing that, I slowly started getting better from the right-hand side. Eventually, I think I hit .300 one year right-handed."[71]

While he never hit for quite as much power from the right side, White did manage to homer from both sides of the plate in the same game five times during his career, something that, up until then, had been done more often by only one other Yankee, Mickey Mantle, who accomplished the feat ten times.

In spite of his many accomplishments and several good years with the Yankees, Roy had to prove himself all over again in 1974, for new manager Bill Virdon. In what would become an all-too-familiar scenario later in his career, White's abilities and overall contributions to the team were underestimated by Virdon, who seemed intent on limiting his playing time early in the season. Over the first two months, he rarely played the outfield, more often than not being used as a designated hitter, or as a pinch-hitter. In Virdon's new outfield alignment, he preferred to use Elliott Maddox in center, Bobby Murcer in right, and Lou Piniella in left. On those rare occasions when White did get the start in left-field, he was frequently replaced in the late innings for defense by Walt Williams. Although he did not possess a particularly strong throwing arm, and, although both Piniella and Williams were proficient as outfielders, White was clearly the best defensive left-fielder that Virdon had at his disposal. Fortunately, the new manager eventually realized that he had misjudged White's abilities and admitted his error.

As Roy tells it: "In spring training of 1974, Virdon came in, and he had never seen me play before. I think I'm one of those guys you gotta' see me play everyday or you probably couldn't appreciate some of the little things that I tried to do as a player. So, I think he formed an opinion of me right away, and he later called me into his office one day — and he even said it to the press— that he underestimated me as a ballplayer when he first got there and didn't realize that I was a good player until after he had seen me play everyday."[72]

Surprisingly, even those who were more familiar with White as a player never seemed to fully appreciate what he was capable of contributing to the team. After leading the league in runs scored in 1976, he received slightly less playing time in 1977, and saw his role diminish even further in 1978. It seemed that the team was always looking to replace him with someone who, they thought, was better. In Roy's own words, "It seemed like, for awhile, they were always trying to find somebody to replace me. I never was a big power guy and they may have just been looking for someone who had more power."[73] As a result, players such as Gary Thomasson and Jay Johnstone, who had been platoon players throughout most of their careers, saw more action in left-field for much of the 1978 season than did White.

Fortunately, for Roy, and for the Yankees, when Bob Lemon replaced Billy Martin as manager that year, he inserted him into the regular lineup. White, who had barely played during the first half of the season, and who had struggled in his part-time role, got hot and raised his batting average from around .200 to .269 by season's end. He was very instrumental in the success the team had during the months of August and September, when they made up a 14½ game deficit to the Boston Red Sox. He also performed exceptionally well in the post-season that year, batting .313 in the ALCS and hitting a game-winning sixth-inning homer against Dennis Leonard in the series clincher. He also batted .333 in the World Series against the Dodgers, hitting a home run, driving in four runs, and scoring the game-winner in the fourth game on a single by Lou Piniella.

The 1978 World Series actually had special meaning for White since he was originally from California, and since it gave him an opportunity to play in front of his family and friends. This is the way Roy tells the

Although surrounded by mediocrity much of his time in New York, Roy White stood out as a solid performer and a class act.

story: "In 1977, I was disappointed because I didn't really get to play in the World Series. I didn't start one game in the Series. I ended up pinch-hitting in a couple of games, but I didn't start any games. I was a little upset because Billy had told me that he was going to use me against right-handed pitchers and that Cliff Johnson was going to DH against left-handers. Anyway, the situation came up where I was supposed to be in there and I wasn't, so, even though we won the World Series, in a way, it was kind of a disappointment because I really didn't get to play in any of those games. And, you know, we were playing the Dodgers, from Los Angeles, and I had grown up in the Los Angeles area. So, my parents didn't see me play in the Series. So it was kind of a bitter-sweet World Series for me. But, 1978 was kind of a redemption for me, getting to play in all the games in the Series."[74]

In spite of the success White had down the stretch in 1978, he, once again, was used sparingly the following season. In 1979, he appeared in just 81 games, collecting only 205 at-bats, and hitting just .215. At the end of the year, White toyed with the idea of signing with the California Angels as a free agent, but ended up going to Japan and playing for the Tokyo Giants for three years. As for his three seasons in Japan, White says, "It was a really good experience. I had an opportunity to play on a championship team in Japan in the second year I was there. So, I'm one of the few guys to have played for a World Series winner and a Japan Series winner. In fact, after playing there, I ended up going back almost every year for about 10 years, doing baseball clinics. I even learned some Japanese. I had a pretty good vocabulary."[75]

It is hard to fully understand why Roy White was so underrated and underappreciated by some of those within the Yankee organization who always seemed to be searching for a replacement for him. From 1968 to 1970, he was the best player on the team, and, in most of the subsequent seasons, he was a major contributor to whatever success the team had. He ranks fifth all-time among Yankee players in games played, sixth in at-bats, eighth in base hits, ninth in runs scored, fourth in stolen bases, and also is in the top 20 in runs batted in and doubles. More than that, though, he always carried himself with dignity and class, and, in his own quiet way, was a team leader.

As the only man to have played on every Yankee team from 1965 to 1975, Roy White, more than anyone, knows what it was like being with the team during that period. Who, then, would be better to talk to about what it was like being a Yankee during that era, what it was like playing on some of those teams, and what qualities some of the players on those teams possessed?

As for what it meant to be a Yankee, Roy says, "It was special being a Yankee. As a kid, I didn't even like the Yankees. I was a fan of the Cleveland Indians and Cincinnati Reds. But, it meant something special being with the Yankees. The first time actually being in the Yankee clubhouse was very special. You're kind of in awe to actually be there. It's something that you read about for so long."[76]

Asked which of those teams, or seasons, stands out the most in his mind, he says, "Personally, 1970 was probably the best year I had in the major leagues. Statistically, that was the best year I had in the big leagues, so that was memorable for that. The team also had a good year, but I think we kind of overachieved. Fritz Peterson had his best season — I think he won 20 games for us that year — and Lindy McDaniel had a big year for us in the bullpen — he saved a lot of games. But, even though we won 93 games that year and finished second in the division, we were never close to the Orioles. So, teamwise, I think 1974 was really a fun year. We surprised everybody in the league and came very close to winning the American League pennant."[77]

During his career with the Yankees, White played for five different managers— Johnny Keane, Ralph Houk, Bill Virdon, Billy Martin, and Bob Lemon. Asked which of those managers he enjoyed playing for the most, without hesitation, he said: "Houk was always my number one guy I enjoyed playing for. He stuck with me through some of those lean years when I was still trying to find myself. I think he must have seen something in me that made him think that, eventually, I might break out and be a decent player. He stuck with me and then gave me my shot. Also, when you played for Ralph and produced, he really stuck by you through thick and thin."[78]

As for which teammates, in particular, stand out in his mind, Roy mentioned Thurman Munson, Catfish Hunter, and Ron Guidry. He says of Munson, "Thurman's locker was right next to mine, so he was one of the first guys I'd see every day coming to the ballpark. We were good friends."[79]

He feels that Thurman was so beloved by his teammates because, "He had a really good sense of humor. He could apply the needle, and he could take it. Also, he was such a great clutch player. With the winning run on second base, Thurman was the guy you'd want to be up there at the plate. You knew he was going to get a base hit. He was such a tough out, especially with a runner on at second. Also, he played hard, and he played hurt."[80]

Roy says of Hunter, "I liked the way Catfish Hunter went about his business. I thought he was very professional. When he came over, I think he lost his first three starts. People were booing, but he didn't panic. He just kept doing the same things. He was always the same guy no matter how he performed."[81]

As for Guidry, White says, "Ron Guidry was amazing ... what he did, and how dominating he was for those years. When he pitched, you just knew you were gonna' win. All you had to do was get just a couple of runs and you knew you were going to win. Nobody was going to hit him."[82]

White says he began to sense that the team was turning the corner and on the verge of becoming a really good team during the 1974 season: "We were starting to get better then. We were picking up some pretty good ballplayers. Gabe Paul was making some really good deals. First Graig Nettles and Chris Chambliss came over. Then we got Willie Randolph, Mickey Rivers, and Ed Figueroa in 1976. Then, some of the younger guys coming through, like Ron Guidry coming into his own. So, you could see us getting better and turning the corner. It was a matter of time before it all came together. You know, getting Sparky Lyle and Goose Gossage. Thurman coming up and becoming the number one catcher."[83]

Having been with the team since 1965, and having gone through some of the worst times in the history of the franchise, no one was more deserving of being there during the late 1970's, when the team finally returned to the top of the baseball world. It is just unfortunate that some of the players who had been with White through so many of those "lean years" — players such as Mel Stottlemyre and Bobby Murcer — were not there to share it with him.

Season Highlights, Outstanding Performances, and Memorable Moments

April 8   On Opening Day at Cleveland's Municipal Stadium, Rachel Robinson, widow of Jackie, throws out the first ball. Then, Frank Robinson, the first black manager in major league history, homers off Doc Medich in his first official at-bat as player-manager of the Indians. Cleveland goes on to win, 5–3.

April 13   After losing their first three games of the season, the Yankees defeat the Tigers in the first game of a doubleheader at Shea Stadium, 6–0, for their first victory of the year. George Medich throws a two-hit shutout. However, Detroit wins the second game, 5–2, dropping New York's record to 1–4.

April 18   At Tiger Stadium in Detroit, the Yankees collect 17 hits in defeating the Tigers, 11–3. Roy White, Bobby Bonds, and Thurman Munson each get three hits, and Bonds and Ron Blomberg each homer. The home run by Bonds is his first as a Yankee.

April 21   The Yankees defeat the Red Sox, 12–1, at Fenway Park, amassing 16 hits in the process. Leadoff hitter Roy White goes 4–for-4, with a homer, four runs scored, and two runs batted in. Thurman Munson, now batting cleanup, goes 3–for-5, with three runs batted in.

April 23	The Yankees lose to Boston at Fenway Park, 11–7, but Roy White homers from both sides of the plate.
April 26	The Yankees defeat the Brewers 10–1 at Shea Stadium. The hitting stars are Elliott Maddox, who collects three hits and two runs batted in, and Thurman Munson and Ron Blomberg, both of whom hit homers and drive in two runs.
April 27	In the second game of a doubleheader split with the Brewers at Shea Stadium, Catfish Hunter earns his first victory as a Yankee, defeating Milwaukee, 10–1, on a three-hitter. The win follows losses in his first three decisions since joining New York. Elliott Maddox and Ed Herrmann are the hitting stars. Maddox goes 4–for–5, with three runs batted in and three runs scored, including his first home run of the year. Herrmann, filling in for Thurman Munson behind the plate, collects three hits, including his first home run as a Yankee, and drives in three runs.
April 30	The Yankees come from behind, scoring four times in the bottom of the ninth inning, to defeat the Orioles, 6–4. The big blow is a game-winning three-run homer by Bobby Bonds with one man out in the ninth.
May 1	At Shea Stadium, the Yankees reach .500 for the first time this season as Catfish Hunter defeats Baltimore, and eventual Cy Young Award winner, Jim Palmer, 5–0. The win leaves New York's record at 10–10.
May 10	At Oakland-Alameda County Stadium, Catfish Hunter faces his old team for the first time. He shuts out the A's, 3–0, on just two hits, to improve his record to 3–4 and end the Yankees' six-game losing streak.
May 20	The Yankees defeat the Royals, 6–0, at Shea Stadium, as Pat Dobson goes all the way allowing just six hits. Roy White goes 4–for–4, and Graig Nettles adds two hits, including his third homer of the year.
May 23	At Shea Stadium, the Yankees defeat the Rangers, 11–7, as Graig Nettles homers twice, collects three hits, scores three runs, and knocks in three others.
May 28	In Kansas City, the Yankees defeat the Royals, 6–2, behind Rudy May. Bobby Bonds has a hand in all six runs, as he homers twice and drives in four runs.
May 31	At Arlington Stadium in Texas, Catfish Hunter throws a one-hit shutout as the Yankees defeat the Rangers, 6–0. Cesar Tovar gets the only Texas hit.

June 7   The Yankees defeat the White Sox, 6–3, at Comiskey Park for
            their seventh straight victory. The red-hot Bobby Bonds goes
            3–for-4, with two homers and three runs batted in. The two
            home runs give Bonds seven in his last seven games.

June 8   At Comiskey Park, the Yankees extend their winning streak to
            eight games with a 4–1 victory over the White Sox. New York's
            record now stands at 28–24, and the eight-game winning streak
            will turn out to be their longest of the year.

June 19   The Yankees defeat the Tigers, 9–2, in Detroit for Catfish
            Hunter's tenth victory of the season. New York collects 16 hits,
            including three each by Roy White, Thurman Munson, and
            Graig Nettles. White and Nettles each homer, and the former
            knocks in five runs as well.

June 24   At Baltimore's Memorial Stadium, the Yankees win their fourth
            of five consecutive games, defeating the Orioles and Mike Tor-
            rez, 3–1. Catfish Hunter gets his eleventh victory of the sea-
            son, improving New York's record to 39–29 and putting the
            team in first place for the first time all year. Unfortunately, they
            will remain there only three more days all season.

July 20   At Metropolitan Stadium, the Yankees sweep a doubleheader
            from the Twins, winning the first game, 14–2, and taking the
            nightcap, 5–4. In the opener, Roy White, Thurman Munson,
            and Bobby Bonds each homer, and White also collects three
            hits and three runs batted in.

August 2   Billy Martin replaces Bill Virdon as Yankee manager. In his first
            game at the helm, New York defeats Cleveland, 5–3, at Shea Sta-
            dium as Roy White hits his ninth homer of the year and Chris
            Chambliss collects three hits.

August 26   At Shea Stadium, the Yankees defeat the Athletics, 7–1, for
            Catfish Hunter's 18th victory of the season. Roy White goes
            4–for-5, and Thurman Munson goes 4–for-4.

Sept. 7   At Baltimore's Memorial Stadium, Catfish Hunter wins his 20th
            game of the season as he shuts out the Orioles, 2–0. Jim Palmer,
            who also has 20 wins, is the losing pitcher.

Sept. 9   The Yankees defeat the Tigers at Shea Stadium, 9–6, as Chris
            Chambliss goes 5–for-5, with three runs batted in and two
            runs scored.

Sept. 11   At Shea Stadium, the Yankees defeat the Brewers, 10–2, as Graig
            Nettles homers twice, collects three hits, knocks in four runs,
            and scores three others.

Sept. 22   Ron Guidry makes his first major league start in a 6–4 loss to the Red Sox at Shea Stadium. Guidry is the loser, while Boston starter Rick Wise picks up his 19th victory of the season.

Sept. 27 At Shea Stadium, Catfish Hunter wins his final start of the year, defeating the Orioles and 20–game winner Mike Torrez, 3–2. The victory is Hunter's 23rd of the year — the most by a Yankee pitcher since Whitey Ford won 24 games in 1963.

1975 American League Final Team Standings and Offensive Statistics

TEAM	G	W	L	PCT	GB	R	H	2B	3B	HR	BB	SO	SB	AVG	OBP	SLG
EAST																
BOSTON	160	95	65	.594	—	796	1500	284	44	134	565	741	66	.275	.347	.417
BAL	159	90	69	.566	4.5	682	1382	224	33	124	580	834	104	.252	.328	.373
NY	160	83	77	.519	12	681	1430	230	39	110	486	710	102	.264	.328	.382
CLE	159	79	80	.497	15.5	688	1409	201	25	153	525	667	106	.261	.329	.392
MIL	162	68	94	.420	28	675	1343	242	34	146	553	922	65	.250	.323	.389
DET	159	57	102	.358	37.5	570	1338	171	39	125	383	872	63	.249	.303	.366
WEST																
OAK	162	98	64	.605	—	758	1376	220	33	151	609	846	183	.254	.335	.391
KC	162	91	71	.562	7	710	1431	263	58	118	591	675	155	.261	.336	.394
TEX	162	79	83	.488	19	714	1431	208	17	134	613	863	102	.256	.332	.371
MINN	159	76	83	.478	20.5	724	1497	215	28	121	563	746	81	.271	.343	.386
CHI	161	75	86	.466	22.5	655	1400	209	38	94	611	800	101	.255	.334	.358
CAL	161	72	89	.447	25.5	628	1324	195	41	55	593	811	220	.246	.324	.328
TOTAL						8281	16861	2662	429	1465	6672	9487	1348	.258	.330	.379

Team Pitching and Fielding Statistics

TEAM	CG	SH	SV	IP	H	HR	BB	SO	ERA	FA	E	DP
EAST												
BOSTON	62	11	31	1436	1463	145	490	720	3.98	.977	139	142
BAL	70	19	21	1451	1285	110	500	717	3.17	.983	107	175
NY	70	11	20	1424	1325	104	502	809	3.29	.978	135	148
CLE	37	6	33	1435	1395	136	599	800	3.84	.978	134	156
MIL	36	10	34	1431	1496	133	624	643	4.34	.971	180	162
DET	52	10	17	1396	1496	137	533	787	4.27	.972	173	141
WEST												
OAK	36	10	44	1448	1267	102	523	784	3.27	.977	143	140
KC	52	11	25	1456	1422	108	498	815	3.47	.976	155	151
TEX	60	16	17	1465	1456	123	518	792	3.86	.971	191	173
MINN	57	7	22	1423	1381	137	617	846	4.05	.973	170	147
CHI	34	7	39	1452	1489	107	655	799	3.93	.978	140	155
CAL	59	19	16	1453	1386	123	613	975	3.89	.971	184	164
TOTAL	625	137	319	17273					3.78	.975	1851	1854

1975 New York Yankee Pitching Statistics

PLAYER	W	L	ERA	G	GS	CG	SHO	SV	IP	H	R	ER	BB	SO
Catfish Hunter	23	14	2.58	39	39	30	7	0	328	248	107	94	83	177
George Medich	16	16	3.50	38	37	15	2	0	272	271	115	106	72	132
Rudy May	14	12	3.06	32	31	13	1	0	212	179	87	72	99	145
Pat Dobson	11	14	4.07	33	30	7	1	0	207	205	105	94	83	129
Larry Gura	7	8	3.51	26	20	5	0	0	151	173	65	59	41	65
Sparky Lyle	5	7	3.12	49	0	0	0	6	89	94	34	31	36	65
Dick Tidrow	6	3	3.12	37	0	0	0	5	69	65	27	24	31	38
Tippy Martinez	1	2	2.68	23	2	0	0	8	37	27	15	11	32	20
Dave Pagan	0	0	4.06	13	0	0	0	1	31	30	16	14	13	18
Ron Guidry	0	1	3.45	10	1	0	0	0	15	15	6	6	9	15
Rick Sawyer	0	0	3.00	4	0	0	0	0	6	7	4	2	2	3
Mike Wallace	0	0	14.54	3	0	0	0	0	4	11	7	7	1	2

1975 New York Yankee Hitting Statistics

PLAYER	AB	R	H	2B	3B	HR	RBI	BB	SO	SB	OBP	SLG	AVG
Thurman Munson	597	83	190	24	3	12	102	45	52	3	.366	.429	.318
Graig Nettles	581	71	155	24	4	21	91	51	88	1	.322	.430	.267
Chris Chambliss	562	66	171	38	4	9	72	29	50	0	.336	.434	.304
Roy White	556	81	161	32	5	12	59	72	50	16	.372	.430	.290
Bobby Bonds	529	93	143	26	3	32	85	89	137	30	.375	.512	.270
Sandy Alomar	489	61	117	18	4	2	39	26	58	28	.277	.305	.239
Fred Stanley	252	34	56	5	1	0	15	15	27	3	.283	.250	.222
Jim Mason	223	17	34	3	2	2	16	22	49	0	.228	.211	.152
Elliott Maddox	218	36	67	10	3	1	23	21	24	9	.382	.394	.307
Ed Herrmann	200	16	51	9	2	6	30	16	23	0	.309	.410	.255
Lou Piniella	199	7	39	4	1	0	22	16	22	0	.262	.226	.196
Walt Williams	185	27	52	5	1	5	16	8	23	0	.320	.400	.281
Rick Dempsey	145	18	38	8	0	1	11	21	15	0	.353	.338	.262
Alex Johnson	119	15	31	5	1	1	15	7	21	2	.297	.345	.261
Rich Bladt	117	13	26	3	1	1	11	11	8	6	.292	.291	.222
Rich Coggins	107	7	24	1	0	1	6	7	16	3	.272	.262	.224
Ron Blomberg	106	18	27	8	2	4	17	13	10	0	.336	.481	.255
Terry Whitfield	81	9	22	1	1	0	7	1	17	1	.274	.309	.272
Ed Brinkman	63	2	11	4	1	0	2	3	6	0	.224	.270	.175
Bob Oliver	38	3	5	1	0	0	1	1	9	0	.154	.158	.132
Kerry Dineen	22	3	8	1	0	0	1	2	1	0	.417	.409	.364
Dave Bergman	17	0	0	0	0	0	0	2	4	0	.105	.000	.000
Otto Velez	8	0	2	0	0	0	1	2	0	0	.400	.250	.250

FOURTEEN

The Legacy Continues

Even though the Yankees had finished a disappointing third in 1975, 12 games behind the first-place Boston Red Sox, many of the pieces were already in place for the team to write the next great chapter in franchise history. Chris Chambliss and Graig Nettles gave New York solid players at both infield corners, while Roy White and Lou Piniella offered the same stability in the outfield. Thurman Munson was the American League's best catcher and the leader of the team. Catfish Hunter was the ace of the pitching staff, and Sparky Lyle was the bullpen closer.

The Yankee front office added to that nucleus with a couple of exceptional deals during the subsequent off-season. First, pitcher George Medich was traded to the Pittsburgh Pirates for a young second baseman named Willie Randolph, and pitchers Dock Ellis and Ken Brett. Randolph would go on to star for New York for the next 13 seasons, providing leadership in the infield and stabilizing the team's inner defense. Meanwhile, Ellis would win 17 games in 1976, helping the team to their first pennant in 12 years.

After just one year in New York, outfielder Bobby Bonds was traded to the California Angels for speedy centerfielder Mickey Rivers and right-handed starter Ed Figueroa. Rivers would give the Yankees speed at the top of the batting order for the next three seasons and serve as the offensive catalyst on all three pennant-winning teams. Figueroa would go on to win 55 games over the next three years and become the first native-born Puerto Rican to win 20 games in the big leagues.

Along with fellow newcomers Oscar Gamble and Carlos May, and role players Fred Stanley and Dick Tidrow, whose roles were expanded in 1976, these acquisitions provided the impetus for New York to win the American League pennant the following year. Although they were swept by Cincinnati's *Big Red Machine* in the World Series, they won the Series in each of the next two seasons, defeating the Dodgers in six games both times. Key acquisitions such as Reggie Jackson, Bucky Dent, Don Gullett, and Mike Torrez, along with the maturation of Ron Guidry, put the team over the top in 1977. Star relief pitcher Goose Gossage was signed as a free agent the following year, but it was really Guidry's incredible season (25–3, 1.74 ERA) that left the Yankees in a position to mount one of the greatest comebacks in baseball history and eventually win their 22nd world championship.

The tragic death of their captain Thurman Munson in early August of 1979 left the team emotionally drained and incapable of mounting another such comeback that year. However, New York returned to the playoffs in 1980, only to be swept in three games by the Kansas City Royals. The following year, the Yankees made it into the World Series, but, in what has to go down as one of the team's most disappointing performances in post-season play, they were defeated by the Dodgers in six games, after winning the first two games in New York.

Reggie Jackson's tumultuous five-year stay in New York ended at the end of the 1981 campaign when he signed with the California Angels as a free agent. Dave Winfield took over as the team's reigning superstar, although he was sarcastically dubbed *Mr. May* by frustrated team owner George Steinbrenner following his poor performance in the World Series that year.

Winfield was joined in 1983 by Don Mattingly, who, the following year, developed into the best first baseman, and one of the finest players in the game. Rickey Henderson arrived in 1985 and gave the Yankees one of the more potent offenses in baseball. With players such as Henderson, Mattingly, Winfield, Don Baylor, Ken Griffey, Willie Randolph, and third baseman Mike Pagliarulo, the Yankees didn't have too many problems scoring runs during the early and mid-1980s, but, unfortunately, their pitching staff often had difficulties keeping the other team's offense off the board. Other than staff ace Ron Guidry and top reliever Dave Righetti, who had been converted from a starter after Rich Gossage left via free agency, the team didn't have any reliable pitchers. As a result, even though their offense usually kept them in the pennant race for much of the season, the Yankees failed to return to the World Series again during the 1980s. Although they finished the decade with more total wins than any other team in baseball, it was the first decade since the team won their first pennant in 1921 in which they failed to win a world championship.

Things only got worse in 1989, when New York began a five-year period of frustration that rivaled anything the franchise had experienced during their "lean years" of 1965 to 1975. The worst of those seasons was 1990, when they finished with a record of 67–95, in last place in the American League East. The team was saddled with selfish players such as Danny Tartabull and Mel Hall, who paid more attention to their statistics than to the ultimate goal of winning.

Things began to change, though, under new manager Buck Showalter. The team rid itself of players like Tartabull and Hall, and replaced them with veterans who had more of a team concept. Paul O'Neill was acquired from Cincinnati, Wade Boggs was signed as a free agent, and Mike Stanley was picked up from Texas. In addition, promising youngsters Bernie and Gerald Williams were brought up from the minor leagues. In 1994, the team seemed poised to make another run at the World Series, but, unfortunately, those hopes were dashed when the players went on strike, ending the season prematurely. Yet, when play resumed the following year, the Yankees continued to play solid ball and made the playoffs as a *wild card*, ending 14 years of futility and giving Don Mattingly his one moment in the sun. Although they lost in the first round to the Seattle Mariners and Mattingly announced his retirement during the off-season, once again, many of the pieces appeared to be in place for another successful period in Yankee history.

There had been a change in philosophy in the front office over the previous few seasons. George Steinbrenner's advisers had finally been able to convince him to hold onto the young talent the Yankees had in their farm system. As a result, at various times during the 1990s, New York was able to promote to the big league roster players such as Derek Jeter, Bernie Williams, Andy Pettite, Jorge Posada, and Mariano Rivera. Added to veterans such as Paul O'Neill, David Cone, and Tino Martinez, who the Yankees acquired prior to the start of 1996 to replace Don Mattingly at first base, these men formed much of the nucleus of the team that would go on to win four world championships in five seasons, beginning in 1996.

In addition, it was finally realized that pitching and defense is what usually wins world championships. The front office always made certain that the Yankee pitching staff was well-stocked with talented arms that would help the team to prevail in a short playoff series. From Andy Pettite and David Cone, to Jimmy Key, John Wetteland, and Mariano Rivera, and, later, to David Wells, Orlando Hernandez, and Roger Clemens, New York has had, over the last seven or eight seasons, a pitching staff capable of rivaling the best in baseball. They have also always had role players and quality people such as Joe Girardi and Mike Stanton, who always put the team before themselves.

Of course, as important to the team's success as anyone has been manager Joe Torre, who brought stability, class, and an attitude of selflessness to the Yankees. Although New York failed to win the World Series in either

2001 or 2002, with Torre at the helm, and with the talent on the Yankee roster, the future seems bright for fans of the team. But, as this group of players carve out their niche in Yankees history, it should be remembered that things were not always this bright and that there were many players who wore the Yankee uniform in the past who were not as fortunate as these men are. While the names of Derek Jeter, Bernie Williams, Paul O'Neill, Andy Pettite, and Mariano Rivera may be more glamorous to Yankees fans of this generation, players such as Bobby Murcer, Roy White, Mel Stottlemyre, Sparky Lyle, and, yes, even Horace Clarke, have just as important a place in Yankees history, and figured just as prominently in the lives of the fans from their era.

Notes

1. Halberstam, David, *October 1964* (New York: Villard Books, 1994), p. 55.
2. Ibid., p. 232.   3. Ibid., p. 233.
4. *New York Yankees: The Movie*. Magic Video Publishing Company, 1987.
5. Todd Newville, "Tom Tresh," online at Baseballink.com (http://www.baseballink.com/baseballink).
6. Halberstam, *October 1964*, p. 288.
7. Ibid., p. 288.   9. Ibid., p. 287.
8. Ibid., p. 287.   10. Ibid., p. 286.
11. *Pinstripe Power: The Story of the 1961 New York Yankees* (New York: Major League Baseball Productions, 1987).
12. Ibid.
13. Francis Kinlaw, "Bobby Richardson," *The Ballplayers*, online at BaseballLibrary.com (http://www.baseballlibrary.com/baseballlibrary/ballplayers).
14. *Pinstripe Power: The Story of the 1961 New York Yankees*.
15. Shalin, Mike, and Neil Shalin, *Out by a Step: The 100 Best Players Not in the Baseball Hall of Fame* (South Bend IN: Diamond Communications, 2002), p. 308.
16. *Roger Maris: Reluctant Hero*. ESPN, 1998.
17. Shalin and Shalin, *Out by a Step*, p. 65.
18. *New York Yankees: The Movie*.
19. *Pinstripe Power: The Story of the 1961 New York Yankees*.
20. *New York Yankees: The Movie*.
21. Norman L. Macht/Christopher Renino, "Roger Maris," *The Ballplayers*, online at BaseballLibrary.com (http://www.baseballlibrary.com/baseballlibrary/ballplayers).
22. *Pinstripe Power: The Story of the 1961 New York Yankees*.
23. Shalin and Shalin, *Out by a Step*, p. 147.
24. Ibid., p. 145.   25. Ibid., p. 146.
26. Conversation with Roy White from 3/5/03.
27. Halberstam, *October 1964*, p. 235.
28. Shalin and Shalin, *Out by a Step*, p. 147.
29. *New York Yankees: The Movie*.
30. "Whitey Ford," *Quotes*, online at Baseball-Almanac.com (http://www.baseball-almanac.com/baseball-almanac/quotes).
31. Ibid.
32. *New York Yankees: The Movie*.
33. *Pinstripe Power: The Story of the 1961 New York Yankees*.

34. "Whitey Ford," *Quotes*, online at Baseball-Almanac.com (http://www.baseball-almanac.com/baseball-almanac/quotes).

35. Ibid.

36. Conversation with Roy White from 3/5/03.

37. Halberstam, *October 1964*, p. 71.

38. Conversation with Roy White from 3/5/03.

39. Todd Newville, "Tom Tresh," online at Baseballink.com (http://www.baseballink.com/baseballink).

40. Ibid.

41. Halberstam, *October 1964*, p. 44.

42. Ibid., p. 45.

43. Conversation with Roy White from 3/5/03.

44. Ibid.   48. Ibid.

45. Ibid.   49. Ibid.

46. Ibid.   50. Ibid.

47. Ibid.   51. Ibid.

52. Shalin and Shalin, *Out by a Step*, p. 228.

53. Ibid., p. 300.   54. Ibid., p. 300.

55. *Yankeeography: Thurman Munson*. Major League Baseball Productions, 2002.

56. *Captain: The Thurman Munson Story*. Estate of Thurman Munson and the New York Yankees, 1992.

57. *Yankeeography: Thurman Munson*.

58. *Captain: The Thurman Munson Story*.

59. Ibid.   61. Ibid.

60. Ibid.

62. *Yankeeography: Thurman Munson*.

63. Shalin and Shalin, *Out by a Step*, p. 58.

64. *Captain: The Thurman Munson Story*.

65. *Yankeeography: Thurman Munson*.

66. Conversation with Roy White from 3/5/03.

67. Ibid.   76. Ibid.

68. Ibid.   77. Ibid.

69. Ibid.   78. Ibid.

70. Ibid.   79. Ibid.

71. Ibid.   80. Ibid.

72. Ibid.   81. Ibid.

73. Ibid.   82. Ibid.

74. Ibid.   83. Ibid.

75. Ibid.

Bibliography

Books

Bouton, Jim. *Ball Four Plus Ball Five.* New York: Stein and Day, 1981.

Cashman, Brian, et al. *1991 New York Yankees Information Guide.* New York: Yankees Magazine, 1991.

Creamer, Robert W. *Stengel: His Life and Times.* New York: Fireside, 1989.

Dewey, Donald, and Nicholas Acocella. *The Biographical History of Baseball.* New York: Carroll & Graf, 1995.

Ford, Whitey, with Phil Pepe. *Few and Chosen.* Chicago: Triumph, 2001.

Golenbock, Peter. *Dynasty: The New York Yankees 1949–1964.* New York: Berkley Books, 1985.

Halberstam, David. *October 1964.* New York: Villard, 1994.

Honig, Donald. *The New York Yankees,* rev. ed. New York: Crown, 1987.

Kubek, Tony, and Terry Pluto. *Sixty-One: The Team, the Record, the Men.* New York: Macmillan, 1987.

Mann, Jack. *The Decline and Fall of the New York Yankees.* New York: Simon & Schuster, 1967.

Mantle, Mickey, with Herb Gluck. *The Mick.* New York: Jove, 1986.

Pepitone, Joe, with Berry Stainback. *Joe, You Coulda Made Us Proud.* Chicago: Playboy Press, 1975.

Shalin, Mike, and Neil Shalin. *Out by a Step: The 100 Best Players Not in the Baseball Hall of Fame.* South Bend IN: Diamond Communications, 2002.

Thorn, John, and Palmer, Pete, eds., with Michael Gershman. *Total Baseball.* New York: HarperCollins Pub, 1993.

Videos

Captain: The Thurman Munson Story. Estate of Thurman Munson and the New York Yankees, 1992.

New York Yankees: The Movie. Magic Video Publishing Company, 1987.

Pinstripe Power: The Story of the 1961 New York Yankees. Major League Baseball Productions, New York, 1987.

Roger Maris: Reluctant Hero. ESPN, 1998.

Yankeeography: Thurman Munson. Major League Baseball Productions, 2002.

Internet Websites

Ford, Whitey. *Quotes*, online at Baseball-Almanac.com (http://www.baseball-almanac.com/baseball-almanac/quotes).

Newville, Todd. *Tom Tresh,* online at Baseballink.com (http://www.baseballink.com/baseballink).

The Ballplayers, online at BaseballLibrary.com (http://www.baseballlibrary.com/baseballlibrary/ballplayers).

The Teams, online at BaseballLibrary.com (http://www.baseballlibrary.com/baseballlibrary/teams).

The Players, online at Baseball-Reference.com (http://www.baseball-reference.com/players).

Historical Stats, online at MLB.com (http://www.mlb.com/mlb/nyy/stats_historical/nyy_historical_team_stats).

Retrosheet, online at Retrosheet.org (http://www.retrosheet.org/boxesetc/index).

Index